CYRUS   SALMANZADEH

9, 50

AGRICULTURAL CHANGE AND RURAL
SOCIETY IN SOUTHERN IRAN

INTRODUCTION by GWYN JONES
POSTSCRIPT by KEITH McLACHLAN

MIDDLE EAST & NORTH AFRICAN STUDIES press limited

Published by Middle East and North African Studies Press Ltd.

Gallipoli House, The Cottons, Outwell, Wisbech, Cambridge, PE14 8TN, England

1980

ISBN   (cased)   0 906559 02 2

ISBN   (paper)   0 906559 03 0

Printed by Whitstable Litho Ltd., Whitstable, Kent

CONTENTS

LIST OF TABLES

LIST OF FIGURES

Page

LIST OF MAPS

LIST OF ILLUSTRATIONS

Acknowledgement is made to Dr C.A.Stobbs for plate 1
to Mr A.K.Sylvester for plates 2 and 5, and to
Mr J.C.Anderson for plates 3,4,6,7,8 and 9

GLOSSARY

adab	good manners	gaave	cow
ahangar	blacksmith	gonjeshk pa	protector of rice
alvari	landless peasants		fields against
amlak–e			birds
saltanati	crown land	gopun	herdsman
amlak–e		hakimbashi	unqualified
khossosi	private estates		doctor
anjoman–e		hama–e–	type of bath
deh	village council	boshgaie	house
anjoman–e		handevaneh	water melon
vahid	unified rural	haq–e alaf	
rustai	council	cher	nominal levy
aqa	sir	haq–e	permanent right
arbab	see **malik**	risheh	of cultivation
bareh		haq–ol	
tarofi	ex–gratia gift	amalkar	dealer
barfurush	fruit and vegetable	hombar	neighbour
	wholesaler	hozeh omran	rural polarization
baq	garden	rustai	programme
baqal	grocer	jersh	see **khin–o–cho**
barzegar	hired labourer	joldoz	saddler
bilan	financial	jow	land measure, 576
	statement		equalling total
bildar	labourer		village area
bist–o–char	24 parts ie total	juft	a traditional
nokhud	village lands		measure of land
boneh	open village **or**		worked by a pair
	peasant work		of oxen
	organization	kadkhoda	headman
bonku	peasant work	kaleh qand	sugar loaf
	team	kaniz	maid servant
chal	field	kar–e gil	mud work
cho	club	kayid	see **kadkhoda**
chopun	shepherd	khaliseh	domain lands
dalak	itinerant barber	khan	chief
darvish	devotee of the	khanevadeh	family
	Imam Ali	khanevar	household
deh	village	kharboozeh	melon
dehsra	village communal	khin	blood
	house	khin–o–cho	informal insurance
delavar	carpenter		scheme
delsozi	enthusiasm and	khish	dry farming area
	devotion to duty	khoda shons	God fearing
doanavice	faith healer	khwushni–	peasant without
dokhtar	patriparallel	shin	land rights
amu	first cousin	kopiter	room adjacent to
domoyar	field supervisor		threshing floor
farman	imperial rescript	kortech	fallow land used
fasel	see **khin–o–cho**		for grazing
gaz	linear measure	kunjed	land measure,
	15 cm approximately		13,824 equalling
			total village area

leaf-o-lafe	brushwood	omal	distributor and supervisor of water
maash	mung beans	omal-e	
madreseh	secondary school	chaltok	rice irrigator
majlis	national assembly	ostan	province
maktab	informal school	oyar	see **sarboneh**
malik	owner or title holder	pakar	footman
malik-e deh	village landowner	pakhtar	picker of crops
malik-o- raiyat	traditional landlord-peasant share-cropping system	papeas	devotees of Shahzadeh Ahmad
mamor-e		pil-e khin	blood money
sabet	registrar	qaleh	walled village
mann	measure of land ordinarily sown by eight kg of wheat	qanat	underground water channel
		quora	resulting production from one cultivation unit
maqtow	fixed rent		
mayandar	see **barfurush**	rabani	see **somkar**
mazraeh	independent farm	raiyat	peasant
minal	dues on public domain lands	rishsefid	village elder
		rodarbasi	reticence
mirab	rice water supervisor	rouzeh khwani	religious festival commemorating death of Imam Hossein
moatamedin	trustworthy men		
mobashir	bailiff		
mohali	non-tribal peasants	sabz-e pa	protector of wheat fields
mohr	large wooden stamp for marking threshed grain	sag pa	protector of rice fields against boars
		sahra	open field
moqani	well digger	sahragard	fieldman
morg	chicken	saleh	temporary dam
mozdi	see **moziri**	salman	see **dalak**
moziri	wage earner	sandoq-e omimi	general communal fund
muassiseh sabzikari	vegetable market garden	saqa	waterman
		sarbildar	foreman
mullah	religious leader	sarboneh	head of peasant work unit
musha	joint ownership of land shares	sarbonku	see **sarboneh**
mushakerat	fixed rent in kind	sayfi	summer vegetable crop
mustajir	lessee		
mutavalli	administrator	sayfikari	summer vegetable crop cultivation
najar	carpenter	sayyid	claimant of direct descent from Mohammad
nalband	farrier		
nasaq	cultivation rights		
nockar	servant		
nokhud	land measure, 24 equalling total village area	shaeir	see **jow**
		shahrak	resettlement centre
		shahristan	urban district
nozulkhor	money lender	sharji	local wind
		sheik	headman
o pa	protector of irrigation water	shish dang	six parts, ie total village lands

sho pa	night watchman	vahid-e	a joint
sohani	team leader	sahami	agricultural unit
somkar	permanent farm	zerai	
	hand	vaqf	endowment land
supur	dustman	vaqf-e amm	land endowed for
			pious purposes
tir-o-goreh	lottery	vaqf-e	land endowed for
tofangchi	rifleman	khass	donor's family
toi zabeton	see kopiter	vasmeh	indigo
tosh kash	young son of		
	a farmer	zabet	landowner's agent and/
tolak zans	female rice		or harvest controller
	planters	zari-e sahib	peasant sharecroppers
torfia	Arabic-speaking	nasaq	
	buffalo herdsmen	zerat-e abi	irrigated farming
		zerat-e dym	dry farming
ulama	religious class	zorji	dry farming area

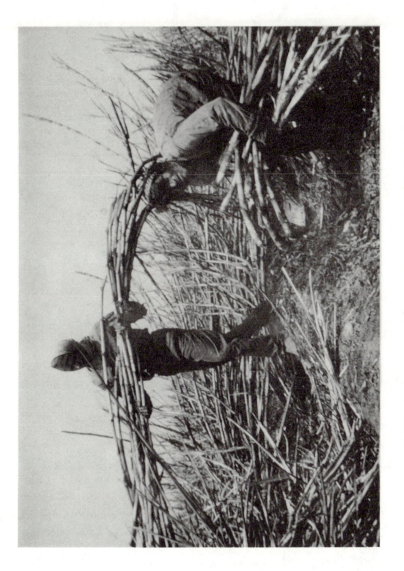

PLATE 1   Sugar cane gatherers at Haft Tappeh

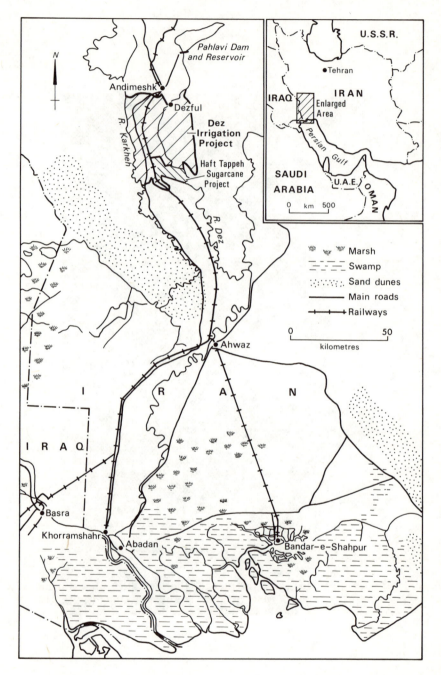

MAP 1   Iran and the Dez Irrigation Project

INTRODUCTION

This volume provides a study of the rural situation and processes of change in a relatively small area of Khuzestan in Southern Iran. Historically, it has been a highly productive agricultural area, using traditional methods of irrigation. The potential for agricultural improvement was dramatically enhanced by the availability of water for irrigation as the result of a dam across the river Dez constructed between 1958 and 1962. In a real and immediate sense, the irrigation and hydro-electric developments in the Tennessee Valley from 1933 onwards, administered by an autonomous Authority, which led to varied rural and agricultural as well as industrial developments, formed the model for the Dez Irrigation Project. A number of development services for agriculture and the rural population were established during the 1960s in many villages in the area. However, these were not expanded, since the emphasis of the project gradually shifted away from the retention and development of peasant agriculture to the establishment of large-scale commercial agriculture in large sections of the area, to the great detriment of rural society there.

In many countries (possibly most), relatively little is known in detail of the characteristics of rural life and of the variations within it. There is a great need for socio-logical and socio-economic studies of rural communities and their ways of life - as it was in the recent past and as it has become today. The availability of such studies could act as a basis for the formulation of relevant rural and agricultural policies, and influence the revision of existing policies. They could also assist in humanizing the rigid character of many policies. However, since development policies of one kind or another have been implemented in the rural areas of most countries in recent years, affecting different rural areas to varying degrees, the knowledge required also needs to take account of alterations which have already occurred due to the implementation of policies. In a very basic sense, this implies an evaluation of the application of particular policies in specific rural areas, and of the adaptions of rural people to the policies.

In this study, Cyrus Salmanzadeh has shown how the Dez development scheme and the changes in policy during its implementation have affected rural society and agricultural output. He has particularly demonstrated the catastrophic social effects of large-scale commercial· agriculture. Ironically, most of these schemes collapsed during the latter part of the 1970s, but by then the damage was done. The old dependency relationships between landowners and peasant farmers have formally disappeared, although in reality there are significant remnants left. In many cases the original inhabitants have simply left the land and, in any case, there is a hiatus between the old, long-established system and the creation of acceptable forms of organization linking the peasantry to their agricultural production and associated pursuits. Modern, but culturally compatible services, to assist the villagers who remain to fully integrate their decision-making on land use with their changing ways of life, are so far largely lacking; the traditional, institutionalized activities and services of the landowners to the villagers, as well as the equally institutionalized responses of the peasants, have yet to be replaced by new forms.

The Islamic Revolution in 1979 has meant that the policies of the previous regime are now open to question and discussion. Many errors, particularly in large-scale schemes such as the Dez Project, have been revealed, although much detailed investigation still remains to be done before they can be corrected. To the extent that this study illuminates the variety of changes, based on detailed sociological and economic enquiry in a number of villages, it contributes to a greater appreciation of the complexities of rural development in a particular cultural environment. It is also indicative of how, and the extent to which, micro-studies can provide a fuller understanding and enlighten the evaluation of national and regional development policies.

Gwyn E. Jones.

Senior Lecturer in Rural Sociology, Agricultural Extension and Rural Development Centre, University of Reading.

1 THE PHYSICAL ENVIRONMENT IN KHUZESTAN

1.1 Introduction

Iran, as a Middle-Eastern country, is in a unique position to benefit from the agrarian experience of both East and West. Agriculture is still the prime occupation of more than one third of her fast growing population – 35 million (1979 estimate) with a growth rate of 2.8 per cent per annum(1). Over half of its 165 million hectares – an area more than six times that of Great Britain(2)- consists of salt desert and barren mountain. Cultivable land forms only a small part of the total area. In 1971-72 only 20 million hectares (about 12 per cent) were under cultivation, 8.3 million hectares being cropped, less than half of which was irrigated.

Agriculture is also of prime importance through its contribution to the national economy. From 1900 to 1970 the agricultural sector (including forestry and fisheries) was the major contributor to the gross national product(3). Even in the early 1970s about half of the total government revenue (excluding oil-related revenue) was derived from direct and indirect taxation on agriculture(4). The importance of agriculture is increasingly evident since demand for agricultural products is rising at an ever-faster rate and domestic agriculture is unable to keep pace. This growing demand is closely linked to rapid population growth and to increasing rural-urban migration. In addition the steady increase in average **per capita** income (from $155 in 1959/60 to $435 in 1971/72 and to $1274 in 1974/75 (5) – calculations based on current prices) means that urban groups have much greater purchasing power.

To meet the accelerating demand, the government has increasingly relied on imports – wheat from Canada; rice and oil seeds from the USA; meat from New Zealand; dairy produce from Eastern Europe; citrus fruits from Lebanon and Jordan. These imports have been financed by the enormous increases in oil revenue (rising from $2.2 billion in 1971 to $20.0 billion in 1974 (6)) but there is no certainty that this will be possible beyond the immediate future and it could lead to a substantial deterioration of Iran's foreign currency balances. Furthermore the recent use of food as a political weapon (ie between the

USA and the USSR) underlines the need for self-sufficiency.

Despite these considerations, agriculture has continued to be one of the least developed sectors in the economy (7). During the Fourth National Development plan (1968-1972) the agricultural sector lagged. While the average annual growth rate for the industrial sector was about 15 per cent, that for agriculture was 3.7 per cent, only marginally higher than the rate of population increase, "but less than the target of 4.4 per cent envisaged in the Plan"(8).

Productivity in agriculture has been low both in terms of labour and of land. According to a Food and Agriculture Organization agricultural survey of 52 countries from 1956 to 1960, Iran ranked 36th in terms of output per hectare and 30th in terms of output per adult farmer (9). This relatively low agricultural productivity has been due to natural, social and economic reasons. Lack of adequate water for irrigation, of water and soil conservation measures and of security in rural areas have acted as deterrents to agricultural development. However, the fundamental problem has been rooted in the traditional landlord-peasant system of land exploitation.

1.2   The traditional landlord-peasant farming system in Iran

Before agrarian reform in the 1960s, some 15.5 million people (65 per cent of the total population) lived in 55,000 villages. Most of the villages were closed to outside influences and had a rigid socio-political structure, being owned by a relatively small number of large landowners. It was not unusual for an influential family to own 100 villages or more (10). The landlords controlled village affairs by employing administrative agents to protect their interests as well as safeguard village stability by supervising local activities. The villages contained some 2.4 million households of peasant sharecroppers who comprised the labour force for the cultivation of nearly all agricultural land (then estimated to be 11.3 million hectares). The average size of the 'farm' cultivated by a sharecropping household was calculated to be 4 7 hectares (11).

Usually the landlord provided land, water and security and oversaw the organization of agricultural production. The function of the peasant was simply to cultivate whichever crops the landlord had decided to grow (12). The system was by no means conducive to progressive agriculture and most landlords had little interest in making a genuine effort to improve rural conditions (13). The peasants often received a relatively small share of the harvest and thus had little inducement to improve productivity or efficiency. They had no voice in village administration and stayed silent, partly because of very low literacy rates (about five per cent in 1961) and were "accustomed to having their landlord think and speak for them and tell them how to vote"(14). The peasant was apathetic about his situation and was felt to represent a serious handicap to rural improvements. At the same time concentration of land in the hands of a few landlords was

seen by the government as a block to its plans which could
only be overcome by drastic reform.

1.3   Agrarian reform

A major element in improving Iranian agriculture would
be land tenure reform. This had been initiated in 1951 by
an imperial rescript (farman) ordering royal estates to be sold
to their peasant tenants (15). In 1958 some of the public domain
lands (khaliseh) were transferred to peasant cultivators
(16). However, landlord resistance and peasant apathy ensured
that the traditional pattern of rural land holding remained
until 1962 when a series of wide-ranging reforms was introduced.
The most significant measures of the initial six-point "White
Revolution", (17) approved by referendum on 26th January 1963,
were those concerned with agriculture and the system of landholding (18). Their primary purpose was to destroy the power
of influential landlords through division of large landholdings
amongst their tenant sharecroppers. The possibility that this
might improve the peasants' standard of living by reshaping
the socio-economic structure of the village (19) was a minor
and incidental consideration. It was clear that land redistribution would only effectively assist rural socio-economic
development if accompanied by appropriate physical and social
services. Since the early 1950s the government had been
involved in minimal improvements in irrigation systems and
rural infrastructure, as well as in the introduction of basic
village-level social and economic services.
The Land Reform Programme was introduced, by a process
of trial and error, in three stages from 1962 to 1970 (20). In
so far as it reduced the power of the landlords, it was a
political success (21), but the new pattern of small peasant
proprietorship did not solve the problem of low productivity.
The average holding was 2.8 hectares in size and has recently
been considered to inhibit the improvement of efficiency through
mechanization (22). Thus alternative systems, such as agribusinesses, farm corporations and production co-operatives
were introduced in selected rural areas.
Agribusinesses resulted from the implementation of the 1968
law on 'The Establishment of Companies for Utilization of Lands
Downstream of Dams'. Here the government purchased land
from landlords and landowning peasants in order to release
it to agribusinesses created by state and/or private domestic
or foreign investment. Peasant cultivation in the areas
concerned was suspended and the land was leased for large-
scale mechanized farming. Sometimes peasants were resettled
in new centres. By 1973, 12 agribusinesses were cultivating
some 94,000 hectares (23) – 1.1 per cent of total cultivated
land – an area that was supposed to have extended to 25
per cent of all irrigated land by 1978 (24).
Farm corporations were established in 1968 for a five-year
trial period. Each was a joint stock company involving several
villages and controlling at least 1,000 hectares. The peasants
involved transferred their landrights to the corporation and

received a proportionate number of shares in return. The corporations were administered by government employees and the peasant stockholders., some of whom are employed by their corporation, received dividends in proportion to their individual stockholdings. By 1973, 43 corporations controlled some 196,900 hectares (25)(2.4 per cent of total cultivated land).

Production co-operatives, which began in 1971, were seen as a middle way between independent small peasant proprietors and the farm corporations. Here, farmers worked, "through joint cultivation while retaining their individual rights of ownership to land; the consolidated lands of the villages are divided among farming groups so that each group has a certain area of land under the various crops cultivated on the village farm lands"(26). By March 1974, 15 production co-operatives worked 17,794 hectares (27) – 0.2 per cent of total cultivated land, too little to have had any effect on agrarian structures.

In addition to the changes described above, a number of measures have been taken to step up agricultural productivity The most important was the rapid expansion of investment in the agricultural sector by 370 per cent to a total of 239.6 billion rials ($3.4 billion) during the Fifth National Development Plan, aimed at expanding large-scale farming in order to create an annual growth rate of seven per cent. This was a major shift away from the emphasis on industrialization present in the first four development plans. The government also offered a number of production incentives to private producers, in addition to the increased investment.

Nevertheless, even with the implementation of all these programmes, Iran is unlikely to be self-sufficient in food by the year 2000 AD, when her population will exceed 60 million. To supply a daily **per capita** diet of 2,800 calories, including 28 grams of animal protein, will require a 100 per cent increase in grain production and a 300 to 500 per cent increase in vegetable, fruit and livestock production(28). As a result, the Ministry of Agriculture in conjunction with two British consultant firms(29), drew up a 20-year national development plan in 1975 designed to promote the best use of land and water for the most suitable crops on a more intensive basis. 19 major areas (poles) were designated throughout Iran where agricultural activity was to be concentrated (polarized)(30) . Some of these, such as the Dez Irrigation Project area and the Dasht-e Moghan, Jiruft and Qazvin development projects had already been developed through regional rural and agricultural development schemes. Farming in these 'poles' was to be large-scale and would have had little to do with traditional peasant sharecropping.

However, peasant agriculture would not altogether disappear and it may well have survived alongside these other systems. The Minister of Co-operation and Rural affairs emphasised in 1978 that traditional farming structures could help to solve some agricultural problems. In 1976 there were proposals for the organization of landowning peasants into groups which would farm 30 hectare units(31). Indeed, peasant farmers are vital to Iranian agricultural productivity and the impact of land tenure changes on village social structure is a matter of considerable importance.

1.4 The Khuzestan region and its natural resources

In 1956, Iran started her first unified regional development plan which was designed to exploit the natural resources – mainly water and land – in the five major river basins in the south west of the Khuzestan region. The region comprises the Khuzestan Plains, an area of some 41,000 square kilometres (32),and the headwaters of the five rivers which drain into the plains – the Karkheh, Dez, Karun, Jarrahi and Hindijan which occupy about 120,000 square kilometres. The region includes all of Khuzestan Province(Ostan)and substantial parts of the four surrounding provinces: Fars, Isfahan, Kirmanshah and Luristan.

The region has always been considered to be one of Iran's well-watered regions (33). With only about one tenth of Iran's total area and a population estimated in 1958 at about 2.5 million (12.7 per cent of the total) of which 65 per cent were settled or semi-nomadic farmers, and in 1976 as four million (11.5 per cent of the total), the region contains nearly one third of the country's annual surface water (32,231 million cubic metres out of an estimated 100 billion cubic metres).

If these rivers were controlled, the current minimum annual discharge of 205 CMS could be raised to 830 CMS, "sufficient to irrigate more than one million gross hectares (at 1.2 CMS per 1,000 hectares) – equivalent to all the better quality lands in the Khuzestan plains. Nowhere else in Iran does an opportunity of this magnitude present itself to regulate and increase water supply systematically for nearby large land areas suitable for intensive food production(34). Another source notes that an annual 20 billion cubic metres of water is available for irrigation and calculates that this would suffice to irrigate 1,750,000 hectares on the assumption that the average water requirement per crop is 12,000 cubic metres per hectare (35). In fact the Khuzestan region possesses some 1,550,000 hectares (7.7 per cent of Iranian agricultural land) suitable for irrigation.

In the past these rich land and water resources formed the basis of local agricultural prosperity(36). However, after the 13th century, Mongol invasions of Iran ended national economic growth and Khuzestan's agricultural prosperity (37), a situation which persisted up to the 20th century. Curzon, writing in 1887, emphasised the richness of the region's natural resources and showed the impact of political instability on their exploitation: "The natural richness of this region is enormous.... it is capable of producing an immense variety of cereal and other crops... with proper care, it might become one vast granary... As it is, tribal warfare and Government oppression have turned it into a desert over which the eye may roam unrested for miles"(38).

Land and water are not the only significant resources in the region. Immense deposits of oil and natural gas, first discovered in 1903, contain much of Iran's petroleum reserves.

TABLE 1

The major rivers in the Khuzestan region 1967/72

River	Source	Discharge into	Amount of discharge CMS *	Total volume MCM +	Hydrological station
Karkheh	Nahavand–Malayer	Hour al–Azim	202	6383	Hamidiyyeh
Dez	Burujird	Karun at Bond–e Qir	278	8789	Dezful
Karun	Yasuz	Shatt al–Arab	419	13241	Gotvand
Jarrahi	Zagros	Swamps at Shadegan	49	1536	Bihbahan
Hindijan	Ardekan	Persian Gulf	72	2282	Deh Mullah

Source: Agricultural Office of Khuzestan, Geografiai Keshavarzi Khuzestan, Ahwaz, Iran, 1352/1973, Table 7.

CMS *: cubic metres per second

MCM +: million cubic metres

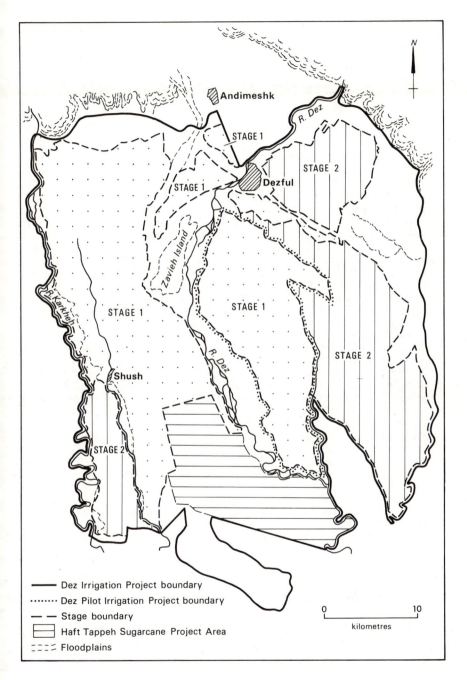

MAP 2   The Dez Irrigation Project – stages of reclamation

in 1974, reserves of oil were estimated to be around 60 billion
barrels, Khuzestan supplying 90 per cent of Iran's daily
production of six million barrels, while reserves of natural
gas amounted to about 270,000 billion cubic feet(39). Until it
was automated, the oil industry in Khuzestan employed some
40,000 workers in 1958 (33 per cent of the country's total
industrial labour force(40)). Oil has also provided the
Khuzestan region with a network of cities, ports roads and
pipelines.

1.5   Rural Dezful and the Dez Irrigation Project

The part of Khuzestan with which this study is concerned
is that covered by the Dez Project area and involves the 169
villages within the area. The Project area includes Dezful
town on its northern boundary and extends for 60 kilometres
south to the ancient town of Susa (Shush) and includes the
Haft Tappeh sugar cane plantation in the extreme south.
In the original 1956 plans the Project extended northwards
to the foothills of the Zagros mountains(41) but in 1958 the
Dezful military airbase was located there so the Project's
northern boundary was modified to exclude it, together with
dry-farming land to the north east of it and the railway town
of Andimeshk. The southern boundary, along the Shaur Hill
Ridge (42) and the Ojirub Southern Agricultural Company estate,
was expanded in 1972, when about 7,000 hectares were added
to the Haft Tappeh sugar cane plantation. The western and
eastern boundaries are formed by the upper part of the River
Karkheh and the intermittent stream of Shoreh or Gelal-e-
Kuhanak respectively. The total current Project land area
is some 167,000 hectares and its use is described in Table
2, together with comparative data for the Khuzestan Province
and Iran.

1.6   Physical structures and soil characteristics

The physiography of the Project area is characterized by
nine rivers and streams, a series of broad alluvial fans
extending from the foothills southwards and two anticlinal
ridges, the Dezful Ridge and the Shaur Ridge, running in
a general east-west direction, roughly parallel to the Zagros
mountain range. It is divided internally by a series of fairly
well-entrenched north-south drainage channels at regular
intervals of four to five kilometres which contribute to the
generally good drainage of the surface and the sub-surface
(43).
Topographically the land, where not eroded along the streams
and rivers, has a slight slope ranging from 1.0 to 0.5 per
cent in the north to less than 0.2 per cent in the south(44). The
area inclines southward from an elevation of about 160 metres
above sea level in the north to some 50 metres in the Haft
Tappeh sugar cane plantations. Generally the high elevation
of the land above the rivers and natural drains provides
sufficient deep percolation(45).

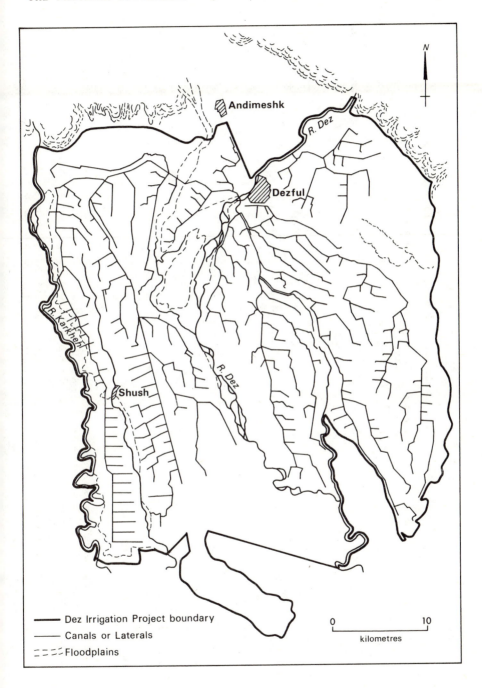

MAP3   The Dez Irrigation Project – canal lay-out

TABLE 2

Land Utilization in Iran, Khuzestan Province and Dez Project Area.

	Iran 1971-72 [a]		Khuzestan Province 1971-72 [b]			Dez Project Area 1958-59 [c]			Dez Project Area 1970-71 [d]		
	Ha. (Gross) '000	% of total	Ha. (Gross) '000	% of total	% of Iran	Ha. (Gross) '000	% of total	% of Iran	Ha. (Gross) '000	% of total	% of Iran
Total area under cultivation	20,200	12.2	1,326.3	20.5	6.6	120	71.9	0.6	128.7	77.1	0.6
Annually cultivated	(8,300)	(5.0)	(910.3)	(14.1)	(11.0)	(92)	(55.1)	(1.1)			
Irrigated farm land and gardens	((3,850))	((2.3))	((494.3))	((7.7))	((12.8))	((72))	((43.1))	((1.9))			
Dry farmed	((4,440))	((2.7))	((416.0))	((6.4))	((9.3))	((20))	((12.0))	((0.4))			
Annually fallowed (during winter cropping)	(11,900)	(7.2)	(416.0)	(6.4)	(3.5)	(28)	(16.8)	(0.2)			
Forests	15,900	9.6	500.5	7.7	3.1						
Permanent pastures and meadows	11,000	6.7									
Cultivable, unused	30,600	18.6	4,638.6	71.8	3.5	47	28.1	0.03	38.3	29.9	0.03
Uncultivable land [e]	87,300	52.9									
Total	165,000	100.0	6,465.4	100.0	3.9	167	100.0	0.1	167	100.0	0.1

Sources: a. Iran Almanac 1973 and Book of Facts, Tehran, 1974, p 221.

              b. "Khuzestan Plan and Budget Office Report", (Ahwaz, Iran, 1971).

              c. Nederlandsche Heidemaatschappij, "Report on the Dez Irrigation Project, Supplement No 1", June 1959, (unpublished) p IV-4.

              d. D & R, Dez Irrigation Project, Stage II Feasibility, New York, USA, D & R 1968, p 23.

Note: e. Including: flood plains, river beds, hilly and eroded water lands, mountains, deserts, lakes, swamps cities, towns, roads etc.

Geologically the Upper Khuzestan Plains are, "only an extension of the great Mesopotamia alluvial plain in south western
Iran"(46)   Originally it was believed that the whole plain was
slowly formed by alluvial soil carried down from the mountains
(47),but more recent views see it as a complex and unstable
geosyncline, "which was produced late in the Pliocene by move-
ments of the earth's crust forcing the Iranian Plateau closer
to the central massif of Arabia" (48).

The Project area soils are calcareous, generally free from
or with only slight salt accumulations and practically no
alkalinity (49). The top soil consists of silt and clay loams,
and the lower layer comprises gravel deposits(50) which prevent
excessive salinity.   The ground water table around Dezful,
Andimeshk and Shush is low, usually far below six metres
(51). The FAO classifies some 70 per cent of the Project area
as good to excellent land (Classes I,II,III), some ten per
cent as good but with limitations such as water needs (Class
IV) and the remaining 20 per cent as having very limited
use for irrigated agriculture (Classes V,VI)(52).

Dezful terrain has traditionally presented no major problem
to its traditional cultivators but the introduction of intensive
agriculture, involving heavy chemical fertilizer and limited
land fallowing, has produced serious land problems such as
salinity and soil structure degradation.   Fundamental land
and water management will be vital if they are to be mitigated.
In this context it should be borne in mind that the decline
of Khuzestan during Abbasid times (750–840 AD) was due mainly
to failure to provide drainage facilities.

1.7   Climate, work and social life

The climate of the northern Khuzestan plains is generally
regarded as semi-arid, with a long, hot and dry summer and
a short, cool and relatively moist winter(53), but it is not
always advantageous to crop growing – rainfall, in particular,
being irregular from year to year. Details are given in Tables
3 and 4. Strong prevailing winds cause dust storms, particularly in spring and early summer, and in July and August
south-easterly winds frequently bring moist air from the Persian
Gulf and create the most oppressive weather – the **sharji**(54).

Although the area can be used for year-round agricultural
production (55), Gremliza's study of the Temperature-Humidity
Index (THI) (56) in 58 Dez Pilot area villages shows that the
peasants suffer physically from the summer heat and this,
in turn, reduces their working capacity and economic earnings
(57). Gremliza also points out that during 115 days of extreme
discomfort, "working capacity as well as ability will be reduced
by 50 per cent"(58) – a loss of 15,160 working hours per day
or a total of 1,743,400 working hours, equivalent to 26,150,000
rials ($373,570) at a rate of 15 rials ($0.21) per hour for
a male farming population of 6,064 working five hours per
day.   In the absence of appropriate means of combating summer
heat (59) Dezfulli peasant farmers cannot be totally blamed for

TABLE 3

Monthly average air temperatures recorded in Dez Project area
(degrees centigrade)

Station	Dezful: 32°24'N, 48°23'E 143 m above sea level 1951 - 1967			Safiabad [c] 1962 - 1966			Haft Tappeh: 32°04'N, 48°21'E [d] 80 m above sea level 1959 - 1971		
Month	Min.1951-67 [a]	Max.1951-67 [a]	Mean 1951-54 [b]	Min.	Max.	Mean	Min.	Max.	Mean
January	7.7	19.2	13.6	4.4	18.0	11.2	5.1	18.0	11.6
February	9.2	21.2	14.6	6.4	20.7	13.6	6.2	19.9	13.1
March	11.6	25.4	15.6	8.4	25.0	16.1	9.4	25.0	17.2
April	16.7	31.3	20.8	12.1	29.5	20.5	14.0	30.1	22.1
May	22.6	38.9	28.5	17.8	37.7	27.6	19.3	38.1	28.7
June	27.6	45.5	34.4	21.2	44.2	32.4	21.7	43.6	32.7
July	29.6	46.9	37.9	22.3	45.5	33.8	23.8	45.3	34.6
August	29.8	46.7	38.5	22.4	45.2	33.6	22.9	44.5	33.7
September	25.7	43.1	36.0	18.2	41.5	29.2	18.4	41.0	29.7
October	16.7	36.2	30.5	13.5	35.6	24.2	14.5	34.8	24.7
November	14.3	27.2	22.3	8.9	27.5	17.8	10.3	25.9	18.1
December	9.1	21.2	15.4	4.8	19.8	12.6	5.7	19.8	12.8
	Yearly average			Yearly average			Yearly average		
	Min.	Max.	Mean	Min.	Max.	Mean	Min.	Max	Mean
	18.4	33.5	25.7	13.4	32.5	22.7	14.2	32.2	23.2

Sources:

a. D & R, Dez Irrigation Project, Stage I, New York, USA, D & R, 1968, Table II-3.

b. Veenenbos, J.S., Unified report of the soil & land classification in the Dezful Project, Khuzestan, Iran, Teheran, Iran, Ministry of Agriculture, 1968, p 50.

c. D & R, Dez Irrigation Project, Stage I, Table II-5.

d. Agricultural Research Department, Haft Tappeh sugar cane Project, Khuzestan Water and Power Authority, Climatological Data Summary 1959-1971 (Haft Tappeh, Khuzestan, Iran: Ag. Research Department, Haft Tappeh sugar cane project, 1972) p 5.

their low agricultural productivity, as is clear from Figure 1.

The adverse climatic conditions also influence certain aspects of social life, such as water conflicts during dry years. The social importance of water is clear in non-irrigated villages of rural Dezful where the amount of rainfall is expressed in the yield of crops and, as some peasant informants claim, is reflected in the level of the bride price. In dry years, crop failures leave little or no surplus for sale and thus bride prices fall or marriages are postponed.

Generally, however, the land, water and climate resources favoured the choice of rural Dezful as a development area, particularly since there were already adequate means of communication available, although other aspects of infrastructure and services were lacking (59).

TABLE 4

Monthly average precipitation recorded in Dez Project area
(millimetres)

Station	Dezful [a] 1951 – 1968			Safiabad [b] 1962 – 1966			Haft Tappeh [c] 1959 – 1971		
Month	Min.	Max.	Mean	Min.	Max.	Mean	Min.	Max.	Mean
January	2.0	231.5	64.1	3.0	156.0	63.3	3.1	260.4	75.1
February	2.5	92.0	46.9	15.5	91.5	44.9	12.3	64.6	32.1
March	0.0	94.0	33.8	1.5	39.5	22.6	5.0	60.1	25.0
April	0.0	84.3	29.5	0.0	70.0	30.0	1.8	95.7	27.6
May	0.0	112.5	11.9	0.0	108.5	22.9	0.0	61.9	10.8
June	0.0	0.0	0.0	0.0	0.0	0.0	0.0	2.5	0.2
July	0.0	0.0	0.0	0.0	0.0	0.0	0.0	0.0	0.0
August	0.0	0.0	0.0	0.0	0.0	0.0	0.0	0.3	0.0
September	0.0	0.0	0.0	0.0	0.5	0.1	0.0	0.0	0.0
October	0.0	26.5	5.3	0.0	28.0	5.6	0.0	22.5	5.0
November	0.0	243.0	51.7	12.0	67.5	34.8	0.1	94.3	42.8
December	4.0	166.0	48.5	5.5	87.5	42.4	3.2	78.4	30.2
Yearly total	Min.	Max.	Mean	Min.	Max.	Mean	Min	Max	Mean
	115.5	543.8	291.7	93.5	333.5	266.6	107.8	525.9	249.2

Sources: a. D & R, Dez Irrigation Project, Stage I, New York, USA, D & R, 1968, Table II, p 1.

b: Ibid., Table II, p 3.

c. 'Agricultural Research Department, Haft Tappeh cane sugar project', KWPA Climatological Data Summary 1959–1971, Haft Tappeh, Khuzestan, Iran, 1972.

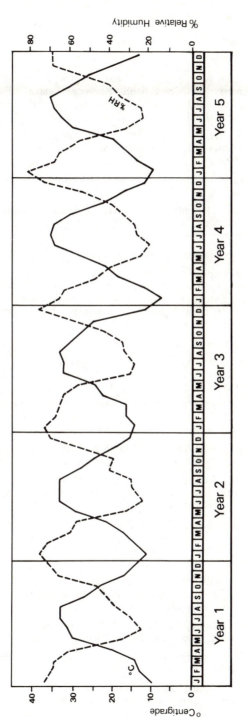

FIGURE 1   Relationship between temperature and relative humidity in the Dez Project area

Chapter Notes

1.   Habibollah Khazaneh and Abulghasem Sadat Darbandi, **Pishbini va Gozashteh Negary Jamiat Shahri va Rustai Iran ta Sal–e 1370**, Tehran, Iran: Statistical Centre of Iran, 1352/1973, p 27.

2.   W.B.Fisher, "Physical Geography", in W.B.Fisher (ed) **The Cambridge History of Iran**, Vol 1, Cambridge UK, CUP 1968, p 3.

3.   Julian Bharier, **Economic Development in Iran 1900–1970**, London UK, OUP 1971, p 131.

4.   Harvey H.Smith **et al.**, **Area Handbook for Iran**, Washington DC, USA, US Government Printing Office 1971 p 379.

5.   **Kayhan Havai**, 3 Esfand 1353 (21st February 1975).

6.   K.S.McLachlan and Narsi Ghorban 'Oil Production, Revenues and Economic Development: Prospects for Iran, Iraq, Saudi Arabia, Kuwait, United Arab Emirates, Oman, Qatar and Bahrain', **Economist Intelligence Unit**, No.18, 1974, p 10.

7.   Bharier, **op. cit.**, p 149.

8.   Mohammed Abdullah, 'Agricultural Extension in Iran: A preliminary Analysis', Tehran, Iran 1973 (unpublished FAO report) p 1.

9.   Hung–Chao Tai, **Land Reform and Politics: A Comparative Analysis**, Berkeley, California USA, University of California Press 1974, p 41.

10. George B.Baldwin, **Planning and Development in Iran**, Maryland USA, The John Hopkins Press, 1967, p 94.

11. Ismail Ajami, 'Land Reform and Modernisation of the Farming Structure in Iran', **Oxford Agrarian Studies**, Vol 2, No 2, 1973, p 1.

12. M.Naeem Butt, 'Development Support Communication Programme for Training and Institutional Services for Land Reform and the Ministry of Co–operation and Rural Affairs', Tehran, UNDP, 1973, (Unpublished) p 4.

13. K.S.McLachlan, 'Land Reform in Iran', in W.B.Fisher (ed), **The Cambridge History of Iran**, Vol 1, **The Land of Iran**, London UK, CUP 1968, p 685.

14. Dana Adams Schmidt, 'The Peasants are Key to Future of Iran', **The New York Times**, 6th August 1961.

15. Lambton, **Persian Land Reform 1962–1966**, Oxford UK, The Clarendon Press 1969, p 5.

16. Reza Moghaddam, 'Land Reform and Rural Development in Iran', **Land Economics**, Vol 48, No 2, 1972, p 160.

17.   James Alban Bill, **The Politics of Iran: Groups, Classes and Modernisation,** Columbus, Ohio USA, Charles E.Merrill Publishing Co. 1972, p 141.

18.   Nasratollah Khatibi, 'Land Reform in Iran and its Role in Rural Development', **Land Reform, Land Settlement and Co–operatives,** No 2, 1972, p 61.

19.   Harvey H.Smith **et al. op. cit.,** p 105.

20.   Ismail Ajami, 'Transformation of the Traditional Agrarian Structure and Development of New Agricultural Production Systems in Iran', A paper presented in the German Foundation for International Development Seminar, Berlin, Germany 1974, p 3.

21.   Ajami, 'Land Reform and Modernisation of the Farming Structure in Iran', **op. cit.,** p 7.

22.   Reza Doroudian, 'Modernisation of Rural Economy in Iran', A paper presented in Aspen Persepolis Symposium, Shiraz, Iran 1975, p 1.

23.   Ajami, 'Transformation of the Traditional Agrarian Structure and Development of New Agricultural Production Systems in Iran', **op. cit.,** p 31.

24.   **Kayhan International,** 2nd February 1974.

25.   Ajami, 'Transformation of the Traditional Agrarian Structure and Development of New Agricultural Production Systems in Iran,' **op. cit.,** p 37.

26.   **Ibid.,** p 42.

27.   **Ibid.,** p 43.

28.   **Kayhan Havai,** 3 Day 1354 (24th December 1975).

29.   The Consultants are: Bookers Agricultural and Technical Services
       Hunting Agricultural Services.

30.   Hassan Shaida, **op. cit.,**

31.   **Kayhan Havai,** 11 Farvardin 2535 (31st March 1976)

32.   Development and Resources Corporation (D & R), **Khuzestan Fertiliser Programme** 1957–1962, Report to the Plan Organization of Iran and the Khuzestan Water and Power Authority, New York, USA, 1962, p 14.

33.   T.M.Oberlander, 'Hydrogeography', in W.B.Fisher (ed) **The Cambridge History of Iran,** Vol 1, **The Land of Iran,** London UK, CUP 1968, p 275.

34.   D & R, **The Unified Development of the Natural Resources of the Khuzestan Region,** New York USA, D & R 1959, p 3.

35.   FAO, **Report to the Government of Iran on the Development of Land and Water Resources in Khuzestan,** Expanded Technical Assistance Programme, FAO Report No 553, Rome, Italy, FAO 1956, p 6.

36. Ibid., p 29.

37. D & R, **The Unified Development of the Natural Resources of the Khuzestan Region,** op. cit., p 29.

38. George N. Curzon, **Persia and the Persian Question,** Vol 2, London UK, Frank Cass & Co. Ltd., 1966 p 364.

39. McLachlan and Ghorban, **op. cit.,** p 10.

40. D & R, **The Unified Development of the Natural Resources of the Khuzestan Region,** op. cit., p 3.

41. The Zagros Mountains are also called the Luristan and Bakhtiari Mountains – being the traditional habitat of these nomadic tribes.

42. This ridge is an arbitrary landmark which separates the Upper Khuzestan Plains (including Dez or the Dezful Plains) from the lower plains.

43. Nederlandsche Heidemaatschappij, 'Report on the Dez Irrigation Project Supplement No 1', June 1959, (unpublished) p IV-4 (Heidemy).

44. D & R, **Dez Irrigation Project, Stage 1, Feasibility Report Supplement,** New York USA, D & R 1968, p II-10

45. **Ibid.** p 1-6.

46. Robert M. Adams, 'Agriculture and Urban Life in Early South Western Iran', **Science,** Vol 136, No 3511, 1962, p 106.

47. Ibid.,

48. Frank Hole, Kent V. Flannery and James A. Neely, **Pre-History and Human Ecology of the Dez Luran Plain, an Early Village Sequence from Khuzestan, Iran,** Ann Arbor, Michigan USA, University of Michigan 1969 p 12

49. D & R, **Dez Irrigation Project Stage I, Feasibility Report Supplement,** op. cit., p II-10.

50. FAO, **op. cit.,** p 73.

51. Ibid., p 80.

52. The classification by the FAO is in six classes and involves consideration of soil chemistry, physical features and drainage.

53. FAO. op. cit., p 44.

54. Veenenbos J.S., **Unified Report of the Soil and Land Classification in the Dezful Project, Khuzestan, Iran,** Tehran Iran, Ministry of Agriculture Soil Institute 1968, p 36.

55. D & R, **Dez Irrigation Project Stage II Feasibility,** New York USA, D & R 1968, p 2.

56. Calculated   from   the   linear   equation   developed   by
     J.F.Rosen:
                 $THI = Td - (0.55 -. 0.55 \frac{R.H.}{100} \times (Td - 58)$
     Td = dry-bulb air temperature in °F, R.H = relative
                                                humidity in, %

57. F.G.L. Gremliza, **Selected Ecological Facts on Health
     in the Dez Pilot Irrigation Area,** New York USA, D & R
     1967.

58. Ibid., p 5.

59. By 1966, only ten out of 58 villages in the Dez Pilot
     Project area had been supplied with electricity –
     Ibid., p 6.

PLATE 2   Construction of irrigation works downstream of Dez dam

2 DEVELOPMENT PLANS IN KHUZESTAN

2.1 Introduction

Almost immediately after World War II steps were taken, "for the development of the resources of the country and towards industrialization " (1). Iran's first long-range national development plan, drawn up in 1948, was followed by four other plans. The 1949/1956 and 1956/1962 plans stressed development of infrastructure while the 1962/1968 and 1968/1973 plans emphasised, "industrialization and assumed a considerable rise in government's share of industrial and mining operations" (2). The Fifth Development Plan (1973/1978) paid more attention to the development of agriculture and the expansion of social services and public welfare. 60 to 80 per cent of the national oil revenues ($215 million in 1963/64, $885 million in 1970/71 and $2,470 million in 1973/74 (3)) has been allocated for plan financing.

In 1947 a semi-autonomous government agency – called the Plan Organization – was established to administer the first Seven Year Development Plan (4). Since 1968 the functions of the agency have been expanded and currently it is entrusted with all development planning and national budgeting, and is now called the Plan and Budget Organization. The Agency's first major regional task was to plan the development of natural resources in Khuzestan.

Originally, Iran had asked the FAO to assist in investigating the land and water in Khuzestan and in 1952 a FAO irrigation team went to Iran, "to give technical assistance with a comprehensive study concerning the development of land and water resources of the Karkheh river basin" (5). The FAO team realized very early on that the whole river basin, rather than just the small Karkheh region needed to be considered. The preliminary study was followed by a soil fertility investigation which became the basis of the fertilizer project, itself part of the unified development programme for Khuzestan (6).

The FAO study was not followed up. Future comprehensive planning was particularly influenced by the Shah's inspection

FIGURE 2

The Tennessee Valley Authority Organization Chart, 1945

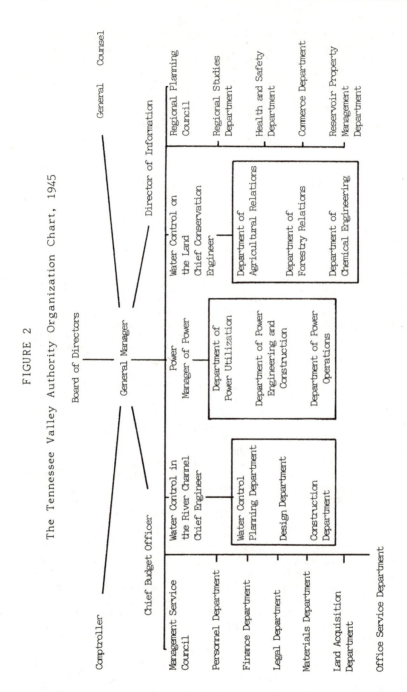

Source: Julian Huxley, **TVA: Adventure in Planning,** London UK, Readers Union/ The Architectural Press, 1945, p. 11.

of the Tennessee Valley Authority (TVA) during his two
month visit in 1954 and 1955 to the United States,(7) where
he learnt that similar development was possible in the
Khuzestan region.   The Shah's interest was matched by
that of Abol Hassan Ebtehaj, then Managing Director of
Iran's Plan Organization, who discussed the prospect for
development in Khuzestan with David E. Lilienthal in September
1955.   Lilienthal, who had been Chairman of the TVA from
1939 to 1945 and one of the original directors of the project,
together with Gordon R. Clapp who had also been Chairman
of the TVA from 1946 until 1954, had recently created a consul-
ting firm - The Development and Resources Corporation of New
York (D & R) - which was to provide planning and administrative services for resource development in foreign countries.
During February and March 1956 Lilienthal and Clapp toured
Khuzestan at official invitation and then presented their preliminary proposals for its overall development along the lines
of the TVA projects.   Their proposals were, "received with
intense excitement, and we were asked to accept responsibility
for the engineering studies that we said were necessary for
providing the operating organization as it gets beyond the
study stage"(8).
On 14th March 1956 the first agreement between the Plan
Organization and the D & R was signed(9) and preparations
for the preliminary survey and the implementation of some
projects began.   The D & R advice was heavily based on
the TVA experience of its leading members and the organization has been chief adviser to the Plan Organization and, on
occasion, has been entrusted with the implementation of its
own proposals.   Essential to its work was the original experience of the TVA.

2.2   The Tennessee Valley Authority

In May 1933 the United States Congress established a
federal agency to handle the overall development of the natural
resources of the Tennessee Valley region(10). President Roosevelt
who strongly supported this early example of 'New Deal'
politics, called the new Organization 'The Tennessee Valley
Authority' (TVA).
The valley which constituted the drainage basin of the
Tennessee River and its tributaries covered an area of about
64,900 square kilometres, nearly four-fifths the size of England
(11). The population, which in 1930 was slightly over 2,800,000,
was made up of large families and fertility was high.   Ten
per cent of it was black although not uniformly distributed
through the rest of the population.
The climate was mild, the rainfall abundant (annual average about 130 cm) (12) and the natural resources - including
coal and water   -   were plentiful.   Yet, "the area was
characterized by backwardness and sub-normal standards ...
The general pattern was that of an exploitative and an
exploited community.   The soil had been mined not cultivated
..... the forest had been wantonly slaughtered ..... resources

FIGURE 3

Organization Chart of the Khuzestan Development Service (KDS)
Period I, 1957-60, D & R entrusted with the execution of the Khuzestan Development Projects

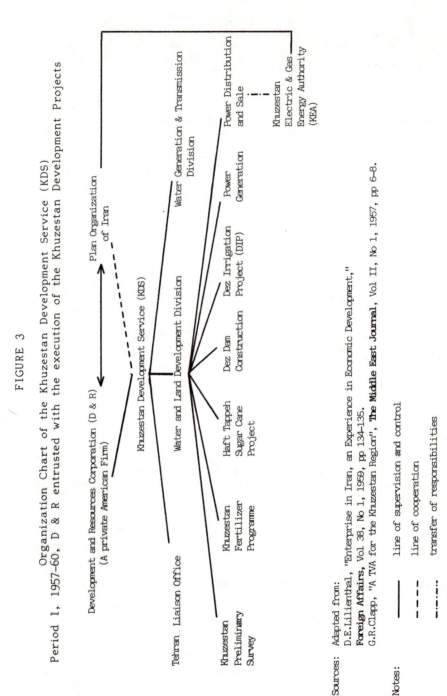

Sources: Adapted from:
D.E.Lilienthal, "Enterprise in Iran, an Experience in Economic Development,"
Foreign Affairs, Vol 38, No 1, 1959, pp 134-135.
G.R.Clapp, "A TVA for the Khuzestan Region", **The Middle East Journal,** Vol II, No 1, 1957, pp 6-8.

Notes: —————   line of supervision and control

                – – – –   line of cooperation

                –·–·–·–   transfer of responsibilities

were shipped out with little margin to the people who did the work and were brought back in fabricated form"(13).

There were most probably three mutually reinforcing reasons for singling out the Tennessee Valley for a massive development programme. Firstly the uncompleted nitrate plants and Wilson Dam at Muscle Shoals, Alabama, built by the US government during World War I, had remained idle for many years and could be used for fertilizer production. Secondly proper control of the Tennessee River was crucial for the prevention of disastrous floods on the lower Mississippi. Thirdly the flood control, "could be readily tied up not only with improved navigation but with profitable generation of electric power",(14) to supply this backward region with cheap electricity.

Government investment in the Muscle Shoals plants and the Wilson dam up to 1918 had been just over $100 million and during the postwar years there was considerable congressional debate over what to do with the plants and the dam – whether they should be utilized by the private or the public sector. The Ford Motor Company and the American Cyanamide Company had shown interest in buying the plants and dam for the large-scale production of mixed fertilizer, but the main argument against the two companies was the suspicion that they, "were in reality primarily interested in the available power and would not give adequate attention to the fertilizer programme"(15). The creation of the TVA in 1933 gave the Federal Government responsibility for the development of resources in the Tennessee Valley and the operation of the Muscle Shoals plants and Wilson Dam.

The TVA activities, in addition to fertilizer manufacturing, have included flood control, navigation and power production, as well as projects relating to agriculture, recreation, conservation, health and education (16). The wide range of the TVA projects underlines the interconnection between water, land and man – the unified approach.

The agricultural programmes were mainly directed towards changing the dominant cropping pattern of the valley from clean-tilled crops, such as cotton and corn, to grass and legume forage crops, thus encouraging the use of phosphoric fertilizer and promoting soil conservation. They were mostly carried out with the cooperation of the state extension services in the region (17) by means of test-demonstration programmes where a selected farm would act as a testbed for surrounding farmers,a supervisory committee of the farmers and the County Agent deciding on planting patterns and the TVA supplying expert help and supervision in the person of the Agent, together with fertilizer. Between 1934 and 1945 over 42,000 farms – many outside the valley – were included in the test-demonstration scheme and some 800,000 farmers were involved (18).

Administratively, the jurisdiction of the TVA, acting as an autonomous body (despite Congressional funding of $669,469,270 from 1934 to 1943), cut across the lines of several federal, state and local bureaux and departments. "A single agency, instead of half a dozen, was to design and build

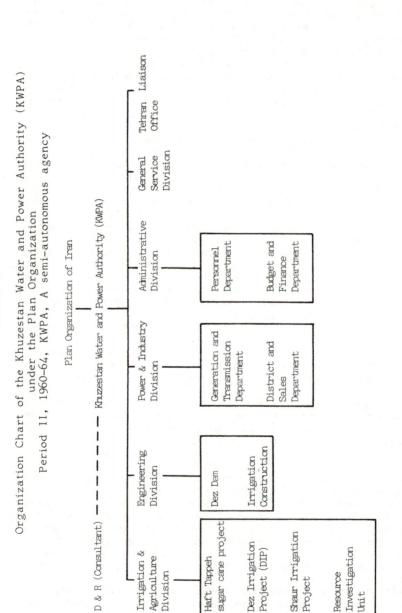

FIGURE 4

Organization Chart of the Khuzestan Water and Power Authority (KWPA)
under the Plan Organization
Period II, 1960-64, KWPA, A semi-autonomous agency

Plan Organization of Iran

Khuzestan Water and Power Authority (KWPA)

D & R (Consultant)

Irrigation & Agriculture Division

Engineering Division

Power & Industry Division

Administrative Division

General Service Division

Tehran Liaison Office

Haft Tappeh sugar cane project

Dez Irrigation Project (DIP)

Shaur Irrigation Project

Resource Investigation Unit

Dez Dam

Irrigation Construction

Generation and Transmission Department

District and Sales Department

Personnel Department

Budget and Finance Department

Source: Field studies

the dams, buy the land, construct transmission lines and
market the power the river produced. One agency was to
envision in its entirety the potentialities of the whole river
system (19).

The general policies and decisions of the TVA were determined by a three-man Board of Directors who were selected
by the President with the consent of the Senate. The Board's
responsibilities are shown schematically in Figure 2, which
shows that the General Counsel and the Controller were
directly responsible to the Board, the former dealing with
legal materials and the latter handling financial responsibilities. The General Manager was the chief executive, but
still subservient to the policies and decisions of the Board.
Under him were five divisions, each consisting of several
departments.

In planning for the development of the Tennessee Valley,
the TVA recognized the importance of 'inter-relationship' –
the unity of land, water and resources. They emphasised
the human dimension in regional development and the application of the unified approach – the TVA ideal – has been taken
into account by many policy-makers in developing natural
resources and in planning socio-economic improvements.
However, as Lilienthal points out, "those who come to have
confidence in the TVA idea and seek to have it put into effect
in their own region should be warned that the task is one
of adaptation and not copying or imitation"(20). Judging from
the outcome of some of the projects carried out in the
Khuzestan region under Lilienthal's supervision, it seems
that not enough attention was always paid to such an
important warning.

2.3 The Administrative Organization of the Khuzestan Development Projects

The regional administrative organization set up in Khuzestan for the implementation of development projects seems to
have been influenced by the general administrative policies
of the TVA.

In 1956 the D & R proposal for Khuzestan regional development was basically for a series of dams to control the five
major rivers, making their water available for irrigation,
power, flood control and navigation (21). The plans involved
the construction of 14 dams – three on the Karkheh, two on
the Dez, seven on the Karun, one on the Marun (tributary
to the Jarrahi), one on the Zoreh (tributary to the Hindijan)
(22) – the production of 6,600 megawatts of electric power and
the introduction of modern (regulated) irrigation on one
million hectares of land in the Khuzestan Plains(23). It was
a plan that would take many years to complete. In 1957
the D & R chose several projects for accelerated development
– the Dez Multi-Purpose Project, involving the construction
of a dam and hydro-electric plant, and the development of
a new irrigation scheme, the Khuzestan Fertilizer Programme,
the sugar cane project at Haft Tappeh, the Electric Power

FIGURE 5

Organization Chart of the Khuzestan Water and Power Authority (KWPA)
under the Ministry of Water and Power
Period III, 1964-74, Transfer of the KWPA to the new Water and Power Ministry

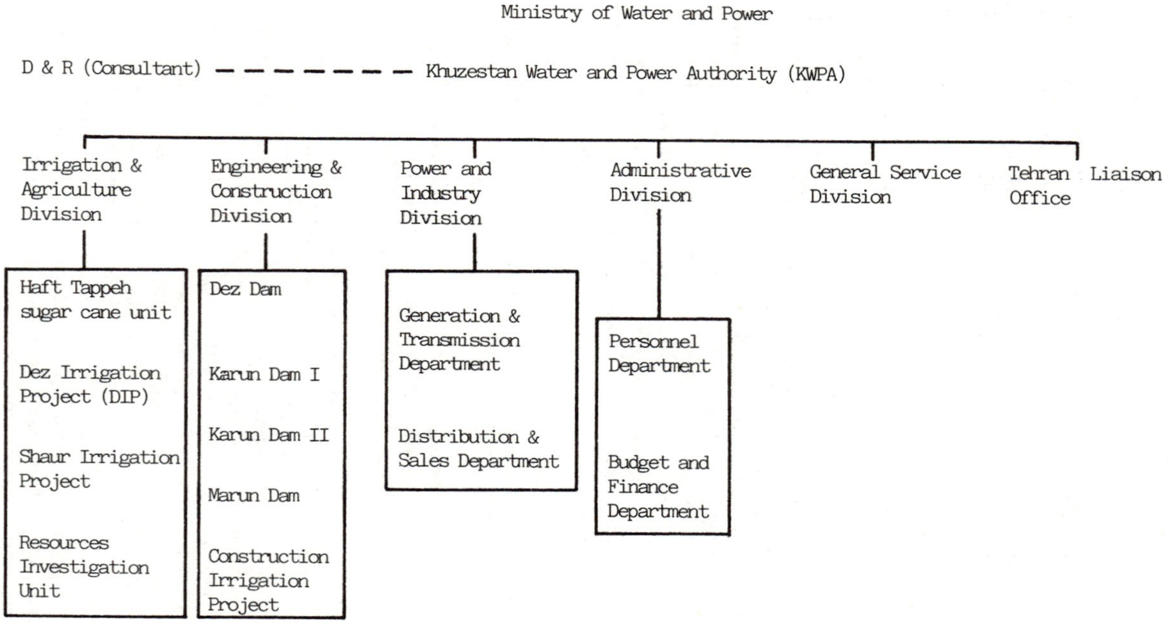

Ministry of Water and Power

D & R (Consultant) — — — — — Khuzestan Water and Power Authority (KWPA)

Irrigation & Agriculture Division	Engineering & Construction Division	Power and Industry Division	Administrative Division	General Service Division	Tehran Liaison Office
Haft Tappeh sugar cane unit	Dez Dam	Generation & Transmission Department	Personnel Department		
Dez Irrigation Project (DIP)	Karun Dam I				
Shaur Irrigation Project	Karun Dam II	Distribution & Sales Department	Budget and Finance Department		
Resources Investigation Unit	Marun Dam				
	Construction Irrigation Project				

Source: Adapted from:
        Development and Resources Corporation (D & R), Dez Irrigation Project, (New York, NY, USA, D & R, 1967), p VI-3.

Development Scheme and the Polyvinylchloride Plastic Plant at Ahwaz. Except for the latter, these projects were authorised and have, in many cases, been completed.
The Khuzestan Development Service (KDS) was first set up by the D & R in 1957 to administer the implementation of the four projects and additional ones in the future. Its structure and functions have changed several times and four different periods can be identified:

Period I   - 1957-60, the D & R was contracted to execute all projects;

Period II   - 1960-64,the Khuzestan Water and Power Authority (KWPA) was created as a semi-independent organization under the Plan Organization;

Period III - 1967-74, the KWPA became part of the new Ministry of Water and Power;

Period IV   - post-1974, the Ministry of Agriculture takes over the KWPA's agricultural functions.

The details of the associated organizational structures are shown in Figures 3 to 6. The significant feature is the way in which the D & R has gradually transferred executive responsibility to the KWPA, although it has retained its consultant capacity after 1960, once the initial planning and construction had been completed usually through foreign contractors. The absorption of the KWPA into the Ministries has not substantially changed its responsibilities or organization, despite the loss of autonomy. Four of the projects that the original KDS was created to administer (in conjunction with the D & R) have now been completed and are reviewed in the rest of this chapter.

2.4   The Khuzestan Fertilizer Programme

In 1956, the Plan Organization entrusted the FAO Khuzestan soil fertility project, which had been started in 1952, to the D & R. In consequence the KDS cooperated with the FAO in a fertilizer test and demonstration programme from 1956 to 1961 (24).The programme was, "to begin to find out by research, test plots and practical farm-field demonstration and experience in the Khuzestan region, workable and economic ways to use chemical fertilizers to increase food and fibre production with benefit to the farmers, the lands and the consumers" (25).
The FAO-KDS team covered 407 villages throughout the Khuzestan region, setting up 54,000 test plots with Government funds,mainly in irrigated areas which could be improved. Most of these test plots were in the Dez Project area, involving 57 villages (almost 100 per cent) in the Pilot area and 72 villages (nearly 65 per cent) in other parts of the Project area (26). The team itself, at the height of its activities in January 1959 consisted of seven American or European soil and fertility experts, 31 Iranian college graduates, each responsible for fertilizer trials in a specific area, and

FIGURE 6

Organization Chart of the Khuzestan Water and Power Authority (KWPA)
Period IV since 1974, Transfer of the Agricultural Responsibility of KWPA
to the Ministry of Agriculture and Natural Resources

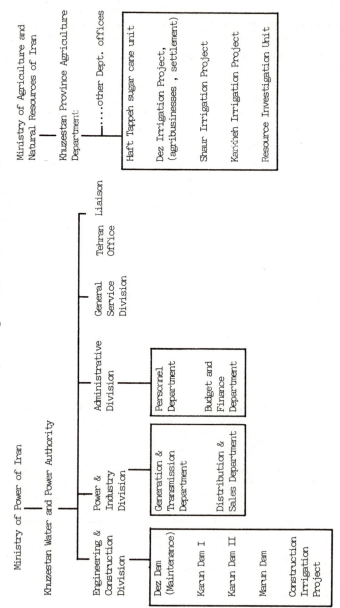

Source: Field studies

77 villagers, each serving as an assistant.
The activities of the team have caused a considerable
increase in fertilizer use. The D & R claims that when the
Fertilizer Programme began in 1958, "hardly a single bag
of fertilizer was used in this vast region" (27) but from 1958
to 1961, "the project called for 9,000 tons of fertilizer"(28).
The fertilizer programmes in Khuzestan and elsewhere in Iran
have led to a greater domestic demand now satisfied by
several recently constructed industrial complexes.

2.5 The cane sugar project at Haft Tappeh

For centuries Khuzestan was known as the land of sugar
cane(29) but by the end of the nineteenth century, or perhaps
two or three centuries earlier, cane cultivation had ceased
and Iran was short of sugar. From 1934 the Ministry of
Agriculture sponsored sugar cane experiments in different
areas of the Khuzestan plains, such as Hamidiyyeh and Ahu-
Dasht, south of the Haft Tappeh, but the Second World War
interrupted the project. During the post-war years, experiments continued in 25 locations throughout the plains under
the supervision of a Japanese team. The area between
Andimeshk and Ahu-Dasht was singled out as a suitable
location for a cane plantation(30).
In 1957 the Plan Organization authorised the re-establish-
ment of a sugar cane plantation in the Dez Irrigation Project
(DIP) area. Some 12,000 hectares around Haft Tappeh were
purchased by the Government from Sheikh Khalf Heidar al-
Kasseir and other landlords. After nearly four years of
preparation in the plantation, sugar mill and refinery,
supervised by the Hawaiian Agronomics Company (under a
sub-contract from the D & R), the first commercial harvest
took place in 1961/62. The plantation was expanded to the
north by 5,000 hectares in 1968/71 and to the south by 7,000
hectares in 1971/74. Currently, of the total 24,000 hectares
in the plantation, cultivable land comprises 11,193 hectares,
of which nearly 10,000 hectares are actually cultivated.
The procedures used in the original 1957 land purchases
are unknown, but a D & R report on the expansion of the
plantation from 1968 to 1974 gives some details(31). A three-
man commission from the Land Registration Department app-
raised the land at $67 per hectare to the landowner and $10
to the farmer for planting rights - a total cost to KWPA of
$77. The farmers who sold land are also guaranteed employ-
ment in the plantation. In fact, in 1974, freehold farm land
in the Dezful area was fetching between $430 and $700 per
hectare.
The mill and refinery have also been enlarged. The mill
has increased production from an original 3,000 tons per day
to 12,000 tons per day in 1974. Refined sugar output is
expected to reach 100,000 tons per year(32). Detailed production
figures are given in Table 5. Two by-products are produced
as well: 30,000 tons annually of molasses and some 2,390
tons daily of bagasse - a fibrous residue(33). Molasses has

TABLE 5

Haft Tappeh Cane Sugar Production

Harvesting & Processing Season	Area, Ha			Production Cane Sugar		Production Refined Sugar tons	Gross[d] Income '000 rials	Operation[e] Costs '000 rials	Net Income '000 rials	Sugar Cost/ton rials
	Total Net	Planted & Harvested	Fallowed	Total '000 tons	Yield tons/ha					
1961-62 (a)	2,314			184	79.4	12,161				
1967-68 (b)	5,589	4,183	1,406	433	103.5	42,423	587,462	492,012	195,450	11,598
1973-74 (c)	9,984	8,793	1,191	1,055	120.0	85,000	1,551,250	1,046,286	504,964	12,309

Sources: (a) Haft Tappeh Cane Sugar Project of Khuzestan Water and Power, Pishraft (Ahwaz, Iran: KWPA, 1952), pp 8-9.
(b) "Amar va Arqam Qasmat Nishekar Haft Tappeh" (Statistics and figures of the Haft Tappeh cane sugar project), 1974, Unpublished report, p 14.
(c) Haft Tappeh Field Record, 1974, Unpublished Data

Notes: (d) Includes income from the factory's two by-products: molasses and bagasse
(e) The cost probably does not include the new 1974 Dez Project water charges of 0.2 rials per litre per second (the water requirement for sugar cane in Haft Tappeh is high. The crop needs to be irrigated 23-26 times annually and each time 1100-1200 cubic metres of water is needed). Quoted in "Amar va Arqam Qasmat Nishekar Haft Tappeh" 1974, Unpublished report, p 12.

been exported while up to 1970 the bagasse was used as a
fuel for steam generators.   In December 1970, the Pars Paper
Company (originally a private concern) opened a factory at
Haft Tappeh and now buys up the bagasse - some 1,600 tons
a day in 1973/74(34). This paper factory is the first in Iran
to use cane fibre and its original annual output of 30,000
tons has now reached 110,000 tons (35) of paper and tissue.
   In the 1973-74 period over 3,000 men (mostly from Dezful
see Table 6) were permanently employed at the plantation
and its associated factories.   From September to April each
year, 3,000 temporary workers were taken on for the cane
harvest. About half of them came from rural areas of Luristan
where there is little agricultural activity during the severe
winter.   These workers, physically stronger than the locals,
settled in the Project Labour Centre, sharing the 200 housing
units with local workers - usually four or five to a room.
The work was contracted to teams of 50 to 60 men of equal
ability.   Team organization was spontaneous and membership
could be changed by individual or group decision if members
were felt not to take an appropriate share in the work.
The team appointed a leader, **sohani** ,who organized the team
and ensured that team knives were sharp, and a waterman,
saqa ,who supplied the team with cold drinking water.
   The amount harvested by each group was recorded daily
and each group member, including the **sohani** and the **saqa**,
was paid every 15 days according to the formula:

$$P = T(26 + T)$$

where P is the payment in rials, T is the average amount
of harvest per head (tonnage) and 26 is a fixed coefficient.
   In 1973 and 1974 the overall average daily harvest was
seven tons and the minimum wage was 88 rials per day, the
rate being set at 33 rials per ton for harvests above 7 tons
per day(36). This provided the average worker with 231 rials
per day, 50 to 100 rials higher than the average wage paid
to workers in the nearby agribusinesses, but still considerably lower than the average Haft Tappeh staff salary in 1974
of 1,428 rials per day (37).
   The sugar cane project offered supplementary benefits to
its permanent employees, such as medical insurance and
housing facilities.   A 430-unit 'plantation village' had been
developed for field workers near the factory and 330 staff
housing units were sited seven kilometres away from the
village.   In addition, Shahrak Shush, 1,200 housing units
with some urban amenities, was being built for field workers
(38).
   Since 1965 workers have also been participating in factory
profits (39) which have provided each worker with an additional
income of between 1.5 and 7.8 per cent of an annual average
salary (estimated to correspond to a daily wage of 330 rials).
The details are given in Table 7.   Since 1974 stock in the
Sugar Mill has been sold to the public - priority being given
to Mill employees - and only one per cent has been retained
in State hands to justify its management function (40).

TABLE 6

Distribution of Haft Tappeh Employees, 1973 – 74

Place of Origin Type of employment	Dezful Area		Shushtar Area		Ahwaz Area		Other areas of Khuzestan		Other Provinces		Total	
	No	%	No	%	No	%	No	%	No	%	No	%
Plantation & Refinery (a)												
Staff (c) (Technical & Administrative)	46	11.5	21	5.3	65	16.5	160	40.5	103	26.1	395	100.0
Non-Staff (Semi and non-skilled)	1,081	51.4	173	8.2	266	12.6	342	16.3	242	11.5	2,104	100.0
Total	1,127	45.1	194	7.8	331	13.2	502	20.1	345	13.8	2,499	100.0
Pars Paper Co. (b)												
Staff (d) (Technical & Administrative)											70	100.0
Non-Staff (e) (Semi and non-skilled)											600	100.0
Total											670	100.0
Grand Total											3,169	

Source: (a) Haft Tappeh Cane Sugar Project, Industrial Relations Office, "Gozaresh Niroii Ensani" (Manpower Report), 1352/1973–74, Unpublished Report, pp 35 – 36.
(b) Pars Paper Company, Personnel Office, Emloyment Record, 1952/1973–74, Unofficial Report.

Notes: (c) Excluding seven foreign consultants.
(d) Excluding 17 foreign consultants and administrators.
(e) An estimated 360 (60%) workers from the Dezful area and the remaining 240 are mainly from Ahwaz, Masdjid-

The sugar cane plantation project at Haft Tappeh has provided Iran with her first successful experience in vertically integrated agro-industry. Despite doubts originally about the plantation's viability, .the generally improved efficiency of the operation, coupled with the increase in the world price for sugar, has made Haft Tappeh production economical. A recent study of state investment in the Haft Tappeh indicates that although investment is high, at 2,200 million rials, in a high-cost, low-profit project, "there have been considerable benefits to Iran's economy, including annual savings of 220 million rials in foreign currency" (41). Iran planned to be self-sufficient in sugar and this led the government to sponsor the Karun sugar cane project in northern Khuzestan, downstream of the new Karun Dam, to the north of Masjed-e Suliman.

TABLE 7

The Distribution of the Haft Tapeh Profits amongst the Non-Staff Workers, 1965 - 73.

Year (21 March- 20 March)	Number of Workers Benefited	Amount of Profit Distributed '000 rials	Average Benefit Rials
1965-66	1,245	3,176	2,551
1966-67	1,306	3,370	2,580
1967-68	1,339	3,594	2,684
1968-69	1,390	3,770	2,712
1969-70	1,596	5,311	3,327
1970-71	2.176	7,543	3,466
1971-72	2,551	10,559	4,139
1972-73	2,885	11,603	4,021

Source: "Amar va Arqam Qasmat Nishekar Haft Tappeh", KWPA 1974, Unpublished, p 8.

2.6   The Electricity Development Programme

Prior to 1960 the electrical supplies for Khuzestan's major urban areas (except for the oil refinery city of Abadan) were generated by a few small power stations which were usually privately owned. The average energy consumption **per capita** was very low as the following figures indicate:

Estimated Energy Consumption of Khuzestan, Iran and some other areas, 1958 and 1973

	1958			1973		
	a	b		c	d	
Area	Population	Electric Production	Per Capita Consumption	Population	Electric Production	Per Capita Consumption
	('000)	(Millions) k Wh	k Wh	('000)	(Millions) k Wh	k Wh
World	2,852,000	1,908,400	669	3,860,000	6,042,000	1,565
Asia	1,592,000	154,200	97	2,204,000	807,700	366
Iran	19,677	720	37	31,298	12,093	386
Khuzestan Region e	(2,500)	(150)	(60)			
Khuzestan Province f				(2,005)	(1,049)	(523)
Egypt	24,781	1,905	77	35,619	8,104	228
Sudan	11,037	60	6	16,901	259	15
Turkey	25,932	2,304	89	37,933	12,289	324
Greece	8,173	1,857	227	8,972	14,817	1,651
Mexico	32,348	9,098	281	54,303	38,084	683

Sources: a Statistical Office, Department of Economic and Social Affairs,
United Nations, **Statistical Year Book 1959,** 11th issue,
(New York, NY USA: United Nations), pp 21 – 39.

b Statistical Office, Department of Economic and Social Affairs,
United Nations, **Statistical Year Book 1961,** 13th issue
(New York, NY USA: United Nations), pp 298 – 306.

c Statistical Office, Department of Economic and Social Affairs,
United Nations, **Statistical Year Book 1974,** 26th issue
(New York, NY USA: United Nations), pp 67 – 73.

d **Ibid.,** pp 372 – 381.

e D & R, **The Unified Development of Natural Resources of the
Khuzestan Region,** New York USA, D & R 1959, p 4.

f "Etalaat Mokhtasari be Manzore Sherakht–Behtar Khuzestan"
(Brief information for better recognition of Khuzestan)
Tahqiqat–e Eqtesadi (Persian ed.) Nos 29 and 30,
1351/1972, p 101.

The D & R proposed to remedy this by a programme calling
for a series of hydro-electric generating stations located at
the 14 proposed dams to supply 6.6 million KWH per annum,
together with new thermo-electric stations using natural gas
and petroleum to generate 3.1 million KWH per annum(42) ,
all linked to urban centres and neighbouring regions by a
power transmission system.
    As a first step, a high-voltage line – the fore-runner of
a transmission system that now extends to Tehran – was
opened between Ahwaz and the Abadan Oil Company generating
plant. Supply from Abadan rose from 4,000 KWH in 1959 to
20,000 KWH in 1963, when the Dez Dam power plant opened
(43). The first two units at Dez Dam produced 130,000 KWH
and output will reach 520,000 KWH once all eight generating
units are in operation. The Dez Dam plant supplies Khuzestan
and surplus power is now transferred to Tehran – 750 km
away.
    The new dam on the Karun river, north of Masjed-e Suliman,
built by a French Company, and two other dams still being
constructed, one on the Karun river and the other on the
Marun will generate over 800,000 KWH per annum(44), bringing
the total hydro-electricity produced in the Khuzestan region
to over 1.3 million KWH per annum. A gas fuelled steam
generating plant, near the village of Zargan eight kilometres
from Ahwaz on the Ramin – Masjed-e Suliman road was completed in 1977 but has not yet achieved full operation. A
second generating plant is being built by a Russian company
near to the village of Waice, 20 kilometres outside Ahwaz,
and is now nearly complete.

2.7 The Dez Irrigation Project

    The Dez Irrigation Project (DIP) has developed in three
stages – the Pilot stage which started in 1960, Stage I which
began in 1969 and Stage II commencing in 1971 – and has
been accompanied by the development of agricultural and
rural services. The original D & R plan for Khuzestan
involved using the River Dez to generate power and irrigate
a large land area. The plan was based on the construction
of a high dam in a canyon 25 kilometres north east of Dezful
which was to create a 6,300 hectare reservoir with a total
capacity of 3.4 billion cubic metres, an average discharge
of 220 cubic metres per second (CMS) (45) and a minimum discharge of 174 CMS – sufficient to irrigate a minimum of
125,000 hectares (a figure that was later reduced to 110,000
hectares on the basis of the minimum flow necessary for effective irrigation being increased to two litres per second during
summer rather than the one litre per second originally
proposed).
    In 1957 some 170,000 gross hectares were designated for
use in a regulated irrigation system to be known as the Dez
Irrigation Project, and the Nederlandsche Heidemaatschappij
(Heidemy) – a Dutch land development firm under contract

to the D & R, began a detailed engineering survey in the
DIP area. Studies revealed that approximately 125,000 ha
were suitable for irrigated agriculture(46)and Heidemy designed
an irrigation project for the area(47) , which closely corres-
ponded to the D & R's 'original proposal' for the DIP area.

The D & R calculated that the Dez Multi-purpose Plan would
cost about $105.9 million which was to be recovered gradually
by selling electricity and introducing water charges. Public
funds (The Plan Organization) were insufficient for initial
financing so loans were sought from the International Bank
for Reconstruction and Development (IBRD) to cover the foreign
exchange requirements – 35 per cent of total public investment
(48)– for the construction of the Dez Dam, power plants and
irrigation facilities.

Initially, the Bank was not in favour as, "They preferred
small operating pumps for irrigation and a thermo-electric
plant for generating electricity, using the gas which had
been flared to the sky" (49) and did not agree with the D &
R original irrigation proposal, with large-scale regulated
flow(50). However, a team of Bank experts examined the project
during October and November 1958(51) and decided that the
peasants would be able to pay the proposed water charges,
on the basis of the Heidemy report which showed that the
average peasant farmer saved about 2,200 rials annually.
After the situation had been further reviewed in August 1959,
the Bank investigators recommended that the D & R proposal
should be tested on a pilot scale and, if economically viable,
it would then be expanded. As a result, in November 1959,
the Plan Organization presented the IBRD with a revised proposal for a small-scale pilot project.

2.8   The Dez Pilot Proposal (DPIP)

The Dez Pilot Project consisted of about 22,000 gross ha.
(20,000 irrigable hectares) on the east bank of the River
Dez and included 58 villages. It was about one sixth of
the original project with the typical physical and socio-
economic conditions of the larger project area so that any
benefits in the pilot scheme would correspond to those possible
in the larger project (52).

A three-year test period with regulated water systems,
starting in 1963, was expected to be adequate and during
this period, "a new type of water-use agreement with landlords and cultivators , involving payment (750 rials per
hectare base charge from 1963 plus a surcharge of 750 rials
per hectare from 1966 – to raise a maximum of 30 million
rials in 1966) by the operators to the government for water
use" was to be made(53)

Definite indications of economic advance were anticipated
by 1966, although it was, "expected to take ten years ...
to obtain the full transition to modern farming methods"
(54). Productivity per hectare by the end of the trial period
in 1966 was to increase by more than 200 per cent over the
1955/1960 figures (5,500 rials per hectare in 1957 (total:110

million rials) to 17,700 rials per hectare in 1966 (total: 345
million hectares)), reaching more than 300 per cent by 1973
(454 million rials overall in the DPIP area), through a series
of supplementary rural and agricultural services including
the extension and training of farmers(55). A 1961 report was
even more optimistic, anticipating a six-fold increase by 1966
- 711.7 million rials for the DPIP area, at 35,600 rials per
hectare(56).

The Bank accepted the proposal and in February 1960 an
agreement for a $42 million loan was signed.   Construction
of new facilities, including regulated flow delivery, would
be restricted·to the DPIP area for a three-year trial period
and the Bank would only consider expansion of the project
area once the trial period was ended and progress had been
evaluated.   The loan was approved by Iran in May 1960.

By May 1963, the Dez Dam had been completed and the new
irrigation system in the DPIP was finished in 1965.   By the
end of 1966, production targets appeared to have been
attained although the southern part of the regulated water
delivery system had not been completed until summer 1965.
In July 1966 Bank investigators declared that, "the Project
has made very encouraging progress in physical and organization terms.   The increase in production by some two and
a half times is impressive.   KWPA has developed an effective
organization, capable of reaching individual farmers, supplying them with the necessary farm requisites and credit, and
persuading them to adopt improved farming methods"(57) . The
Bank agreed to support further extension of the irrigation
project.

In 1967 the D & R presented plans for irrigation extensions
into the remaining DIP area and asked the Bank for a second
loan.   The Bank required that the irrigation facilities should
be confined to the west bank of the River Dez(58) , so the
D & R modified its plans, restricting them to a 54,000 net
hectare area on the west bank - the DIP Stage I proposals.
These were accepted and in 1969 the Bank offered Iran a
$30 million loan(59).

The Stage II plan for the remaining DIP area - 29,000 ha
on the East Bank - was prepared by D & R in 1971(60) and
was due for completion in 1975.   The total area under regulated water flow by 1973-74 was about 103,000 net hectares.

2.9   Agricultural and Rural Services

Under the terms of the first IBRD loan peasants and landowners were expected to pay for water from their increased
incomes and to aid in this, local cultivators were to be
assisted in establishing land and water rights and in stabi-
lising the peasant land assignment system.   Here the annual
lots, drawn through the traditional tir-o-goreh system, involving lot rotation and thus lack of investment incentive, were
to be stabilised so that there would be an incentive to take
measures to increase productivity.   Modern methods of land
and water use were also to be adopted and other rural

matters, such as education, health and village improvements,
were to be aided.
The pilot project therefore anticipated the establishment
of a field farm, a training centre, an agricultural extension
service - the Village Production Service - a credit unit, an
agricultural equipment service, a marketing assistance
programme and a unit dealing with village health, sanitation
and education. The units that were established were dissol-
ved in 1968, when it was decided to replace peasant farming
with a large-scale agricultural scheme.

(a) The Field Trial Farm, Research Station and Training
     Centre

Project authorities planned to substitute traditional crops
and cultivation methods with new varieties and techniques.
In order to determine comparative adaptability for different
crop varieties and cultural practices, the Project sponsored
local experiments and trials. Between 1958 and 1962, over
80 varieties of new crops were tested in five locations
scattered throughout the Project area at Amalieh Taymoor,
the Haft Tappeh sugar cane plantation, Qaleh no Askar, Qaleh
Sheikh and Kutian(61).
In 1960, Heidemy recommended that these activities be
concentrated in a permanent and centrally located farm where
demonstrations for local producers and training courses for
staff and field workers could also be held(62). A research
station - the Safiabad Agricultural Research Centre, named
after the then Managing Director of the Plan Organization,
Safi Asfia - was established on a 200 hectare site at Kutian
village. Other locations were abandoned. The Safiabad
Centre has undertaken applied research designed to prevent
or correct "serious pathological, cultural, weed, varietal
and chemical problems which may occur in the Dez Irrigation
Project Area"(63).
The training centre was established first at the Haft Tappeh
crop trial farm in February 1961, mainly to prepare personnel
for the new Village Production Service, but in 1962 training
activities were transferred to the new Safiabad Centre. These
terminated when all agricultural and rural services were
stopped in 1969. When the Khuzestan Fertilizer Programme
was discontinued in 1962, the Dez Project employed some of
its trained personnel after giving them a brief orientation
course. A further group of field workers (Village Agents)
was recruited mainly from local areas and trained at the
Safiabad Centre. They were all "to participate in the job
of translating Western know-how into the Iranian language"
(64) - adapting Western agricultural technology to Iranian
conditions and transmitting this knowledge to the peasantry.

(b) The Village Production Service and Associated Programmes

On-site technical assistance to peasants and landowners was first suggested during work on the Khuzestan Fertilizer Programme, and soon after the Pilot Project was approved, organizational activities began for a 'mass application' of proven agricultural ideas and practices(65). A university of California extension agent was contracted to design an extension-type programme for the villages in the DPIP and, during summer 1961, he was in charge of the Haft Tappeh field trial farm. The experience gained there, together with his background experience would, it was felt, ensure that "an effective production service similar to the Netherlands' type"(66) could be organized at least one year before the regulated flow system began.

The resulting programme emphasised multiple practices – simultaneous fertilizer use, improved irrigation and new crop varieties – for the necessary three-fold productivity increase to be obtained by 1966(67). The programme – known as the Village Production Service – had two main functions. First it set up plots on peasant farms to demonstrate the benefits of improved practices. Second it organized peasant production, providing access to agricultural credit and the hire of farm equipment. The Agricultural Credit Unit and the Agricultural Equipment Service were thus closely associated with the programme.

The Credit Unit, created in 1962/63, offered three types of credit: long-term for land purchase or improvement, intermediate for machinery purchase and short-term for mechanized production. The Equipment Service was formed in 1962 to replace "a moderate amount" of hand farming methods by mechanized techniques (68) so that the soil could be properly prepared for the introduction of new crops and particularly so that the sowing period for winter crops could be reduced. These crops – wheat and barley – must be sown in Dezful during a 30-day period for maximum yield to be obtained.

(c) Other Rural Services

From the start, the KDS assumed responsibility for government services essential to the Project(69) – roads, education, health and sanitation. Since then a 419 kilometre all-weather road system has been developed for the project (70), providing "access for farm operation, public thoroughfare and project operation and maintenance activities" (71) and allowing general access to the Tomb of Daniel, an important local pilgrimage centre. In 1962 the Project also initiated a ferry service linking the Pilot area with the Haft Tappeh sugar cane plantation.

In 1960, the KDS financed a study of Khuzestan's educational needs which, together with KDS staff reports, stressed the need for community schools where adult farmers could get elementary education and younger people could obtain

technical instruction. Based on this study the KDS and the
Ministry of Education constructed 29 schools in the DPIP
between 1960 and 1966(72). However, as elsewhere in rural
Iran, these concentrate purely on providing formal instruction
for youth and not on technical education for adults.

Health and sanitation programmes began in the DPIP in
1959 with a survey. Following the survey, Gremliza,a German
physician with over ten years experience of rural Khuzestan,
supervised a diagnostic and preventative medical programme
in all 58 villages. From 1960 to 1966 he operated a Mobile
Health Unit there (73). Efforts were made to drain and fill in
stagnant pools, remove dung heaps, gravel streets, supply
purified water and relocate livestock away from living quarters. Attempts were also made to control some of the endemic
diseases of the area, such as schistosomaiasis and malaria.
These measures were intended to double indigenous work
capacity (74).

2.10   An Evaluation of Development in Khuzestan and Dezful

Development is a multi-dimensional process and improvement
of the physical environment is only one and perhaps the
easiest dimension. Another, perhaps more important and
certainly more difficult, are human resources. Indeed, in
the case of Khuzestan, plans with a broader spectrum and
a greater emphasis on human elements seem more vital to
future prosperity than the plans actually adopted with their
concern with land and water projects. The 1974 International
Conference on the Social Sciences and the Problems of Development at Shiraz (75), realised this and emphasised the necessity
for comprehensive planning and "development with a human
content" (76).

In addition, Khuzestan clearly differs vastly from the
Tennessee Valley. Khuzestan has its own problems for which
new solutions - particularly culturally compatible solutions
must be worked out. Indeed, a programme of physical works
"unrelated to the culture, traditions, skills, aspirations of
local people can be disruptive instead of beneficial"(77)

Another shortcoming in Khuzestan was public lack of understanding and participation. The D & R initial activity
resulted in rapid physical changes and programme planning
and implementation did not adequately involve the local
population and community leaders, nor had there been information available in a language that local people could understand. The seven-man Preparatory Commission for the
Khuzestan Region, created in 1956 "to lead the way to public
understanding of the regional plan and to contribute ideas"
(78) , had little effect on the D & R since the latter were
entrusted with all aspects of planning and execution and
were most receptive to suggestions from official sources.
Moreover the Commission, under the chairmanship of the
Managing Director of the Plan Organization, included top-
ranking officials who were unfamiliar with rural Khuzestan.
Clapp felt that this was a sign that the region was not ready

for a full-scale plan and needed a period of careful and speedy preparation beforehand (79). However, little seems to have been done. As far as the Dez Irrigation Project is concerned, the D & R has evaluated the costs and benefits involved - usually reporting on the project as a whole. Recently, M. Rabbani, an Iranian economist, has studied the costs and benefits of individual schemes within the overall project. According to Rabbani, up to 1973, "15.310 million rials has been spent to irrigate an eventual 109,000 hectares"(80) - 140,500 rials or $1,870 per hectare. Further details are given in Table 8 and show that the total construction costs of the Project stand at 9,385 million rials (90,000 rials ($1,200) per hectare).

The life span of the dam was originally estimated at 80 years in 1960, but erosion prevention measures were not taken so that mud flow into the reservoir will, it is estimated, silt it completely by 1991, despite dredging. Irrigation and power production will then completely stop (81). An official KWPA view claims that the life span may range from 80 to 120 years, however(82) , but Rabbani observes that, "the whole plan has been extremely expensive and that, in particular, a very large portion of the total expenses has gone on administrative expenses and the costs of the Development and Resources Corporation"(83). The D & R has justified this investment and has emphasised a number of social and economic benefits.

In its report to IBRD, the D & R drew a grave picture of the living conditions in the 58 villages of the DPIP in 1959, but claimed that six years after the beginning of the programme and only three years after the introduction of regulated flow, this grave situation had changed (84). The entire population of 13,500 was enjoying changes in many phases of rural life. Crop productivity had more than doubled by 1964 and livestock had significantly increased. Mechanized agriculture had become accepted practice - in spring 1966, 13 KWPA-owned combines and 20 custom-operated combines were working in the DPIP. The Project administered a credit system designed to help the small farmers who had been steeped in debt and thus mortgaged their harvests in advance. By 1966, virtually all old debts had been paid and the only money owed by the peasants was to the Dez Project Revolving Credit Fund. Provision of the regulated water had led to a fuller employment in agriculture and to higher incomes (from 9,000 rials **per capita** in 1960 to an astonishing 30,000 rials in 1966)(85). There were increased opportunities in education, the number of schools having risen from two in 1961 to 31 in 1966, accommodating 900 boys (26 per cent of the total, as opposed to only three per cent in 1961) and 71 girls. The Project's road system brought all villages within a, "one hour ride of Dezful which has enormously increased the ability of the area with regard to supplying the markets in Dezful, all of Khuzestan and Tehran"(86).

All of these developments had created a profound and lasting change amongst the rural population. Much of the earlier distrust and antagonism had disappeared. The peasants

TABLE 8

Estimates of the real costs of the Dez Irrigation Scheme [e.]

Item	Million Rials	Equivalent 'ooos US dollars ($=75 rials)
The Pilot Stage		
Survey of Resources [a.]	308	4,106
34.5 per cent Cost of Shell of Dam[b.f.]	1,244	16,587
Cost of Irrigation Scheme [c.]	1,579	21,053
Stages I and II [d.]		
Re-regulating and Diversion of Dams	398	5,308
Canals, Pump Stations,Other structures	2,556	34,075
Roads, Drains, Flood Protection, Land Preparation etc.	3,300	44,004
Total	9,385	125,133

Sources: a. Rabbani, **op. cit.**, p 160.

b. "Etalaat Mokhtasari be Manzore Shanakht Behtar-e Khuzestan", **Tahaiqat-e Eqtesadi** Nos 29 and 30 1351/1972, p 114.

c. "Basic Legal Documents, Dez Irrigation Pilot Project", New York USA, D & R 1968, p 30.

d. D & R, **Dez Irrigation Project**, New York USA, D & R 1968, p V-30.

Notes: e. Excluding the administrative expenses and the costs of operation and maintenance.

f. An official report counted 34.5 per cent of the costs of the dam towards the expenses of the irrigation scheme.

had begun to do some planning on their own with regard to the selection of crops, farming rotations and marketing, and no longer waited for the government to initiate action.

All these seem to be major achievements. Why then did the Project sharply shift from developing traditional peasant farming to large-scale non-peasant agriculture?

Originally, and during the Pilot Stage of the DIP, traditional peasant farming was seen as the basis of lasting economic prosperity in the area with some 9,000 farms planned for 98,800 irrigable hectares(87). Despite the success of the Pilot Stage, Stage I proposed the introduction of large-scale commercial agriculture along with small-scale farming, with ten hectares of irrigable land to be allocated to each juft (88)(amounting to 31,000 hectares overall) and the remaining 50,000 hectares to be handed over to foreign and Iranian agro-industrialists (89).Stage II aimed at extending large-scale farming to all of the irrigable land. In little more than a decade, policy had drastically changed from improving peasant farming to expanding a non-peasant agriculture. The basic reasons for this are unknown but sources do hint at some of the factors involved.

Iran's Fourth Development Plan (1968-1973) called for a fuller utilization of lands watered by dams to increase agricultural prosperity. A close examination of the DIP showed that, despite production increases, land preparation, "was slow so that utilization of the irrigable lands was unsatisfactory". Although Stage I had scheduled 10,000 hectares for preparation by the second quarter of 1974, in July 1970 only 900 hectares had actually been prepared for irrigation. In fact, only if, "intensive commercial farming could be introduced on all of the irrigable area,'(90) could the plan targets be met in the DIP area.

Thus the D & R proposed the introduction of agribusinesses in their 1967 report. More generally, enthusiasm for the rapid increase of agricultural production, coupled with the desire for a non-peasant farming system, led to the 1968 law for "The Establishment of Companies for the Utilization of Land Downstream of Dams". Here the Ministry of Water and Power could "acquire irrigable lands, consolidate holdings and develop farm projects", (91) and so 68,000 hectares of the DIP area were purchased for release to agribusinesses (92). By 1974-75, four such companies had set up.

The Dez Irrigation Project has been criticised by students of agriculture both at home and abroad. Lambton, who visited three villages in the Pilot area during 1966, claims that peasants in Dihbar, "were dissatisfied with the Authority, as apparently were all the 50 or so villages in the area in which it was running irrigation and supervising agriculture. In matters of cultivation, it (the Village Production Service) allowed no freedom to the peasants, who complained that their expenses had increased more than the productivity of the land" (93). Because farming practices were controlled by the Authority, "the benefits of the land reform have not been felt by the peasants to the same extent as in other areas such as Shushtar. The peasants fear that they have

TABLE 9

The Growth of Urban and Rural Population Centres 1900-1976
(population in thousands)

Year	Urban				Rural [e]				Iran	
	Population	% of total pop.	Settlement Centres		Population		Settlement Centres (Estimate)		Population	Settlement Centres (Estimate)
	No.		No.	%	No.	%	No.	%	No.	No.
1900 a.	2,040	21.0	100	0.7	7,820	79.0	15,200[f]	99.3	9,860	15,300
1926	2,491	21.0			9,369	79.0			11,860	
1956 b.	5,900	31.4	186	0.5	13,000	68.6	39,099[f]	99.5	18,900	39,285
1956 c.	9,800	38.0	223	0.3	16,000	62.0	66,757[g]	99.7	25,800	66,980
1976 d.	14,900	42.8			19,900	57.2			34,800	

Sources: a. Bharier (1900 and 1926 data) "The Growth of Towns and Villages in Iran", **Middle Eastern Studies**, Vol 8, No 1, 1972, pp 52-59.

b. Khazaneh H. and Darbandi A.S., **Pishbini va Gozaghteh Negary Jamint Shahri va Rustai Iran ta Sal-e 1370**, Tehran, Iran, Statistical Centre of Iran, 1352/1973, p 22.

c. Khusrou Khusrovi, **Jameeh-shenasi-e Rusta-e Iran**, (Rural Sociology of Iran) (Tehran, Iran: University of Tehran 1351/1972), p 9.

d. Khazaneh and Darbandi, **op. cit.**, p 26 (Estimates, population only)

Notes: e. Including nomad population

f. Excluding hamlets (ie places of less than 50 inhabitants)

g. Including 21,624 hamlets.

merely exchanged one master for another"(94).

Lambton also criticised the Project for trumpeting their economic achievements and for a lack of social consideration. The Project Authority "had elaborate table and statistics in the office at Dezful, showing the use of water, but seemed entirely to neglect the human element. They appeared to have little care for the well-being of the peasants, whom they seemed to regard simply as instruments in the experiment ... " (95).

Rabbani, focussing on the economic aspect, also criticises the Project on similar grounds to Lambton. He also remarks that "although it would be quite acceptable to create agro-industry in previously barren land on which there are no rights of **nasaq**, it does not seem to be such an acceptable project for the Dez lands where, at first, action was taken to create experimental farms in order to acquaint local culti-vators with modern methods. But despite these initial steps, agro-industry has taken over the land on the grounds that Iranian farmers are not capable of using modern methods or of setting up producers' cooperatives" (96).

He also points out that agribusinesses' acquisition of the peasants' lands has led to an employment problem. Peasants affected by the scheme have no further interest in the village and their only possibility of employment is to move to the urban areas. As to recovering the cost of the Project through water dues, Rabbani mentions that agro-industrial companies were to pay 750 rials per hectare per year, "but this sum is so tiny that it is impossible to regard it as being of any economic significance at all"(97).

The really significant consideration, though, is the control of land - a factor that has undergone considerable evolution as a result of the land reforms of the 1960s - and, to a lesser extent, control of water.

Chapter Notes

1. D & R, The Unified Development of the Natural Resources of the Khuzestan Region, New York, D & R, 1959, p 3.

2. Jane Perry, Clark Carey and Andrew G. Carey, 'Industrial Growth and Development Planning in Iran", The Middle East Journal, Vol 29, No 1, 1975, p 1.

3. McLachlan and Ghorban, op. cit., p 16.

4. Smith et al., op. cit., p 634.

5. FAO Report to the Government of Iran on the Development of Land and Water Resources in Khuzestan, op. cit., p 9.

6. FAO Interim Report on Soil Fertility Investigations in the Khuzestan Region and Headwaters, Rome, Italy, FAO, 1959, p (i).

7. 'Chronology - Iran', The Middle East Journal, Vol 9, No 2, 1955, p 169.

8. David E. Lilienthal, The Journal of David E. Lilienthal - The Road to Change 1955-1959, New York, USA, Harper and Row, 1969, p 77.

9. Ibid., p 82.

10. C. Herman Pritchett, The Tennessee Valley Authority: A Study in Public Administration, University of North Carolina Press, USA, 1943, p 3.

11. Ibid., p 18.

12. Selznick P., TVA and the Grass Roots: A Study in the Sociology of Formal Organization, University of California Press, USA, 1949, p 85.

13. Pritchett, op. cit., pp 118-119.

14. Julian Huxley, TVA: Adventure in Planning, London UK, Reader's Union/The Architectural Press, 1945, p 9.

15. Selznick, op. cit., p 87.

16. Huxley, op. cit., p 12.

17. Selznick, op. cit., p 86.

18. Huxley, op. cit., p 31.

19. Lilienthal D.E., TVA: Democracy on the March, Penguin Books, London UK, 1945, p 62.

20. Ibid., p 143.

21. D & R, The Unified Development of the Natural Resources of the Khuzestan Region, op. cit., p 9.

22. Ibid., p 36.

23. D & R, **Dez Irrigation Project, Stage I Feasibility Report Supplement**, New York, USA, D & R, 1968, pp 1-2.

24. D & R, **Khuzestan Fertilizer Project Program for the Period 1 December 1957 - 1 October 1959**, D & R, New York, USA, 1959, p 2.

25. D & R, **The Unified Development of the Natural Resources of the Khuzestan Region**, op. cit., p 22.

26. D & R, **Khuzestan Fertilizer Project Program**, op. cit., p 14.

27. D & R, **The Unified Development of the Natural Resources of the Khuzestan Region**, op. cit., p 23.

28. Ibid.

29. Adams, **op. cit.**, p 118.

30. Personal Interview with Sayyid Murtaza Khunsari, an operator of the Shush Modern Farm, a large mechanized farm in Haft Tappeh, 6 September 1974.

31. D & R, **Dez Irrigation Project, Stage I, Feasibility Report Supplement**. op. cit., p VI-5.

32. "Amar va Arqam Qasmat Nishekar Haft Tappeh" (Statistics and Figures of the Haft Tappeh sugar cane project), 1974, Unpublished Report, p 11.

33. Ibid. p 11.

34. Ibid. p 11.

35. **Kayhan**, 30 July 1974.

36. "Amar va Arqam Qasmat Nishekar Haft Tappeh", **op. cit.**, p 15.

37. Ibid. p 9.

38. **Kayhan International**, 11 May 1974.

39. **Kayhan**, 30 October 1973.

40. **Kayhan International**, 11 May 1974.

41. H. Refahiyat, 'Sozialökonomische Bedeutung von Agro-Industriellen Kombinations projekten in Entwicklungsländern am Beispiel eines Zuckerrohrprojektes in Iran', **World Agricultural Economics and Rural Sociology Abstract**, Vol 15, No 5, 1973, p 256.

42. D & R, **The Unified Development of the Natural Resources of the Khuzestan Region**, op. cit., p 42.

43. Ibid.

44. Iran Almanac 1973 and Book of Facts, **op. cit.**, p 221.

45. "Etelaat Mokhtasri be Manzor-e Shanakhat Behtar-e Khuzestan", (Brief Information for Better Recognition of Khuzestan), **Taqiqate Eqtesadi** (Persian Ed.), Nos 29 and 30, 1351/1972, p 102.

46. Nederlandsche Heidemaatschappij (Heidemy), "Report on the Dez Irrigation Project Supplement 1" June 1959 (unpublished), p 1.

47. D & R, Dez Irrigation Project, Stage I, Feasibility Report Supplement, op. cit., p V-1.

48. Khuzestan Water and Power Authority, "Basic Legal Documents, Dez Irrigation Pilot Project", 1960 (unpublished), p 30.

49. Lilienthal, The Journal of David E. Lilienthal, The Road to Change 1955 - 1959, Vol III, op. cit., p 177.

50. R.F.Kriess and G. Jan Koopman, "Plans for Agricultural Development in the Khuzestan Plains", 1962, (Unpublished), p 5.

51. Nederlandsche Heidemaatschappij, "Report on the Dez Irrigation Supplement No 1", op. cit., p 1.

52. KWPA, "Basic Legal Documents, Dez Irrigation Pilot Project", op. cit., p 17.

53. Ibid. p 17.

54. Ibid. p 18.

55. Ibid. p 34.

56. Ibid. p 34.

57. D & R, Dez Irrigation Project, op. cit., p I-8.

58. Ibid.

59. D & R, Farm Corporations for the Dez Irrigation Project, Part I, New York, USA, D & R, 1968, p 5.

60. D & R, Dez Irrigation Project Stage II, Feasibility, D & R, New York, USA, 1968.

61. Khuzestan Development Service (KDS), "Status of Dez Irrigation Pilot Project", Brief Papers for IBRD Representatives, April 1961, (unpublished), p 24.

62. Nederlandsche Heidemaatschappij (Heidemy), "Short Note on Activities for the Establishment of a Field Trial Farm and Training Centre", 1960, (unpublished), p 1.

63. D & R, Dez Irrigation Project, op. cit., p IV-24.

64. KDS, Status of Dez Irrigation Pilot Project, op. cit., p 27.

65. KDS, Dez Irrigation Pilot Project Work Plan for Production Service, 1962, (unpublished), p 1.

66. KDS, Status of Dez Irrigation Pilot Project, op. cit., p 31.

67. KDS, Dez Pilot Irrigation Project Village Production Service, 1963, (unpublished), p 5.

68. KDS, Status of Dez Irrigation Pilot Project, op. cit. p 32.

69. KWPA, "Basic Legal Documents, Dez Irrigation Pilot Project", op. cit., p 28.

70. "Etalaat Mokhtasari be Manzore Shenakht-e Behtar-e Khuzestan", op. cit., p 103.

71. D & R, Dez Irrigation Project, Stage I, Feasibility Report Supplement, op. cit., p VIII-15.

72. Dez Pilot Irigation Project (DPIP), "Agriculture and Irrigation Report to IBRD", 1966, (unpublished), p 3.

73. Ibid. p 3.

74. "Basic Legal Documents, Dez Irrigation Pilot Project", op. cit., p 28.

75. Organized jointly by the Plan and Budget Organization, Tehran University and Princetown University.

76. Shaul Bakhash, "Development Must Be Human", Kayhan International, 5 June 1974.

77. Gordon R. Clapp, "Iran: A TVA for the Khuzestan Region", The Middle East Journal, Vol II, No 1, 1957, p 4.

78. Ibid. p 8.

79. Ibid.

80. Mehdi Rabbani, "A Cost Benefit Analysis of the Dez Multi-Purpose Project", Tahqiqat-e Eqtesadi, (Eng. Ed.) Vol VIII, Nos 23 and 24, 1970, p 162.

81. Ibid. p 137.

82. "Etalaat Mokhtasari be Manzore Shanakht Behtare Khuzestan", op. cit., p 110.

83. Rabbani, op. cit., p 162.

84. DPIP, "Agriculture and Irrigation Report to IBRD", op. cit., p 1.

85. Informal lecture on the Extension Activities of the KWPA by the Head of the Agricultural Division of the DIP, 6 February 1970, Safiabad.

86. Ibid.

87. Nederlandsche Heidemaatschappij, "Report on the Dez Irrigation Project, Supplement No 1", op. cit., Table VI-7.

88. D & R, Dez Irrigation Project, Stage I, Feasibility Report Supplement, op. cit., Table VI-1.

89. Ibid. p IV-17.

90. D & R, Farm Corporations for the Dez Irrigation Project, Part I, op. cit., p 4.

91. Ibid. p 9.

92. "Etalaat Mokhtasari be Manzore Shanakht Behtare Khuzestan", op. cit., p 104.

93.   Lambton, **The Persian Land Reform**, London, UK, OUP, 1969, p 156.

94.   **Ibid.** p 280.

95.   **Ibid.** p 281.

96.   Rabbani, **op. cit.**, p 158.

97.   **Ibid.** p 162.

3 SETTLEMENT, LAND REFORM AND IRRIGATION
IN KHUZESTAN

3.1 Ancient Settlement and the Village in the Upper Khuzestan Plains

The Upper Khuzestan Plains have been "the home of earliest civilisation of Persia"(1) , but agricultural settlement there long predates the Persian Empire. Agricultural man first appears in the northern Khuzestan several millennia before the ancient Elamite capital of Shush (around 3000 BC). Archaeological investigations show that from 8000 to 4000 BC "man in southwest Iran was a semi-nomadic herder who sub-sisted partly on domestic goats, sheep, wheat and barley, and partly on wild animals and seasonally-available wild plants" (2).

Adams, however, identifies 130 population sites - towns and villages (3) - in the northern Khuzestan plains in the period from 6000 BC to the Ninth Century AD. Although the towns of Shush and Jundi Shapur (an old Sassanid capital) were particularly prominent, the typical settlement was the village, a view confirmed by Lambton in more recent times(4).

The **deh** (village) has dominated as settlement in Iran because it has conferred freedom from extortion and attack, facilitated corporate work - such as irrigation - and has been encouraged by government policy, as it eased adminis-tration(5). The domination of village settlement from 1900 to 1976, shown in Table 9, is a feature which is repeated in the Dez Project area. Of about 180 scattered population centres there, only two are urban centres: Dezful (113,000 inhabitants in 1972) and Shush (9,000 in 1972) (6).

In Iran and rural Dezful, the siting of villages is usually dictated by the availability of water(7). Most villages are located along the main rivers or water diversion canals. This would be normal in a semi-arid environment , but in Dezful water is relatively abundant, so villages were estab-lished wherever there was suitable farmland. Water was then diverted to the new cultivable areas. This happened in the early 1920s at Qaleh Shahrukni, on the east bank of the

Karkheh River where the late Hadji Abdul Hassein Shahrokni, a member of an influential landowner group, owned about 700 hectares of land. He decided to use peasant share- croppers to cultivate it, so he extended the canal already supplying some of his farm land and recruited peasant farmers, assigning each an appropriate number of **jufts**, assisting them to build homes, thus creating a new village.

3.2 Village Structure

Normally a village has two main components: a residential area - the village or **deh** - and land for farming - in Dezful called the **sahra** (open field).
The layout of the villages in the Project area is not uniform. Two types can be identified: the walled villages or **qaleh** (literally 'castle') and open villages or **boneh**. **Boneh** is also used for a peasant farmers' work organization.

TABLE 10

The Distribution of Walled Villages (**Qaleh**) and
Open Villages (**Boneh**) in the Dez Project Area, 1958.

Types of village configuration	Frequency of occurrence among the DIP villages	
	No.	%
Qaleh villages	52	30.8
Boneh villages		
Attached	23	13.6
Independent	94	55.6
Total	169	100.0

Source: Field studies

A **qaleh** is characterized by its rectangular plan surrounded by high walls and a single narrow entrance gate. The walled enclosure is usually divided into two sections: the village homesteads - clustered peasant dwellings, each with its own courtyard for family use and a livestock shelter (8) - and the landlord's garden or orchard. Each dwelling typically consists of one or more rooms around the courtyard, each with one window or a small opening for ventilation and light. The walls are of mud and straw, and the roofs of timber and brush covered by a thick layer of mud. These materials are relatively low conductors of heat and are cooler than bricks and metal. Formerly each **qaleh** had a gate house occupied by the village **gopun**, herdsman, who was responsible for guarding the gate at night.

The open villages have neither defensive walls nor gates, and extend according to prevailing housing needs. Since space is not restricted, roads are wider and the dwellings are larger. Open villages are either attached to a larger village or they are separate. Most attached villages resulted from the extension of irrigation facilities from larger villages which had tracts of uncultivated or less intensively cultivated land. Independent open villages such as Amaleh Sayf often resulted from the 1930s nomad settlement programme, when the use of tribal tents was prohibited in an attempt to settle the Lur and Bakhtiari tribes that had used the Dezful plains as a wintering place. There are also some Arabic tribal groups in open villages.

Qaleh No Shomsabad, the satellite village to Shomsabad, began 60 years ago when the landlord extended the Shomsabad irrigation canal to some of his uncultivated land, which was then assigned to some **khwushnishins** (peasants without land rights) in Shomsabad. They gradually built their own houses on the new land to protect their fields and to be nearer their work. At the same time, they continued to use facilities such as the mosques and the school in the parent village.

The fortified villages or **qalehs** arose as a response to local physical conditions and security. De Planhol has suggested that "the **qaleh** village is the product of pastoral civilisation that was fraught with insecurity; it reflects the settled people's need to defend themselves and their cattle against repeated incursions of the nomads"(9). With the establishment of a strong central government and nomad control programmes "the recent progress towards a more peaceful way of life would seem to imply the end, sooner or later, of this (**qaleh** type of) village; and in fact many **qaleh** are to be found in varying stages of dilapidation"(10). In Bonvar Hossein for example, dwellings were crowded inside **qaleh** before 1970 but in recent years over half the peasant families (26 out of 50) have left their former living quarters – many now used as grain stores – building new houses outside the defensive wall. The new houses are protected by walls "far less formidable than the habitable (defensive) wall of the village, and this fact in itself gives evidence of the greater security of life today"(11).

Outside both the **qaleh** and the open village residential area is the threshing ground and farm land. The threshing ground covers one to two hectares, usually adjacent to the dwellings and is considered 'communal land'. Seasonally each farmer is assigned an area on it where he accumulates his harvest. The village farm land consists of several scattered **chals** (12) (fields) of different sizes. In Bonvar Hossein the cultivated land area comprises 50 **chals**, ranging from one hectare to 20 hectares.

The amount of land for each village can only be roughly estimated, varying from as little as 70 hectares in Miyan Choghan Salehipour, to as much as 3,015 hectares in Bonvar Nazer. The reasons are complex. Most village boundaries used to be imprecise using land marks such as 'a row of trees at the end of the village' or 'the village irrigation ditch'. Some of these disappeared over time and were not replaced, although the limits of village land were well known to villagers. Also the local land measure, the **mann**, could not be used to determine the land hectarage. A **mann** was the area which could ordinarily be sown with one **mann** or eight kilograms of wheat and this area varied with the quality of the land. In Dezful, one **mann** would be adequate to sow 1,000 square metres of fertile irrigated land or as little as 770 square metres of less fertile land. In any case in most villages no cadastral survey had been carried out.

Traditionally, both irrigated and dry farming were practised. Irrigated farming, the dominant pattern of agriculture, involved intensive land use through double cropping. Dry farming involved more extensive land use with single cropping in winter. However, since 1958, the new agricultural schemes - the Haft Tappeh sugar cane plantation, farm corporations and agribusiness enterprises - have covered the majority of the villages in the Project area.

3.3 Land Ownership in Traditional Dezful

Iran's traditional agrarian structure was dominated by the concentration of land in the hands of a few large, and often absentee, landlords who had little interest either in improving the land or the conditions of the peasant share-croppers who worked it. Rural Dezful was no exception to this national pattern. Landlordism was long considered a major obstacle to creating a progressive agricultural system and a transformation of land ownership was widely acknow-ledged to be the key to agrarian reform.

The common unit of land ownership was, until very recently 'the village' - an imprecise concept since villages vary considerably in area and population, figures which "vary from say ten families in the small clusters of houses in the mountain valleys .... to over 400 families in the large villages on the plain" (13). Traditionally the village could be divided into six arbitrary parts, or shares as it was physi-cally indivisible, and ownership was called **shish dang**, ('ownership of six parts'). However, in rural Dezful it was more common to divide a village into 24 equal parts; each being called a **nokhud** ('a pea'), overall ownership then being called **bist-o-char nokhud** ('ownership of 24 parts (peas)'). There was no term to describe the **land** owned because it was the produce **from** the land which interested the traditional landlords. Each **nokhud** could be subdivided into 24 **jow** or **shaeir**, ('barley') and each **jow** further sub-divided into 24 **kunjed**, ('sesame'). Thus a village or any part of it could be divided into 24^3 (13,824) parts and each part could have a different **malik**, (owner or title holder). In fact, the system meant that the ownership structure of a village did not affect peasant sharecroppers, for there were no physical boundaries, each landowner's harvest portion being calculated in terms of the number of parts he held.

The landownership system was also compatible with the Islamic law of inheritance permitting division of land amongst all heirs of a deceased landowner (in the ratios of son: daughter:widow = 8:4:1), without disturbing its cultivation by peasant sharecroppers. In Bonvar Hossein, for instance, repeated division amongst heirs has resulted, within living memory, in the single original owner being replaced by 33 owners in 1962 when the Land Reform Programme started.

The system was further complicated by **musha**, the joint ownership of undivided shares (eg. three brothers and a sister might jointly own two **nokhuds** of village A and one **nokhud, three jows and five kunjed** of village B).

The absence of clear and comprehensive records of land ownership was a further complication. Although a property registration law was passed in 1928-29,(14) it had never been fully implemented. In the Dezful **Shahristan**, the registration office was only opened on 1st March 1937(15). Even then landowners commonly transferred part of their holdings to their children or sold it without fulfilling the legal procedures. Instead, a recognized religious leader authorized such transactions as a non-civic 'notary public'. In any case property registration records were rarely kept up to date. Furthermore, until the 1960s, most rural areas of Iran had never undergone a detailed cadastral survey, so land boundaries were vague. Land area was seldom expressed in hectares or other conventional units, different local systems being used instead. In Khuzestan the only lands which had been 'surveyed' were those areas of interest to oil companies. The first agricultural land survey in rural Dezful was conducted by Heidemy in 1957 in connection with the Dez Irrigation Project (DIP) (16).

The ultimate result of lack of ownership records and of ill-defined property boundaries was that land taxation records were inaccurate. Land taxes had been levied since the 19th century but its assessment and collection were subject to bribery and default so that the local tax office records were unreliable.

In short, the cumulative effect of these inter-related factors is that land ownership typology and distribution in rural Dezful can only be determined approximately.

3.4 Categories of Land Ownership

Before Land Reform, there were four broad categories of land ownership:

1. **Kaliseh**, (public domain) either confiscated by the State in lieu of taxation or acquired by state purchase (17).

2.   **Amlak-e Saltanati,** (Crown Land) acqui-
      red by the monarch and belonging to
      the royal family.

3.   **Vaqf,** (endowment land) was alienated
      to support a foundation for "a group
      of 'poor men' or an institution of
      public interest"[18] for pious purposes,
      (**vaqf-e amm**)[19]   or for the donor's
      family, (**vaqf-e khass**).

4.   **Amlak** or **amlak-e khossosi,** (private
      estates) belong to individuals, families,
      or firms.

In considering these types of ownership, it should be noted
that before the 1928/29 Land Registration Law it was not
always easy to establish 'ownership' and often 'holding'
or occupying a property for a period of time was sufficient
to acquire ownership status.

The distribution of villages in Iran within these categories
is difficult to establish, partly because, "the exact number
of villages in Persia is still something of a mystery" [20]   ,
estimates ranging from 48,500 to over 70,000 in addition to
22,000 **mazraehs** (independent farms)[21]. In the 1956 Census,
however, Crown Lands contained about four per cent of all
villages, Public Domain about ten per cent, endowment lands
about ten per cent and private holdings the remaining 76 per
cent [22].

Despite discrepancies, numerous reports indicate that before
the Land Reform Programme in the 1960s, land ownership was
"highly concentrated in the hands of a small number of
individuals"[23]. Hobbs suggests that in January 1962, about
90 per cent of the arable land in Iran was owned by less
than five per cent of the population[24].   Baldwin mentions
that before Land Reform there were 200 families owning more
than 100 villages each (a total of one third of all villages
in Iran).   Another 10,000 villages were owned by landlords
possessing between five to 100 villages each and approximately 7,000 villages were owned by landlords holding between
one to five villages each[25]. In fact, "In 1962 an estimated
60 per cent of Iranian farmers owned no land and another
23 per cent owned less than one hectare of cultivated land"[26].

Traditional land ownership in Khuzestan Province was unusual in that many villages were **khaliseh,** (public domain)
and Manoutcher Nezam-Mafi divides land ownership in Khuzestan into **khaliseh, vaqf,** and private holdings[27]. The **khaliseh**
lands were mostly in Southern Khuzestan and in the Dezful
area, the State owned two groups of villages: Chogha Mish
and its immediate neighbours, and a number of villages in
Sar Dasht sub-district, to the north of Dezful town, as well
as about 3,600 hectares of the 212,660 hectares of agricultural
land in Shushtar **Shahristan** and about 75 per cent of the
4,000 hectares of agricultural land in the rural districts of
Masjed-e Suliman **Shahristan** in the north of the Province
[28]. The 972 public domain villages in Khuzestan Province
were distributed by 1971,   (25.5 per cent of the total) there

having been 90 **vaqf** villages in Khuzestan prior to the land redistribution programme (2.4 per cent of the total) and more than 2,700 privately-owned villages (72.1 per cent of the total).

It is clear that, before the recent reform, Khuzestan was predominantly in the hands of large landed proprietors (30) - former governors, tribal leaders and local Arabic-speaking sheikhs. Nezam al-Saltaneh for example was appointed the Governor of the Province by Nasir al-Din Shah from 1887 - 1891 and 1895 - 1896, acquiring large tracts of land in the Jarrahi River district, and between the Karun and Karkheh rivers (31), including a vast area in Hosseinabad sub-district near Shush. The Bakhtiari chiefs had bought the Rumaz (Ram Hurmuz **Shahristan**) in about 1896, in 1898 they acquired the plain of Aqili and later a large area between Shushtar and the Dez River and a tract between the Karkheh and Shaur rivers to the north of Shush. Sheikh Khazal and a few Arabic-speaking sheikhs controlled many villages in the coastal areas of the Persian Gulf intermittently during the 19th and early 20th century. Peasant proprietorship in Khuzestan was rare and probably did not exceed more than five per cent of the total private holding.

3.5 Land in Rural Dezful

The situation in Dezful is summarized in Table 11. Crown Lands did not exist but there were two **khaliseh** villages: Boneh Fazili and Chogha Mish (Boneh Dolati). Before the irrigation scheme started, both were dry farmed by share-croppers. The dues on **khaliseh**, referred to as **minal**, (the State's landowner's harvest share) were fixed in Chogha Mish for example at 20 **manns** (160 kilograms) of wheat, seven **manns** (56 kilograms) of barley plus 50 rials per **juft** per annum. They were paid to the **kadkhoda**, (headman) who was in reality the village-level Government agent.

Eight villages were endowed: five publicly and three privately. Of the five, two were wholly endowed, (Biatian Raffat and Zavieh Mashali) and three only in part: (Bonvar Nazar, Seyheh and Ganjeh). Of the three villages privately endowed, Qaleh Agha Hassani was endowed in whole and Jeibar and Qaleh Robe-e Kuyekh were partly endowed. The purpose of endowment varied; Biatian Raffat was endowed to benefit the local theological school, Zavieh Mashali was endowed for the Javad ul-Aameh Hospital in Mashad. The three partly publicly endowed villages benefited mosques in Dezful or Andimeshk and the shrine of the Prophet Daniel in Shush. The privately endowed villages were for specific individuals or families but could not be further divided amongst inheritors. Each endowed village had a **mutavalli**, (administrator) with functions similar to those of a 'typical' landowner. However, for publicly endowed villages, the Endowment Office for Dezful **Shahristan** would act as 'compt-roller', taking 15 per cent of the endowment income as a service charge (10 per cent supervision fee and 5 per cent

TABLE 11

Estimates of the Distribution of Village Ownership in Iran, Khuzestan Province and the Dez Project Area Before the Land Reform Programme

Form of Ownership	Iran, 1956 [a]		Khuzestan Province, 1961 [b]		Dez Project Area, 1961 [c]			
	No. of villages	%	No. of villages	%	No. of Villages (in Whole)	(in Part)	Village Equivalent [d] No	%
Public Domain Lands	5,500	10.0	970	25.5	2		2.0	1.2
Crown Lands	2,200	4.0						
Endowment Lands	5,500	10.0	90	2.9	3	5	5.3	3.1
Public					(2)	(3)	(3.1)	
Private					(1)	(2)	(2.2)	
Private Ownership	41,800	76.0	2,740	72.1	159	5	161.7	95.7
Total	55,000	100.0	3,800	100.0	164	10	169.0	100.0

Sources: a. Ajami I, "Land Reform and Modernization of the Farming Structure in Iran", Oxford Agrarian Studies, Vol 2, No 2, 1973, p 1.
b. Adapted from: Iran Almanac and Book of Facts 1962, (Tehran, Iran:Echo of Iran, 1963), p 387.
c. Field studies

Note: d. The 'Village Equivalent' refers to a whole village or parts of villages (that might not necessarily be of the same hectarage) which would be equal to one complete village.

for administrative costs). Endowed lands were worked, like private land, by sharecroppers according to customary rates but the **mutavallis** usually had less interest in village conditions than did large landowners.

Most DIP villages were privately owned before the Land Reform Programme - 159 villages of the 169 studied in toto and five in part. The size of an individual holding could not be easily established because of the prevailing pattern of joint and undivided ownership and in the entire DIP area only two villages were owned entirely by one person, the others being undivided estates owned by more than one person but a single person, usually family or clan head, acting as representative. Moreover, the number of owners and the size of their holdings continually changed because of property transactions and inheritance.

Nevertheless, Heidemy in 1950 estimated that about 100 DIP villages (65 per cent of the total) were owned by ten families. (Qotb, Asaf, Mostofi, Al-Kassir, Shahrokni, Sohrabi, Rashidian Tahmasabi, Samsam Bakhtiari and Sagvand.) On average, individual holdings exceeded three villages or village equivalents even if widely scattered over several villages. Nearly 40 villages (25 per cent of the total) were held by 20 landowning families each with individual holdings from one to three villages. There were then some 250 small owners whose cumulative holding equalled 25 villages (15 per cent of the total). Peasant freeholdings existed only in the region around Dezful and in the dry farming Sabili Khaki, to the north of Dezful (32).

Land ownership in rural Dezful had several other charac-teristics. Firstly, the most holdings were usually widely scattered in the form of shares in a number of villages. Secondly, land ownership in irrigated areas was always accompanied by and often integrated into water rights. Thirdly, most landowners were local, living in Dezful, Andi-meshk or Shush or even in their own villages, and some personally managed their own estates, thus differing radically from the vast majority of Iranian landlords, often absentees leaving village management to agents. Fourthly, large proprietors were often members of inter-related families. The four major landowning families - Qotb, Asaf, Mostofi and Rashidian - were inter-related by numerous marriages which helped to keep land within the landed class and acted as a means of 'boundary maintenance'.

There appear to have been five main ways through which the 'original owners' acquired their land; on occasion land was acquired through official posts, (Nezam al-Saltaneh, a former Governor General of Khuzestan Province) or by being 'court favourites', (Sayyid Hashim). An alternative was by inheritance, marriage with landed families or entrepreneurial skills (Bareh Qotb), or as a tribal leader acquiring land by seizure or through purchase from the central government. The remaining large landowners were craftsmen, merchants and/or money lenders who acquired their estates by purchase or in lieu of unpaid debts.

However, for their successors, inheritance was the primary

source of land.   By 1962, Bonvar Hossein for example, was
'owned' by a group of 33 small landowners, some of whom
were related but had, according to village sources, originally
belonged to one Karim, an ordinary government office clerk.
The 'owners' holdings varied in size from two **nokhuds**,
13 **jows**, and six **kunjeds** – the largest share – down to 19.2
kunjeds.   Chogha Sorkh in 1962 was held on a **musha** basis
by 13 members of the Rashidian family through inheritance.
Shalgahi Sofla, however, had belonged to a major Bakhtiari
tribal chief, Morteza Qali Samsam Bakhtiar.   In 1962 it was
owned by seven descendants of Morteza Qoli, of whom Jahan
Shah (a former Governor of Khuzestan Province), Amir Bahman,
and Iraj each held four **nokhuds**, Hossein Qoli five, Amir
Qoli three and Parvin and Azar each held two **nokhuds**.

3.6   Early Attempts Towards Land Reform

Between 1906 and 1960 a number of ineffective land reform
laws were passed, although the Crown Land Distribution
Programme (1951 to 1963) was claimed to be successful.
According to official sources, the royal estates with their
2,100 villages were sold to their peasant cultivators in lots
large enough to support their families and for a price ten
times the value of the landowner's harvest share, paid over
a 25 year period(33). From 1951 to 1962 some 517 villages (25
per cent) were redistributed, and in 1963 a further 289
villages (14 per cent) were sold to residents(34).

The 1951 royal decree was also intended to set an example
for other landed proprietors and in 1955 the government
responded by preparing for a distribution of the **khaliseh**
(35). Previous governmental attempts from 1927 to 1950 to redistribute **khaliseh** land in Sistan, Khuzestan, Luristan,
Kirmanshah and Dasht-e Moghon, had been unsuccessful
because the land was often misappropriated and subsequently
acquired by landowners and merchants rather than the
peasants.

The 20 December 1955 law for the sale of **khaliseh** land
changed all this, authorising the distribution of all public
domain except pastures, natural forests and buildings or
properties needed by government agencies.   The law was
based on the transference of land to its cultivators in maximum units of ten hectares in irrigated areas and 15 hectares
in dry farming regions.   Minimum unit size depended on the
relationship between the cultivable village land area and
the number of persons eligible to receive it.   In villages
where land was insufficient, only resident farmers received
it, whereas in larger villages, other groups including the
resident farmers' male children, and **khwushnishins** (landless
peasants) did.

Payment was to be made over a 20 year period and the
price was fixed according to the land area and fertility,
by a Ministry of Agriculture provincial supervisory committee,
and it could not be sold or transferred for ten years.
Supporting services were to be financed by a co-operative

fund to which each peasant landowner was to contribute in proportion to his annual income. This law was only implemented in 1958 and had a very limited impact. By January 1963, only 157 **khaliseh** villages had been distributed, benefiting a total of 8,366 families (36).The passage of the land reform laws in 1962 and administrative reforms in the Ministry of Agriculture in 1967 speeded up the process, so that by 1971 a total of 1,536 whole villages and 263 part villages had been distributed amongst 90,413 recipients, 972 of the whole villages (63.3 per cent) being in Khuzestan(37). The experience gained in redistribution of **khaliseh** land turned out to be of little use in organizing the redistribution of privately-owned land because the original law did not allow for land ownership complexities and traditional cultivation patterns.

The initial land reform law of 16 May 1960 – "the Abortive Land Reform Law of 1960" (38) limited private holdings to a maximum of 400 hectares of irrigated or 800 hectares of dry farming land, excess land being sold to the government for redistribution to landless peasants. The law proved to be unworkable because of innumerable loopholes; rural Iran had never been surveyed cadastrally and estate size was unknown, even to proprietors, and most were held in **musha**. Before the law was amended, it persuaded landowners to divide land amongst relatives and friends in order to reduce the size of their holdings and thus gain exemption(39).

3.7   The Three Phases of the National Land Reform Programme

Iran's first nation-wide land tenure reform was inaugurated on the 9th of January 1962 when the Council of Ministers amended the initial 1960 land reform law to make it compatible with the traditional system where the village constituted the land holding 'unit'.

The amendment limited the maximum land holding to one 'full' **shish dang** village – a whole village or selected parts of villages equivalent to a whole village. Excess land was to be sold to the government for redistribution to sharecroppers. Excluded from the law were orchards, tea plantations, woodlands, homesteads and mechanized farming areas using wage labour. The exemption of mechanized farms was apparently intended to encourage their expansion and to encourage improvements in the level of farm technology.

Compensation was paid for surplus land by the Land Reform Organization in amounts depending on the taxes paid and a 'multiplier'. The multiplier took into account factors such as the distance from village to city, village revenue and peasant/landlord crop division patterns. In general, compensation was some 100 to 180 times the amount of the last tax payment prior to 1962 (40) – a method which was particularly disadvantageous to tax defaulting owners! Since most landowners had under-paid their tax they received correspondingly less for their land(41). Compensation was paid over 15 years in annual instalments corresponding to seven per cent of the principal sum plus six per cent interest by the Agricultural Bank. However, payments could only be used to purchase shares in government factories, to pay taxes, or as a security against bank credit for investment in mining, industry or agriculture.

Suitable recipients (who had to be members of a local co-operative society) for expropriated land were defined as, **inter alia**, **zari-e sahib nasaq** – peasant sharecroppers, who provided a factor of production in addition to their own labour, their heirs if death occurred within 12 months of redistribution; other sharecroppers, agricultural labourers and non-farming villagers who wished to become farmers, (42) although in reality the beneficiaries were nearly always former sharecroppers and their heirs. This system of allocation did not disturb the field layout of the village, where each peasant cultivator held ownership rights on a **musha** basis. The Land Reform Programme actually gave him a land-title and not unconditional 'absolute' land ownership rights.

The price paid by recipients was the government purchase price plus a maximum ten per cent service charge over a 15 year period. The redistribution process was thus substantially self-financing. Holdings could not be transferred or sold until the full price had been paid.

The first phase of land reform only affected 9,000 villages (about 16 per cent of the total) and the status of the vast majority of peasants remained unchanged. However, "it was neither fair nor wise to ignore the difference created among those who received land and the majority of the peasants who had been left without land"(43).The government, therefore, further amended the Land Reform Laws through the "Additional Articles" (17th January 1963) which when put into effect in February 1965, formed the second phase of the land reform. The new land ceiling was defined as from 20 to 150 hectares, varying from region to region, presumably because of differences in land fertility and water availability as well as proximity to the market. Landowners were offered five alternatives for redistribution and landowners **and** peasants had mutually to agree on one of them.

1. The land could be let on a 30-year lease to share-croppers in occupation for a fixed (**maqtow**) rent, equivalent to average annual net income of the owner over the previous three years and reviewable every five years, payable in cash or kind.

2. The owner could sell his land to the tenants at a mutually acceptable price.

3. The owner could divide the land between himself and the cultivators in proportion to their respective crop shares, selling the portion equivalent to the peasants' shares to them and receiving payment over ten years.

4. Here a joint agricultural unit (**vahid-e sahami zerai**) was farmed by mutual consent. The management was the responsibility of a committee of three, one peasant appointed, one appointed by the landlord, and the

third mutually selected by both parties.

5. The landowner could purchase the peasant farmers'
    haq-e risheh (root rights) or rights of cultivation
    provided that the consequent land holding did not
    exceed the Government limits.

The exemptions under the second phase were similar to
those of the first phase except that mechanized farms were
generally limited to 500 hectares.

Most landowners, not surprisingly, preferred to lease land
to their sharecroppers, a procedure which defeated the
purpose of the amended law. As a result a further amendment
was made on 7th March 1969, thus making the third phase
of land reform.

According to the amendment, landowners who had leased
their lands or who had set up joint farming units were now
required either to sell all their lands to tenants, or to divide
them in accordance with the proportions prevailing under
the previous traditional sharecropping agreements. For outright sale tenants were to pay an equivalent to ten years
rent or 12 annual instalment payments equal to 12 times the
annual rent. For land division the cash price was to be
two-fifths of ten years' rent, less 15 per cent or payment
in 12 annual instalments at two-fifths of 12 times the annual
rent.

Despite the new amendment some landowners were reluctant
to comply so, on 30th January 1971 a law was passed fixing
22nd September 1971 as a deadline by which time all unre-
solved settlements were to be completed. "If by that time,
the landowners had not agreed with the tenants in the
villages how to divide the land, a vesting process was put
into motion. As from Farmers' Day, September 23, 1971, the
land was deemed to have been sold to the tenants and the
rental payment next due and the subsequent payments were
to be accepted as instalments of the purchase price to be
paid for the land"(44).

All three phases of land reform treated private endowments
as 'ordinary' private holdings, and the Government was
authorised to purchase private endowments from the mutavalli,
(endower's agent) the capital obtained being used for investment to fulfil the endower's bequest(45). Public endowed estates
were transferred to tenants on a 99-year basis under the
second phase of the land reform and then sold to tenants
by a special law passed on 4th May 1971.

3.8 The Land Reform at National Level

Although much data on the practical application of the
land reform laws is unreliable, conclusions based on official
sources and using fairly consistent data may provide a rough
idea of how the reforms progressed. The results obtained
during the first phase - up to October 1972 - are   summarized in Table 12.

Data on the Second Phase are too vague to admit any

TABLE 12

Villages and Villagers affected by the First Phase of the Land Reform

Item	Iran 1972 [a]	Khuzestan Province 1972 [a]	Dez Project Area 1974 [b]
Villages			
Total Number	55,000	3,800	169
Villages exempted (mechanized farming)	1,100	–	–
Number of villages affected	14,290	708	58 [c]
– In whole	3,887	256	4
– In part	10,403	452	54
Number of village equivalents	9,088.5	482.0	18.3
Per cent of total	16.5	12.9	10.8
Peasants with Land Rights			
Total number	2,530,000		6,927
Number of Beneficiaries	690,500	22,460	2,404
– In villages distributed in whole			215
– In villages distributed in part			2,189
Per cent of total	27.3		34.7

Sources: a   Adapted from D.R.Denman, **The King's Vista,** Berkhampstead, Berks
               USA, Geographical Publication Ltd, 1973, **op. cit.,** p 120.
           b. Field studies

Note   c. Including two public domain villages, Boneh Fazili and Chogha Mish,
               redistributed in accordance with the law concerning the sale of
               khaliseh, of 20 December 1955, amended 9 February 1963.

effective analysis, mainly because of the complex arrangements
for disposal of land. However, it seems that about two thirds
of the landowners leased their holdings for a 30 year period
thus retaining control over their land(46)·. Ajami indicates
that 72 per cent of estates (villages) were leased and 18
per cent were organized into joint farming units, six per
cent were divided between landowners and only 1.4 per cent
were sold outright to peasant cultivators. Peasant root rights
were sold to landowners in 2.6 per cent of the estates
(47). The vast majority of both public and privately endowed
estates were similarly leased, the former for 99 years and
the latter for 30 years.

Under the third phase leased land was sold outright to
peasant tenants, and a comparatively small percentage of
landlords divided their holdings with their tenants. Up to
March 1972 over 281,000 landowners (87.2 per cent of the
total affected by the third phase) are believed to have sold
their lands outright while approximately 41,000 (12.7 per
cent) divided their estates(48). By 18th September 1973, some
3,540 villages and farms endowed for charitable purposes
had also been transferred to 112,741 peasant families(49).

In short, an estimated 1.4 million peasants with cultivation
rights (approximately 70 per cent of the total 2.5 million
sharecroppers in Iran) had by September 1971 received ownership of the land they cultivated(50).

3.9   Land Reform in Khuzestan

The redistribution of private holdings and endowed villages
in the Khuzestan Province, differed little from the general
national pattern, as can be seen from Table 12. The percentage of 12.9 per cent redistributed villages in phase one
is less than that nationally (16.5 per cent) partly because
in Khuzestan more villages were in the public domain (25.5
per cent against ten per cent nationally). A relatively large
number of **khaliseh** villages were transferred to private
ownership under the 1955 law. Under the second phase more
than 96 per cent of recorded transactions were tenancy
arrangements, and of the remainder 3.5 per cent involved
land division and in only 24 out of a total 82,000 transactions was there an outright sale(51). Information concerning
the third phase is unavailable but most landowners probably
preferred outright sale to land division.

3.10   Land Reform in the Dez Irrigation Project Area (52)

The 169 villages in the DIP area fell into the following
categories before the land reforms were applied:

1.   Public domain (two villages)

2.   Villages wholly publicly endowed (two villages)

3.   Villages wholly privately endowed (one village)

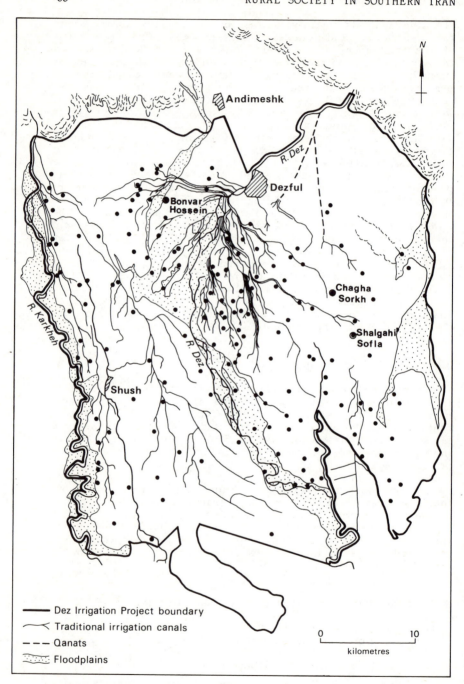

MAP 4   Location of villages and traditional systems

4. Villages endowed in part publicly and partly owned privately (three villages).

5. Villages privately endowed in part and partly owned privately (two villages).

6. Villages privately owned and partly mechanized (16 villages) and

7. Villages privately owned with no mechanization (143 villages).

The 16 villages which were mechanized in part were exempted from inclusion in the Land Reform Programme – the mechanized parts being equivalent to 3.9 villages (2.3 per cent). The two public domain villages, Boneh Fazili and Chogha Mish were distributed among 175 peasant sharecroppers under the 1955 **Khaliseh** law.

The first phase of land reform affected 56 privately owned villages, two completely (Qaleh Chiti and Zavieh Hamoudi) and the other 54 only in part – a total of 342.9 **nokhuds** (14.3 village equivalents). Thus, by the end of the first phase, public domain and privately owned villages distributed amount to 18.3 village equivalents (10.8 per cent of all the villages in the DIP area). The actual number of peasant beneficiaries is shown in Table 13 for all three stages of the land reform.

Under the second phase, land owners in the DIP area only availed themselves of the two options (out of five possible ones) of leasing the land for 30 years, or dividing it between themselves and the peasants. 14 villages were divided; 13 in full. One was divided in part – to an extent of 17 **nokhuds**, seven **nokhuds** out of the 24 having already been distributed during the first phase. The divided villages made up 13.7 village equivalents, equal to 8.1 per cent of the villages in the DIP area.

The remaining 148 privately owned villages were leased for 30 years, 76 in whole and 72 in part. Of the latter, two were partly mechanized and had also been affected by the first phase. A further 14 villages were partly mechanized and were included in the programme for the first time. Another 51 villages had already been involved in the first phase. Two villages (Jeibar and Qaleh Robe-e Kuyekh) partly privately owned and partly privately endowed, together with the three remaining villages (Bonvar Nazer, Seyheh and Ganjeh), which were partly privately owned and partly publicly endowed, were also leased for 30 years.

In addition, Qaleh Agha Hassani, which was wholly privately endowed, and the remaining partly endowed parts of Jeibar and Qaleh Robe-e Kuyekh, were leased for the same terms as the privately owned villages. Thus, the total village shares involved equalled 1270.2 **nokhuds** (nearly 53.0 village equivalents). These, together with 76 villages leased in whole, amounted to 130 village equivalents (76.9 per cent of the total DIP villages).

The two villages wholly publicly endowed (Biatian Raffat and Zavieh Mashali), and the three partly publicly endowed

TABLE 13

Beneficiaries of Land Reform, Dez Project Area
(169 villages)

Phase of Land Reform	No. of Peasant Beneficiaries		First time beneficiaries in villages			Second time beneficiaries in villages			Third time beneficiaries in villages partly affected
	No.	% of total (6,927)	Wholly affected	Partly affected	Total	Wholly affected	Partly affected	Total	
First Phase	2,404	34.7	215	2,189	2,404				
Second Phase — Division Option	505	7.3	480		480		25	25	
Second Phase — Lease Option	6,205	88.6	2,916 a	1,127 b	4,043		2,162	2,162	
Third Phase — Division Option	2,984	43.1				1,624	759	2,383	601
Third Phase — Sale Option	3,115	45.0				1,310	244	1,554	1,561
1971 Law — Sale of Public Endowments	316	4.6				106	210	316	

Source: Field studies

Note: a Includes two wholly public endowed villages, leased for 99 years to 106 peasants.
       b Includes three partly endowed villages for charitable purposes, leased for 99 years to 210 peasants.

villages (Bonvar Nazer, Seyheh and Ganjeh) were leased for 99 years. These made a total of 3.1 village equivalents - 1.8 per cent of the total.

Under the third phase, all the leased villages had to be either sold to the tenants or be divided between them and the landowners. Those opting for division included the owners of 39 whole villages who had previously leased their holdings as well as owners of 30 villages which had been leased in part. The aggregate of parts thus divided under the third phase amounts to 23.3 village equivalents which together with the wholly affected 39 villages amounts to 62.3 village equivalents, or 36.8 per cent of all the villages in the DIP area.

The leased village lands which were sold included 38 whole villages and 42 part villages. Of the 38 leased whole villages, one was the privately endowed village of Qaleh Agha Hassani and the remaining 37 villages belonged to private owners. Of the villages sold in part, four were partly mechanized, 36 had been affected by the two previous phases and two villages, (Jeibar and Qaleh Robe-e Kuyekh) were partly privately owned and partly endowed for private purposes. The aggregate amounted to 67.7 village equivalents (40.1 per cent of the total).

The two wholly endowed villages (Biatian Raffat and Zavieh Mashali), and the three partly endowed villages (Bonvar Nazer, Seyheh and Ganjeh) had all been leased for 99 years under the second phase and were subsequently sold to their cultivators under the May 1971 law for the Sale of Public Endowments - being equivalent to 3.1 villages, (1.8 per cent of all the DIP villages).

3.11   Evaluation of the Land Reform

The first phase reform law was explicitly aimed at re-distributing large holdings to sharecropping tenants - 'land-to-the-tiller', in fact. But its primary objective was political rather than solely social and economic, through the destruction of centuries of landowner domination and rural control. The law was formulated with considerable understanding of traditional land holding patterns and, because of its basic simplicity, it was implemented with considerable speed. From January 1962 to January 1963, 1,524 villages were redistributed among 51,720 peasant cultivators,(53) a considerable achievement, in view of the opposition from landowners with a voice in government and fundamental bureaucratic inefficiency. The new-found efficiency was mainly due to Dr Hassan Arsanjani, the Minister of Agriculture who successfully organized a crash programme of reform in remote rural areas.

It is, therefore, not surprising that many comentators explicitly acknowledged the importance of the reforms in 1962. Even a critic such as Mahdavy, admitted in 1965 that "from a social point of view, land reform has had the effect of shaking the foundations of feudalism in Iran"(54). However, the second phase of the land reform lacked the simplicity

of its predecessor and was characterized by a clause permitting owners with holdings below the maximum size to purchase
peasants' root rights - a reversal of the 'land-to-the-tiller'
principle. The second phase was also implemented more
slowly, starting two years after it was legally instituted
on 17th January 1963.

Apparently, one of the reasons for this was that reform
was 'unpopular' with middle-size landowners - numerically
the largest group and threatened directly by the second
phase. "Army officers, government officials, merchants and
others who had made small investments in land resented being
lumped together with major landowners as a target for reform.
In addition, landlords who had lost all but one village
resented being subject to further expropriation of land.
Because of the controversy, the reform was stalled for a time"
(55).

The third phase of land reform was "the logical outcome
of a reform in the interest of a true peasantry, and was
directed against those landlords who either still maintained
a foothold through the agricultural unit or were party to
tenancy contract"(56). Although the third phase was to end
the land redistribution programme by 22nd September 1971,
the many problems involving **musha** and the land right
inheritance system among peasants required much more time
and the deadline was extended to 9th January 1977(57) - the
15th anniversary of the original Land Reform Law.

The programme as a whole has also been criticised for
discriminating between the various classes of peasant-share-
croppers received land but agricultural labourers did not,
although their needs were far greater. Also, the reform
discriminated between types of tenants since cultivators of
small areas received less than did cultivators of large areas.
Land evaluation formulae also created 'unfair' price differentials since they were based on land tax previously paid.
Corrupt landowners, since they were paid correspondingly
less on acquisition, thus ensured that their sharecroppers
could buy land at a much lower price than sharecroppers
of 'honest' landowners who had paid their tax in full.
Finally, as Jones in his 1964-65 case study of the economic
impact of the Land Reform in a Hosseinabad Sub-district
village, near Shush, suggests, the reform did not increase
the general level of agricultural output, although it did
improve income and income distribution. "The level of agricultural output remained unchanged because the farmers of
Hosseinabad continue to employ the same production techniques
as were used prior to land reform"(58).

3.12   Traditional and Modern Irrigation Systems in Rural
        Dezful

The Dez Project area lies in a well-watered region of Iran,
traditionally served by a series of nine rivers and streams
together with numerous ancient waterways. Intricate systems,
involving 36 privately owned open and underground canals

watered more than two-thirds of the Project area. The new irrigation system which has now replaced them has not been created or controlled by the rural communities - it is externally directed change - and has influenced aspects of rural Dezful economic and social life.

The traditional irrigation system had generally required both the landlord's financial involvement and his considerable communal influence as, according to the former landlords, peasants in the Dezful area had not been directly involved in managing it. They have also claimed that if a government-sponsored irrigation system had not replaced the traditional one, peasant farming would have collapsed after land reform - the two, land and water reform, were interdependent. This view is supported by those land reform critics who have maintained that "the peasants to whom the land was transferred would not be able to run the irrigation system"(59).

3.13   Ancient Irrigation Methods

Much of the region now in the Dez Irrigation Project was irrigated in ancient times and most of the ruins of canals and associated equipment is in an area beween Karkheh, Shaur, Dez and Karun - the "heart land of Northern Khuzestan"(60). The ruins include the 80-kilometre Darius canal (about 500 BC) which carried water from the Karkheh River southward, a dam built by Sassanian (226 - 651 AD), on the Karkheh River, and Sassanian water conduits delivering water from Dez to Jundi Shahpur. Rawlinson indicates that Jundi Shahpur "was watered by some magnificent aqueducts, excavated at an immense depth in the soil rock and derived from the river of Dezful about five miles (eight kilometres) above the town"(61).

Although dry farming was the main form of agriculture, irrigation was also practised in the areas surrounding towns. The ancient system was "a communal way of irrigation by which the water from the rivers (Dez and Karkheh) was led through canals to the land where it was left spilling freely to irrigate large areas"(62) - a system quite unlike the one in use from historic times until immediately prior to the DIP.

3.14   The Traditional Irrigation System

The traditional system which had been in operation for the past 70-100 years (63) consisted of a series of 36 open canals and qanats (see Table 14), watering some 90,000 hectares (60 per cent) of the DIP area.

Qanats are gently sloping underground tunnels bringing water by gravity from upland sources. Built for the past 2,500 years as a series of interconnected wells, dug at intervals of 30 to 100 metres, the vertical shafts also serve as a means of ventilating the tunnel during seasonal cleanings. Seven major qanats were originally used in the DIP area,

TABLE 14

Distribution of the Water Channels
within the Dez Project Area, 1959.

Irrigation Districts	Number of Channels			Area Irrigated Gross[a]	
	Open Canals	Qanats	Total	Ha.	%
Dez, East Bank	13	5	18	35,000	38.9
Dez, West Bank (Incl.Bala Rud)	6	2	8	14,300	15.9
Karkheh	5	0	5	31,300	34.8
Shaur	2	0	2	6,040	6.7
Sish Mansour-Lureh	3	0	3	3,390	3.7
Total	29	7	36	90,030	100.0

Source: Nederlandsche Heidemaatschappij, "Report on the Dez Irrigation Project
Supplement No1", June 1959 (unpublished), p IV-1.

Note: a. The area adjusted according to current boundaries.

leading from the Dez River at a point ten kilometres from
Dezful and watering three villages eight kilometres away
(Shahabad, Bonvar-e Shami and Siah Mansoor) and two farm
areas (Qumish Hadjian and Qumish Muminan), while two others
branched off from the west bank of the River Dez at Dezful,
and irrigated two villages (Sanjar and Jateh).
    The open canals were filled by directing water into them
through temporary weirs - brush and stone dams, called
salehs locally, made from interlocking timber comb-shaped
baskets filled with brush and stone.   Traditionally, each
peasant juft-holder supplied one donkey load of brush, leaf-
o-lafe, as the dam was rebuilt annually.   Water was subsequently sub-channelled to appropriate farming areas and
fields rather than spilling freely over large surfaces as it
had in ancient practice.
    According to custom, since landowners also owned the canals
and qanats, they were allowed to obstruct the river temporarily to fill their own canals to the maximum.   Thus landlords upstream had the special privilege of satisfying their
maximum water requirements, while those downstream could
not obtain sufficient water.   In dry years, the resulting
competition to save the summer crops (landlords received

50 per cent harvest share here) was serious and could lead to conflict. Apparently downstream landowner agents would remove upstream stone and brush dams, upstream landowner agents then reacted and clashes could result.

Only a few landlords had sufficient influence and power in the community to manage the traditional irrigation system. These water managers themselves represented the interests of a large number of landowners. The landowners were also responsible for maintaining the main canals from river to village farm lands. In most cases they usually hired semi-professional foremen, **sarbildars**, and several hundred labourers, **bildars**, for one to two weeks for the annual canal cleaning – a process that involved heavy financial investment.

The procedures involved are well illustrated by the case of the village of Bonvar Hossein which shared its canal with two neighbouring villages: Aliabad and Ali-Bol-Hossein. The canal inlet in the River Dez was about two kilometres downstream from Dezful and, before the 1960s, some 70 landowners had delegated their responsibilities for water to one Hassan Asaf.

The canal was typically cleaned twice a year: in May to supply the rice nursery and in July to supply the rice fields. First the costs involved were estimated and funds accumulated. Traditionally, estimates were made by a **sarbildar**, a local canal service foreman, and then the representative would divide the cost between all landowners in terms of their holdings. Each would deposit his share in a designated bank account and then work would commence.

The canal was some 12 kilometres long and ten metres wide at the river inlet, narrowing to about three metres just at the village farm land and required 300–400 labourers, **bildars**, working in teams of three to four, for ten to 15 days, removing two **gazs** (roughly 30 centimetres) of silt deposit along its length. The cost per man of 50 to 60 rials in 1962 per six-hour day (6 am to 12 noon) amounted to about 250,000 rials. In addition at least three canal foremen and one head foreman were paid a total of 10,000 rials at 120 to 200 rials per day. Finally, **saleh** construction costs – one third of total labour cost (90,000 rials) were included, to reach an overall total of 350,000 rials ($4,667) per year. This was equivalent to a landlord's net share harvest income from 900 hectares in 1958/59.

3.15   The New Irrigation System

The new government-sponsored irrigation system which has replaced the traditional, privately controlled system consists of perpetual gravity flow of regulated water from a re-regulating dam and a diversion dam to two main canals on each side of the River Dez, and a series of laterals and distributaries which extend to headgate (farm) units of approximately 100 hectares (64) where flow is controlled by a lockable sluice-gate. The project is divided into 20 irrigation blocks, nine on the east side and 11 on the west side

of the River Dez. The total net irrigable area is 91,762
hectares, (65) but an additional 10,000 hectares of Haft Tappeh
sugar cane plantation are also supplied. In comparing the
irrigated land area in the new and traditional systems, it
needs to be mentioned that only about 38,650 hectares (gross)
of land which were dry farmed traditionally are now irrigated
instead by the new system – 30 per cent of the total area
irrigated by regulated flow.

Initially regulated water was made available to 58 villages
of the pilot area, supply facilities being extended to the
west bank of the River Dez (Stage I) in July 1967 and supply
starting in February 1970. This was followed by the final
Stage II programme to cover the east side of the Project
which was still in progress in the Summer of 1974. Table
15 gives details of the progress of the project.

3.16   Economic and Social Effects

There are two economic features in the new irrigation
system – restricted water measurement and water charges –
which are unfamiliar to local peasants. Traditionally
peasants did not pay for the water they used, nor was the
amount controlled. Instead the landlords' financial burden
of canal maintenance was compensated by the size of their
harvest portions (50 per cent). Thus peasants had no concept
of 'value' in the context of irrigation water and practised
no conservation of it.

Now, water discharge is measured in cubic metres, and
charges are imposed accordingly, with consequent awareness
of cost on the part of the peasant user. General policy by
the KWPA has been to recover any pre-project water costs
and local economic capabilities were taken into account.
Thus, water charges consisted of base charges and surcharges. The base charges (750 rials per hectare per annum)
were an average of pre-project costs ranging from 638 to 855
rials. The surcharge of 0.1 rials per cubic metre corres-
ponded to an estimated 15 per cent of the increase of agricultural product values because of regulated irrigation. In
the pilot area villages the charges were limited to 750 rials
per hectare without surcharge, water being supplied at two
cubic metres per second per hectare. In Chogha Sorkh, for
example, in 1963 charges of 9,120 rials (for a 12 hectare **juft**)
were paid in two equal instalments after winter and summer
harvests (66).

After March 1974 the base and surcharges were combined
and the new rate of 0.2 rials per cubic metre, although
acceptable for agribusinesses, was too much for the peasants.
This is because the main traditional summer crop is rice,
which requires large quantities of water and substitution
of another crop more economical in water requires special
technical aid – currently non-existent or very rudimentary.
Moreover, fields are mostly unlevelled and water efficiency
(67) is relatively low, ?5 – 45 per cent(68). To level the land
would cost more than 20,000 rials ($286) per hectare, an

TABLE 15

Land Area and Number of Vilages Incorporated in
the Three Stages of Regulated Flow of
The Dez Irrigation Project

Stages of the Irrigation Project	Date Scheme Introduced	Area d.				Villages Incorporated	
		Gross		Net			
		Ha.	%	Ha.	%	No.	%
Pilot, Dez East [a]	July 1963 to June 1965	22,000	17.1	20,000 18.9		58	34.3
Haft Tappeh plantation [c]	1958	24,000 [e]	18.7	11,163	10.5	3	1.8
Stage I Dez West	Feb 1970 to May 1972	47,100 [f]	36.6	42,669	40.3	66	39.0
Stage II Dez East [a] [b]	1973 to 1975	32,240 [g]	25.1	29,093	27.4	36	21.3
Not covered – ie Trad. Irrigation no regulated flow	–	3,340 [h]	2.5	3,095	2.9	6	3.6
Total	–	128,680	100.0	106,020	100.0	169	100.0

Sources: a. D & R, Dez Irrigation Project, Stage II, Feasibility,
New York USA, D & R, 1968, p 20.

b. D & R, Dez Irrigation Project, Stage I, Feasibility,
New York USA, D & R, 1968, Table III-1.

c. Letter from Y.Rahmani, Director of Haft Tappeh Cane Sugar
Division, KWPA, 12th September, 1974.

Notes: d. Gross hectarage includes the farm roads, village homesteads, etc.,
while the net hectarage contains only the cultivated land area.

e. The area includes north and south expansions –
The Plantation was initially (1958-69) pump irrigated,
gravity flow was introduced in 1970.

f. The Karkheh Flood Plain and Qomaysh of Dez East are included.

g. The Dez Flood Plain is included.

h. The agricultural lands of the Zavieh Island on Dez West are
not supplied with the new canal water.

impossible   cost   for   the   average   peasant.   Agribusiness
enterprises, however, have the technical and financial means
to grow cash crops – cotton or asparagus – and have levelled
their lands raising irrigation efficiency to 60 per cent(69).

In Bonvar Hossein, peasants have indicated that payment
of the new water charges would leave them with smaller
incomes than those from traditional sharecropping. In fact,
water for rice crops in Bonvar Hossein is estimated at seven
litres per second per hectare for 90 days, a total of 54,432
cubic metres per hectare.

At the suggested water charge rate this would cost about
11,000 rials per hectare but average rice yields per hectare
there in 1973 were about 1,800 kilograms, valued at 36,000
rials (at the wholesale average price of 20 rials) per hectare
in summer 1974. Thus the water cost is nearly one third
of gross return, almost equivalent to the traditional landlord's harvest share because he also paid the rice water
supervisor, **mirab** – now paid by the peasants (in 1973/74
this was 1,900 rials per **juft**). As a result of the high water
costs, rice plantings in summer 1974 were restricted to 50
per cent of the 1968/69 figure of 77 hectares(70).

There have also been certain social changes, most noticeably the prevention of conflicts over irrigation water and a
reduction in manual jobs connected with irrigation. The
traditional competition between landlords over scarce water
in dry years has vanished with regulated flow and the new
canals are dredged by mechanical dredgers, thus depriving
the **sarbildars** and **bildars** of a traditional livelihood.
However, the expansion of orchards and gardens has, to some
extent, mitigated the loss of traditional activities.

Chapter Notes

1.   Percy Sykes, **A History of Persia**, Vol 1 (London UK: Routledge and Kegan Paul, 1969), p 38.

2.   Hale, Flannery and Neely. **op. cit.**, p 1.

3.   Adams, **op. cit.**, p 109 - 122. (In Adams's study, a village is defined, in the ancient context, as a settlement occupying less than four hectares; while a small town is referred to as an inhabited ares of four to five hectares and a large town to as much as ten hectares.)

4.   Lambton, **The Persian Land Reform 1962 - 1966**, op. cit., p 6.

5.   Ibid.

6.   The population figures are based on unpublished estimates of the Khuzestan Plan and Budget Office, 1974.

7.   Lambton, **The Persian Land Reform 1962 - 1966**, op. cit., p 6.

8.   X de Planhol, "Geography of Settlement", in W.B.Fisher, **The Cambridge History of Iran, Vol I, The Land of Iran**, (Cambridge, UK: Cambridge University Press, 1968), p 426.

9.   De Planhol, **op. cit.**, p 426.

10. Ibid., p 425.

11. De Planhol, **op. cit.**, p 428.

12. A **chal** is a farming area (field) with more or less uniform topography and fertility.

13. P.H.T.Beckett, "Persia's Need for Land Reform", **Fortnightly Review,** No 171, 1957, p 100.

14. Nikki R. Keddie, **Historical Obstacles to Agrarian Change in Iran,** (Claremont, California, USA: The School of Oriental Studies, 1960), p 11.

15. Personal interview with Semnani, Head of the Dezful **Shahristan** Property and Document Registration Office, 22 January 1974.

16. Nederlandsche Heidemaatschappij (Heidemy), **Dez Irrigation Project Report of Land and Water Rights,** (Arnhem, Holland: Heidemy 1960).

17. Lambton, **Landlord and Peasant in Persia,** op. cit., p 238.

18. **The Cambridge History of Islam,** Vol II, 1970, p 519.

19. Endowment lands belong mainly to religious shrines, the income being used to maintain them.

20. M.A.Katouzian "Land Reform in Iran, a Case Study in the Political Economy of Social Engineering" **The Journal of Peasant Studies**, Vol 1, No 2, 1974, p 229.

21. Ibid.

22. Ajami, "Land Reform and Modernization of the Farming Structure in Iran", **op. cit.**, p 1.

23. Assadollah Alam, "The Land Tenure Situation in Iran" in K.H.Parsons, R.J.Penn and P.M.Roup **Land Tenure, Proceedings of the International Conference on Land Tenure and Related Problems in World Agriculture** (Madison, Wisconsin, USA: The University of Wisconsin Press, 1956), p 95.

24. John H. Hobbs, "Land Reform in Iran: A Revolution from Above", **Orbis**, Vol 7, No 3, 1963, p 619.

25. George B.Baldwin, **Planning and Development in Iran**, (Baltimore, Maryland USA: The John Hopkins Press, 1967), p 94.

26. Paul Ward English, **City and Village in Iran: Settlement and Economy in the Kirman Basin** (Madison, Wisconsin USA: The University of Wisconsin Press, 1966) p 141.

27. Manoutcher Nezam-Mafi, "Une Region Agricole de l'Iran Le Khuzestan" (An Agricultural Region of Iran, Khuzestan), (Unpublished Docteur des Sciences, Université de Lausanne, Switzerland, 1961), pp 81 - 86.

28. Ibid.

29. Hadi Shams Zandjani, "Allocation of Resources under Agrarian Reform in Iran", (Unpublished Ph.D. Dissertation, Sidney Sussex College, University of Cambridge, UK, 1973), p 34.

30. Lambton, **Landlord and Peasant in Persia, op. cit.**, p 269.

31. Lorimer, **op. cit.**, p 1754.

32. Nederlandsche Heidemaatschappij, "Report on the Dez Irrigation Project", **op. cit.**, p 111 - 16, 17.

33. Alam, **op. cit.**, pp 95 - 100.

34. Yahya Armajani, **Iran** (Englewood Cliffs, JJ, USA: Prentice-Hall Inc., 1972), p 16 and McLachlan, **op. cit.**, p 692.

35. Shams Zandjani. **op. cit.**, p 40.

36. McLachlan, **op. cit.**, p 691.

37. Shams Zandjani, **op. cit.**, p 49.

38. Lambton, **The Persian Land Reform 1962 - 1966, op. cit.**, p 30.

39. Nikki R. Keddie, "The Iranian Village Before and After Land Reform", **The Journal of Contemporary History**, Vol 3, No 3, 1968, p 88.

40.   Hossein Mahdavy, "The coming Crisis in Iran", **Foreign Affairs**, Vol 44, No 1, 1965, p 138.

41.   Smith **et al. op cit.**, p 412.

42.   **Ibid..** p 411.

43.   Khatibi, **op. cit.**, p 65.

44.   D.R.Denman, **The King's Vista** (Berkhamsted, Herts, UK: Geographical Publications Limited, 1973), p 147.

45.   Khatibi, **op. cit.**, p 65.

46.   R.R.Hoeppner, "Aspekte der Agrarreform Irans" (Aspects of Agrarian Reform in Iran) **Orient**, Vol 14, No 1, 1973, pp 37 - 40.

47.   Ajami, "Land Reform and Modernization of the Farming Structure in Iran", **op. cit.**, p 6.

48.   Shams Zandjani, **op. cit.**, p 112.

49.   Kayhan, 26 Mehr 1352 (18 September 1973).

50.   Ajami, "Land Reform and Modernization of the Farming Structure in Iran", **op. cit.**, p 7.

51.   Denman, **op. cit.**, p 339.

52.   For a detailed account of land reform in the Dez Irrigation Project Area see:
Cyrus Salmanzadeh and Gwyn E. Jones, "An Approach to the Micro Analysis of the Land Reform Program in Southwestern Iran", **Land Economics**, Vol 55, No 1, 1979, pp 108 - 127.

53.   Ajami, "Land Reform and Modernization of the Farming Structure in Iran", **op. cit.**, p 4.

54.   Mahdavy, **op. cit.**, p 141.

55.   **Ibid.**

56.   Shams Zandjani, **op. cit.**, p 105.

57.   **Kayhan Havii**, 12 Khordad 2535 (2 July 1976).

58.   Royal Maurice Jones, "The Short-Run Economic Impact of Land Reform on Feudal Village Irrigated Agriculture in Iran", (Unpublished Ph.D. Dissertation, University of Maryland, College Park, Maryland, USA, 1967), p 11.

59.   Lambton, **The Persian Land Reform 1962 - 1966, op. cit.**, p 274.

60.   Hale, Flannery and Neely, **op. cit.**,p 12.

61.   Rawlinson, **op. cit.**, p 72.

62.   **Ibid.**

63.   Veenenbos, **op. cit.**, p 58.

64.   D & R, **Dez Irrigation Project, op. cit.**, p V-8.

65.   D & R, **Dez Irrigation Project, Stage I, Feasibility Report Supplement, op. cit.**, p 111 - 1.

66.   Juft: the right given to a peasant to cultivate a portion
       of the village land as a sharecropper – hence, by
       association, the actual portion of land allotted to a
       peasant sharecropper. This is now the usual meaning.

       The estimated cost of water distribution was reported
       around $34,075,000. a)   However, the level of water
       charges was to be fixed with a view to recovering the
       following:

       i.   the allocatable capital costs of the project:

       ii.   administrative and operating costs of the project,
             including cost of: servicing of loans, water
             management, maintenance, repair and improvement
             of dams, canals and other facilities;

       iii. costs of research, studies and services and agri-
             cultural and marketing services and studies,
             training and education programmes b).

             a) D & R, **Dez Irrigation Project, op. cit.**, p
             V–20.

             b) D & R, **Dez Irrigation Project, Stage I, Feasi-
             bility, op. cit.**, p XI–1.

67.   Water efficiency is referred to as the percentage of
       irrigation water retained for the plant use, thus it
       excludes the seepage, run–off etc.

68.   Nederlandsche Heidemaatschappij, "Report on the Dez
       Irrigation Project Supplement No 1". op. cit., p IV–4.

69.   D & R, **Dez Irrigation Project, Stage II, Feasibility
       Report**, op. cit., p 70.

70.   Dez Irrigation Project Crop Survey Records, Unpublished
       1970.

4 THE DEMOGRAPHY OF DEZFUL SHAHRISTAN AND SELECTED VILLAGES IN THE DEZ IRRIGATION PROJECT AREA

4.1 Introduction

Until 1956 there was little information on rural and urban populations in Iran. However, the 1956 and 1966 national censuses have provided demographers with basic data on Iran's urban and rural populations and for projections of future trends. In Dezful there has only been a general population survey by Gremliza(1) and a study by Ehlers (2) but no extensive comparative demographic studies.
The population generally has high fertility and relatively low and declining mortality. In 1971, the birth rate was estimated at 48 per thousand and the death rate at about 16 per thousand, equivalent to a current annual increase of about three per cent, one of the highest in the world (3). This is mainly due to early marriage, for although the pre-1974 minimum legal marriageable age of 15 years for girls and 18 years for boys, has been raised to 18 and 20 years respectively, the restrictions are rarely observed and village girls aged about ten or 12 are often given in marriage. The consequence is a high birth rate, on average seven live births per woman, and larger households in rural areas than in towns: in 1956 the average household in urban centres had 4.9 members but in rural areas totals reached 5.2 members (4).
The rapid population growth has been paralleled by rapid urbanization(5). Two decades ago, less than one third of the population lived in urban centres, but by 1976, this proportion had almost reached 50 per cent, and is currently increasing at 4.3 per cent per annum – double the rate of increase in rural areas. The differential is partly due to rural–urban migration which itself may lead to greater urban unemployment and affect agricultural productivity by inflating the rural dependency ratio, (inactive population/active population) estimated at 0.99 in 1966, as compared with 0.658 in the United States(6).

TABLE 16

Demographic Change in Iran and Khuzestan
(Population in thousands)

Population Feature	Iran [a] (Area 1,650,000 sq.km)			Khuzestan Province [b] (Area 64,654 sq. km.)			Dezful Shahristan (Area 4,775 sq. km.)						Dez Project Area [c] (Area 1,670 sq. km.)	
	1956	1966	1976 [g]	1956	1966	1972	1956 [g]	1956 (adjusted) [d]	1966	1966 (adjusted) [e]	1972 [f]	1976 [g]	1966	1972
Population Total (Approximate	18,900	25,800	33,591	1,138	1,587	2,005	180.5	147.6	175.5	180.3	238.0	301.3	135.0	122.0
Population Urban	5,900	9,800	15,715	610	896	1,265	60.9	60.9	105.2	105.2	148.0	160.5	89.0	
Population Urban % of total	(31.4)	(38.0)	(46.7)	(53.6)	(56.5)	(58.1)	(33.7)	(41.2)	(60.0)	(58.4)	(62.2)	(53.3)	(65.9)	
Population Rural and Nomads	13,000	16,000	17,876	528	691	911	119.6	86.7	70.3	75.1	90.0	140.8	46.0	
Population Rural and Nomads % of total	(68.6)	(62.0)	(53.3)	(46.4)	(43.5)	(41.9)	(66.3)	(58.8)	(40.0)	41.6	(37.8)	(46.7)	(34.1)	
Average Rate of Annual Increase, Total, %		3.1	2.7		3.6				2.0					
Average Rate of Annual Increase, Urban, %		5.1	–		4.1				5.8					
Average Rate of Annual Increase, Rural, %		2.1	–		2.9				1.7					
Average Population Density (persons/sq. km.)	11.5	15.6	20.4	17.6	24.5	31.0		30.9	36.8				80.8	

Sources: a. The 1956 and 1966 population figures for Iran are based on the 1st and 2nd national census reports respectively and the 1976 estimates (projections) are based on Khazaneh H and Darbandi A.S., see Chap.1.13 for full reference (No 1), p. 26.
b. The 1956 and 1966 population figures for the Khuzestan Province and Dezful Shahristan are also based on the 1st and 2nd national census reports. The 1972 population estimates are derived from: Khuzestan Plan and Budget Office, "Khuzestan Urban and Rural Population", unpublished report, 1973.
c. The 1966 population figures of the Dez Project area are based on: D & R, Dez Irrigation Project Stage I, Feasibility Supplement, New York, USA, D & R, 1968, p 11 – 13.

Notes: d. The area included in the Dezful Shahristan changed both between 1956–1966 and between 1966–1972. Between 1956 and 1966, six dehestans, sub-districts, were detached from the administrative authority of the Dezful Shahristan and transferred to Khurramabad and Izeh and Dehluran Shahristans; and
e. Between 1966 and 1972, the Sardasht Bakhsh, district, including four dehestans (administratively) detached from the Izeh Shahristan and transferred to the Dezful Shahristan. Because of these changes adjustments have been made in the Dezful Shahristan population records both in 1956 and 1966.
f. The rural population records of 1956 and 1966 national census classified Shush as a rural area (since its population in both censuses was less than 5,000). However, its population has since increased to over 5,000, thus it is now classified as an 'urban centre'. In the above table, the population of Shush has been included in the population of urban centres and not rural.
g. 1976 figures drawn from the preliminary results of the Census of 2525.

4.2 Urban and Rural Population in Dezful

The general population features of Iran, Khuzestan Province, Dezful **Shahristan** and the Dez Project area are shown in Tables 16 and 17. Generally, in contrast to the national pattern, more people in Khuzestan live in towns than in villages. perhaps because of the development of the oil industry which has created new urban centres, and the urban population almost doubled between 1956 and 1972 while rural areas grew at less than three per cent per annum.

The Dezful **Shahristan** has shown a similar increase, the urban population between 1956 and 1972 in Dezful, Andimeshk and Shush, growing annually at five per cent, 8.2 per cent and 10.6 per cent respectively since 1966. Currently the fastest growing town in the Dezful **Shahristan** is Shush. This is mainly due to the expansion of the Haft Tappeh sugar cane operation and the consequent increase in technical and field staff who tend to live in Shush. The growth of Andimeshk could be related to an increase in administrative staff living there and to an influx of army personnel from the base nearby. Dezful may have grown recently as a consequence of the government's purchase of land downstream from the dam for agribusiness use. 22 villages have been demolished and many inhabitants have migrated to Dezful and taken up urban employment, rather than settle in a **shahrak** (resettlement centre). In addition, the growing population of Dezful Air Base nearby has presumably, been included in the Dezful population figure. Records for the Dez Project area only began in 1966 and show population patterns similar to the Dezful **Shahristan** as a whole.

4.3 Village Populations

Table 18 summarizes total populations, average size and total numbers for villages and hamlets in Iran, Khuzestan and Dezful. The striking features are, first, the decline in nomadic populations, as a result of the 1930s settlement programmes, and, second, the disparity in size between villages in Iran generally and those in the Dez Project area. In 1966, the mean rural settlement size in Iran was about 236 persons. The corresponding average for Khuzestan Province was 183 persons and for Dezful **Shahristan** it was 193. In the Dez Irrigation Project area, however, it was 315 – considerably higher than the national, provincial or **Shahristan** average.

This could be due to several factors, such as availability of water and land, and soil fertility. Khuzestan Province has a high percentage of low fertility land despite the abundance of water , and soil salinity in the vast lower Khuzestan plains is considerably higher than that in the upper plains (of which the Dez Project is a part)(7). Productivity is further lowered by an inadequate land drainage and thus there is a 'mild' population pressure on land

TABLE 17

Growth of Urban and Rural Population Dezful **Shahristan**

Year	Towns in Dezful **Shahristan**			Urban Population		Rural and Nomadic Population		Total Dezful **Shahristan**	
	Dezful	Andimeshk	Shush	No.	%	No.	%	No.	%
1900 (a)	16,000								
1915 (a)	45,000								
1956 (b) (unadjusted)	52,121	7,324	1,433	60,878	33.7	119,582	66.3	180.464	100.0
1956 (adjusted)	52,121	7,324	1,433	60,878	41.2	86,731	58.8	147,609	100.0
1966 (c) (unadjusted)	84,499	16,195	4,548	105,242	60.0	70,261 (e)	40.0	175,503	100.0
1966 (d) (adjusted)	84,499	16,165	4,548	105,242	58.4	75,081	41.6	180.323	100.0
1972 (d)	113,000	26,000	9,000	148,000	62.2	90,000	37.8	238,000	100.0

Sources: (a) Bharier, J., Economic Development in Iran 1900-1970, London UK, OUP 1971.

(b) General Statistical Department of the Ministry of Interior, **Gozaresh Mashruh-e Hozeh Sarshomary Dezful**, (Detailed Census Report of the Dezful Region) Vol 19, (Tehran, Iran: General Statistical Dept., 1959), p 1.

(c) Statistical Centre of Iran, Plan Organization, **National Census of Population and Housing**, 1966, Vol 77, Dezful **Shahristan**. (Tehran, Iran: Statistical Centre, 1968), pp 11 – 18.

(d) Population estimates of 1972 are based on the report of: Khuzestan Plan and Budget Office, "Khuzestan Urban and Rural Population", unpublished report, 1973.

(e) The boundaries of the Dezful Census District in 1956 were not the same as the boundaries of Dezful **Shahristan** in 1966. Six **dehestans**, sub-districts, with a population of 32,851 or 18.2 per cent of the total population of the district in 1956 were detached from the Dezful Census District and added to the Izeh, Dehloran and Khurramabad **Shahristans**.

reflected in the average village size in Khuzestan Province. There is a similar disparity between Iran and Dezful Shahristan on the one hand, and the Dez Project area on the other in terms of village size distribution. Table 19 shows that the percentage of larger villages is comparatively higher in the Dez Project \area than elsewhere - a further indication that there is a direct relationship between soil fertility and mean village population size.

4.4   Population characteristics of Dez Irrigation Project villages

The 145 villages in the Dez Project area can be classified in terms of four demographic factors:-

(1) population size

(2) changes in population size between 1966 and 1973,

(3) mean household size

(4) change in household size between 1966 and 1973.

(1) Approximately half of the villages in the DIP area have a population of less than 250 - an 'unofficial' cut-off point to distinguish between "non-viable" and "viable" villages. Those under 250 are implicitly considered too small to be served by government-sponsored services. The smaller villages will probably be phased out either by merging them into larger villages or by moving their inhabitants to re-settlement centres.
Village population size in 1973 varied from a minimum of ten (Miyan Choghan-e Salehipur) to a maximum of 3,085 (Hashieh Sheikh Khalaf), the mean being 369. In 1966 the average population was 310 and village size varied from a minimum of 11 (Miyan Choghan-e Salehipur) to a maximum of 2,344 (Amlieh Taymour).

(2) Changes in village population size (see Table 20) between 1966 and 1973 are more complex. Some 15 per cent of villages decreased in size while the remainder increased, in some cases by more than 100 per cent. In Qaleh Seyyid and Qaleh No Shamsabad for instance population increase during this period has been 116 and 91 per cent respectively. This rapid increase is partly due to the influx of inhabitants from villages affected by the agribusiness scheme - with consequent effects on the price of village housing land. In Qaleh No Shamsabad land price in the village residential area increased from 50 rials per square metre in 1967 to 500 rials in 1973. In those villages covered by the agri-business scheme peasants were eventually to be evacuated and moved to new resettlement centres so percentage population changes would have been lower, although it is likely that these plans will now be changed .

(3) The mean household size has been calculated from the 1973 Malaria Eradication Department Village Survey where

TABLE 18

Rural Population Distribution in Iran, Khuzestan Province,
Dezful Shahristan and the Dez Irrigation Project Area

Area	Year	Total popu-lation '000	Rural popu-lation '000	Nomadic popu-lation '000	Hamlets (50 inhabitants)			Villages (50 inhabitants)			Rural Settlements	
					Popu-lation '000	No. of Hamlets	Mean Hamlet size	Popu-lation '000	No. of villages	Mean village size	No. of settle-ment centres	Mean size
Iran	1900 [a]	9,860	7,820	2,470	182			5,168	15,200	340		
Iran	1956	18,900	13,000	240	561			12,760	39,099	312		
Iran	1966	25,800	16,000	240	484.14	21,624	22	15,760	45,133	338	66,757	236
Khuzestan Province	1966 [b]	1,587	695.18								3,800	183
Khuzestan Province	1972 [c]	2,005	839.36								3,800	221
Dezful Shahristan	1966 [d]	175.5	75.10								390	193
Dezful Shahristan	1972	238	90								390	231
Dez Irrigation Project Area (Existing villages excluding shahraks)	1966 [e]	135	44.1								140	315
	1973 [f]		52.82								143	370

Sources: a. Bharier J., Economic Development in Iran 1900-1970, London UK, OUP 1971, pp 58-60, (data 1900-1966).
b. Statistical Centre of Iran, Plan and Budget Organization, Amar Nameh Ostan-e Khuzestan (Statistical Records of the Khuzestan Province) (Tehran, Iran: Statistical Centre, 1973), p 4.
c. Khuzestan Plan and Budget Office, "Khuzestan Urban and Rural Population", 1974, unpublished.
d. Ibid., (adapted).
e. Derived from: Statistical Centre of Iran, Plan and Budget Organization, Village Gazetteer, Vol 20, Khuzestan Province, (Tehran, Iran: Statistical Centre, 1971).
f. Derived from: Malaria Eradication Department of Khuzestan Province"1972-73 Village Survey Report", unpublished, 1974.

the average household size per village in nearly one half of the DIP villages was six persons or less. In most of the remaining villages it was between 6.1 and 6.5 persons with a minimum of 4.3 (Boneh Ghaisor) to a maximum of ten persons (Miyan Chogan-e Salehipur, which consisted of only one large household). The overall average in 1973 was 6.1 persons while in 1966 it had been 5.4. Miyan Chogan-e Salehipur, whose total population of 11 in 1966, formed three separate households, produced the lowest mean household size (3.9), while in 1973 the total population was considered as a single household. The general picture is given in Table 21.

(4) There has been a general tendency in rural Dezful during the past 20 years towards a larger average household size. The household mean size in 1956 for the Dezful Shahristan was five(8) while the corresponding average in 1966 was 5.5(9). There has been a similar trend in the DIP villages recently. The mean household size in 1966 being 5.4, and increasing by 1973 to 6.1, as shown in detail in Table 22. The increase is related to the same factors which have led to a rapid increase in the national population, - high fertility rates and, more recently, to relatively low mortality rates. Family planning programmes in rural Iran have had little influence because of a complex set of socio-economic factors, including high illiteracy rates, low rural income levels, demand for more household labour, and, most important of all, fatalism.

4.5 Relationships between Demographic Variables

Apart from the four categories mentioned earlier -population size, household size and population and household size changes, two other variables may be used to categorize the villages in the Dez Irrigation Project area. These are the level of physical and social services (PSS) and the percentage degree of literacy(10). Figure 7 shows the results of these analyses in diagrammatic form. Four strong relationships exist. Three of them are between village population size, the level of PSS and the degree of literacy. In general, in villages of larger relative population, the levels of PSS and degree of literacy are correspondingly higher. In fact villages that are better served with PSS are the ones which have often had formal elementary schools for a number of years, thus giving younger villagers greater opportunity to achieve literacy. Conversely, the level of PSS and degree of literacy in a proportionately larger number of small villages is low for several reasons. Official policy in recent years has been to provide small villages only with rudimentary services as they will eventually be merged with other villages. The number of job opportunities in smaller villages is often limited and younger men, who are relatively more literate than their older colleagues, leave, thus maintaining a low literacy level in the village.

Another strong association exists between average household size (1973) and change in average household size between

TABLE 19

Size distribution of villages in Iran, Dezful Shahristan and Dez Irrigation Project Area

Population Range	Iran [a] 1966		Dezful Shahristan [b] 1972		Dez Project Area [c] 1973–74	
	No. of places	%	No. of places	%	No. of places	%
50 Hamlet	21,624	32.4			21	14.5
51 – 124 Village			286	73.3		
125 – 249 Village	27,367	41.3			52	35.8
250 – 499 Village	10,140	15.2	63	16.2	43	29.7
500 – 999 Village	5,170	7.7				
1,000 – 2,499 Village	1,863	2.8	41	10.5	27	18.6
2,500 – 4,999 Village	593	0.9				
Not known					2	1.4
Total	66,757	100.0	390	100.0	145	100.0

Sources: a. Khosro Khosrovi Jamaeh-Shenasi-e Rustai Iran (Rural Sociology of Iran) (Tehran, Iran: University of Tehran, 1351/1972–73), p 9.
b. Khuzestan Planning and Budget Office, "Khuzestan Urban and Rural Population", 1974, unpublished.
c. Field studies

TABLE 20

Distribution of villages in the Dez Project Area on the basis of percentage population change, 1966–73.

Percentage of change in population size	Frequency of occurrence among existing villages No.	%
Decreased (D) 0	22	15.2
Slight increase (SI) 1 – 15	47	32.4
Moderate increase (MI) 16 – 30	38	26.2
High increase (HI) 31	32	22.1
Not known (NK)	6	4.1
Total	145	100.0

Source: Field studies

1966 and 1973. Over this period a large proportion of villages with a relatively large average household size have experienced a large increase. Conversely, over the same period, only a small proportion of villages with a relatively small average household size have experienced such a large increase. This is probably because villages with a relatively small average household size have lower economic possibilities and the male members of these households often move out to look for employment and housing elsewhere. Such a tendency over time would lead to a decrease in average household size. This is probably also the reason why there is an association between the change in average household size and the percentage change of village population between 1966 and 1973. Here a larger proportion of villages whose population size has decreased, fall into the category of villages whose average household size has also decreased – probably because villagers who have left their households have also left their village and taken up residence elsewhere.

There is also a link between the village population size in 1973 and its percentage change between 1966 and 1973. This link is due to the fact that a larger proportion of villages with very small population sizes have decreased in size and, conversely, a higher proportion of villages with a large population have had a proportionately higher population increase. Furthermore, a proportionately lower number of very small villages than would be expected have experienced a moderate population increase. In general smaller villages are becoming smaller and larger ones are becoming larger. Again this is due in part to the relatively limited economic possibilities in smaller villages so there is gradual population depletion, whereas in villages with larger populations there are relatively more employment opportunities. This has not only prevented a loss, but might have also attracted peasants from other smaller villages. Official policy has aided this process recently by gradually phasing out smaller villages, either by merging them into larger ones, or by resettling the peasants in larger villages. In the latter, social and physical services are better and possibly act as an added inducement in attracting residents from the smaller villages. This would help to explain why villages with a larger population size have had a proportionately higher population increase.

4.6   Living conditions in a Dezful village

Village living conditions are fairly uniform throughout rural Dezful. Bonvar Hossein in 1974 was typical of traditional village life and will be taken as an archetype for Dezful at that time, although there had been few qualitative changes in the intervening period to the end of 1978.

Bonvar Hossein is a **qaleh** village and residence was kept inside the walls until recently. However, since 1970, about 50 per cent of the dwellings (23) have moved outside this protective wall, the result of the gradual improvement in

TABLE 21

Distribution of Villages in the Dez Project Area
on the basis of their average household size in 1973.

Categories for analysis	Village mean size of household (persons/household)	Frequency of occurrence among existing villages	
		No.	%
Relatively small (S)	6.0	72	49.7
Relatively large (L)	6.1	71	49.0
Not known (NK)		2	1.3
Total		145	100.0

Source: Field studies

TABLE 22

Distribution of Villages in the Dez Project Area
on the basis of the absolute changes of
average household size, 1966–1973.

Categories for analysis	Changes in village mean size of household (persons/household)	Frequency of occurrence among existing villages	
		No.	%
Decreased or No Change (D)	0	15	10.3
Slight increase (SI)	0.1 – 0.9	75	51.7
High increase (HI)	1.0	49	33.8
Not known (NK)		6	4.1
Total		145	100.0

Source: Field studies

the security of rural Dezful during the past 50 years. In
terms of its physical and social services, Bonvar Hossein
is in the 'medium' category. Nevertheless, the village still
lacks many basic public facilities such as piped water and
a communal bath house. During the summer villagers bathe
in nearby streams, an activity more convenient for men than
for women who, for reasons of modesty and religion are
restricted to bathing in the late evening, sometimes fully
dressed. In winter streams are too cold and bathing is more
difficult. Some households wait to use public baths on visits
to Dezful. Four of the more enterprising villagers have
devised crude but effective domestic bath facilities known
as **hama-e-boshgaie**, (literally drum bath house) consisting
of a 45-gallon drum placed on the roof and connected to the
bath house below by a pipe. However water must be carried
in buckets from the stream several hundred metres away,
poured into the drum and then heated with a wood or dung
fire (although butane gas is now used by one family instead)-
a lengthy and laborious process. It should be noted that
under Muslim religious law, ceremonial bathing is obligatory
after sexual intercourse or menstruation.

Drinking water is brought daily by the women from the
nearby stream in which they also wash clothes and cooking
utensils. Except for seven houses (less than 15 per cent
of the total), which have private toilets, the inhabitants
share five outdoor latrines located around the village.

All cooking is done in the open courtyards on brush fires,
and bread is baked daily in simple mud ovens. Six households have bought butane gas cooking units but they serve
more as status symbols and are rarely used.

Domestic furniture usually consists of one or two storage
trunks, and perhaps a wardrobe. Bedding consists of single
cotton filled mattresses, cotton quilts, and feather-filled
tubular shaped pillows. A fairly recent introduction is the
presence of Persian rugs which, most probably, reflects the
improved standard of living and financial situation, since,
until two decades ago, Persian rugs were rarely, if ever,
found in villages. They are used mainly to honour a visitor,
particularly if he should come from town.

Similarly, transistor radios are now found in more than
half of the households. Apparently, the first radio was
introduced in 1946 by a German railway engineer working
at nearby Sabz-ab Station, who gave it to the late village
headman (**kadkhoda**). It ran on a re-chargeable battery
which had to be taken to Dezful every few days for re-
charging. Today villagers listen mainly to music or the news
but not to the agricultural programmes which they find irre-
levant to their farming problems. Among the radio owners,
Mash Aidi, the **kadkhoda** in 1974, is, surprisingly, very much
aware of international affairs. His information on current
events is up to date and he listens to BBC World Service
broadcasts in Persian.

Paraffin lamps are used for lighting in Bonvar Hossein
because, although the village is only 20 kilometres from the
hydro-electric plant at Dez Dam, it is not included in the

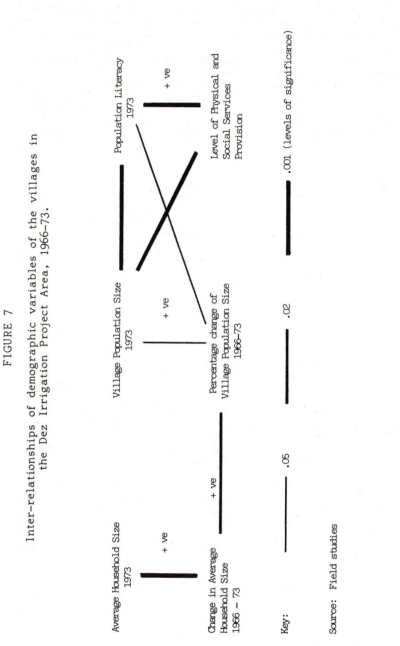

FIGURE 7

Inter-relationships of demographic variables of the villages in
the Dez Irrigation Project Area, 1966–73.

Source: Field studies

electricity supply network which serves mainly urban rather
than rural consumers. Most households possess one or two
paraffin lamps. Electric light is reserved for special
occasions such as weddings and religious festivals, when
a portable diesel operated electric generator is hired by the
particular household for the event they are celebrating at
a cost of as much as 2,000 rials ($29) per day.
In fact, physical and social services found in Bonvar
Hossein are rather limited, and living conditions are still
rudimentary.

4.7 Demographic Characteristics of three Dezfulli Villages

The population of rural Dezful consists predominantly of
non-tribal peasants, referred to in Dezfulli dialect, as
mohali. However, peasants with tribal ties are found in
almost all the DIP villages. There are also a number of
predominantly tribal villages populated by Bakhtiari, Lur
or Arabic-speaking peasants, probably as a result of the
government tribal sedentarization programme of the 1930s.
The Bakhtiari villages are mostly located near the foothills
of the Zagros mountains on the east bank of the River Dez,
while the Lur villages are mainly situated in the area between Dezful and Shush on the west bank of the River Dez.
Arabic-speaking peasants occupy some of the villages on the
Karkheh Flood Plain, between Shush and the Qumat area in
the south of the DIP area.
The number of households with a tribal background varies
in the three case study villages of Bonvar Hossein, Chogha
Sorkh and Shalgahi Sofla. In Bonvar Hossein there are five
households (out of 50) with a Lur tribal background, and
in Chogha Sorkh there are eight households (out of 64) with
a Bakhtiari tribal tie. In Shalgahi Sofla - the village
originally owned by Morteza Qulikhanm a Bakhtiari tribal
chieftain - there are 21 households with a Bakhtiari tribal
background as well as two Arabic-speaking households, (out
of 85 households). In all these three villages, there seems
to be little or no segregation because of ethnic differences,
and nowadays inter-marriage among peasants with different
origins is not uncommon. However, some of the traditional
tribal practices, such as the lineage protective insurance
scheme khin-o-cho, have linked peasants in different villages.

(a) Bonvar Hossein

The traditional village of Bonvar Hossein consists of 50
households with a total population of 295, an average of 5.9
persons per household. The village population distribution
according to age and sex is given in Table 23 and also in
Figure 8. Both show that the population is a young one -
the population pyramid has a broad base and fertility rates
(the number of children less than five years, per 1,000 women
in the child-bearing age group of 15 to 49) are high at 913.

TABLE 23

Population of Bonvar Hossein by Sex and Age
1973-74

Age Group	Male		Female		Total	
	No.	%	No.	%	No.	%
5	22	15.3	31	20.5	53	18.0
5 - 9	25	17.4	25	16.6	50	17.0
10 - 14	16	11.1	20	13.3	36	12.2
15 - 19	19	13.2	15	9.9	34	11.5
20 - 24	9	6.3	8	5.3	17	5.8
25 - 29	4	2.8	10	6.6	14	4.7
30 - 34	7	4.9	7	4.6	14	4.7
35 - 39	5	3.4	6	4.0	11	3.7
40 - 44	7	4.9	5	3.3	12	4.1
45 - 49	5	3.4	7	4.6	12	4.1
50 - 54	5	3.4	2	1.3	7	2.4
55 - 59	6	4.2	1	0.7	7	2.4
60 - 64	5	3.4	6	4.0	11	3.7
65 - 69	2	1.4	1	0.7	3	1.0
70	7	4.9	7	4.6	14	4.7
All Groups	144	100.0	151	100.0	295	100.0
%	48.8		51.2		100.0	

Source: Field studies

Unlike the other two villages there are more women than men
in Bonvar Hossein.   The sex ratio is 95.4 as compared with
122.0 in Chogha Sorkh and 107.4 in Shalgahi Sofla.   The
sharp decrease in the number of males in the 20 - 30 age
group is mainly due to men being drafted into the armed
forces or emigrating to urban centres in search of employment.
This pattern is also observable in the two other villages.

FIGURES 8, 9 and 10

Population pyramids, 1973–74, of the villages of
Bonvar Hossein (top), Chogha Sorkh (middle)
and Shalgahi Sofla (bottom)

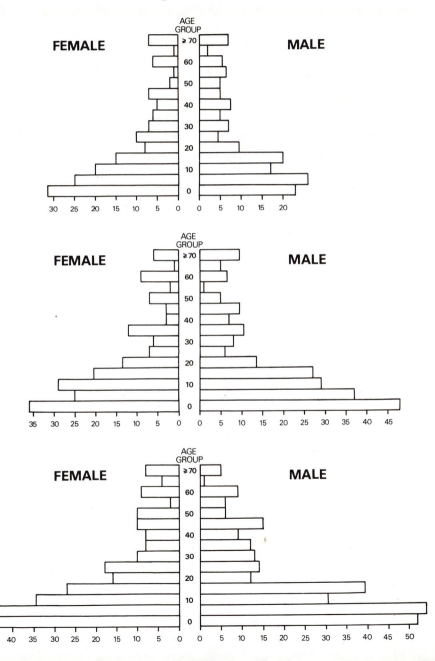

(b) Chogha Sorkh

Chogha Sorkh forms part of a farm corporation and is a
community of 52 households with a total population of 392,
an average household size of 6.1 persons. The population
distribution of the village based on age and sex is presented
in Table 24 and Figure 9 and shows a similar pattern to
that of Bonvar Hossein – a young population and a sharp
decrease in the number of males in the 20 – 30 age category.
However, the village fertility ratio of 1,281 is considerably
higher than the corresponding ratio in Bonvar Hossein or
Shalgahi Sofla. The high fertility ratio could be related
to a decline in child mortality brought about by the introduction of health and sanitation programmes in all 59 DIP
pilot villages (of which Chogha Sorkh was one) in the 1960s.
The sex ratio of 122 is also higher than that for either of
the other two villages, but no socio-economic explanation
of this could be established during field studies.

TABLE 24

Population of Chogha Sorkh by Sex and Age
1973-74

Age Group	Male		Female		Total	
	No.	%	No.	%	No.	%
5	47	21.8	35	19.9	82	20.9
5 – 9	36	16.7	24	13.6	60	15.3
10 – 14	28	13.0	28	15.9	56	14.3
15 – 19	26	12.0	20	11.4	46	11.8
20 – 24	13	6.0	13	7.4	26	6.6
25 – 29	6	2.8	7	4.0	13	3.3
30 – 34	8	3.7	6	3.4	14	3.6
35 – 39	10	4.6	12	6.8	22	5.6
40 – 44	7	3.2	3	1.7	10	2.6
45 – 49	9	4.2	3	1.7	12	3.1
50 – 54	5	2.3	7	4.0	12	3.1
55 – 59	1	0.5	2	1.1	3	0.7
60 – 64	6	2.8	9	5.1	15	3.8
65 – 69	5	2.3	1	0.6	6	1.5
70	9	4.1	6	3.4	15	3.8
All Groups	216	100.0	176	100.0	392	100.0
%	55.1		44.9		100.0	

Source: Field studies

PLATE 3   Rice transplanting in Safiabad

(c) Shalgahi Sofla

Shalgahi Sofla is affected by an agribusiness enterprise and consists of 85 households with a total population of 531, averaging 6.2 persons per household. The village population distribution according to age and sex is shown in Table 25 and Figure 10 which, as in the other two villages shows the population to be a young one with nearly half aged below 15 years. Furthermore, the decline in numbers of the male population in the 20 - 30 age category, is slightly greater than that of either Bonvar Hossein or Chogha Sorkh probably because the rate of emigration from Shalgahi Sofla has been higher than in the other two villages. From 1969 to 1974, 49 peasants (9.2 per cent of the total population) emigrated to Dezful. Most of these were in their early 20s and moved out of the village after 1973. The corresponding figure in Bonvar Hossein was 16 (5.4 per cent of the population) and in Chogha Sorkh 28 (7.1 per cent of the population). The village fertility ratio of 1,000 lies almost exactly between those for Bonvar Hossein (913) and Chogha Sorkh (1,281). Similarly the sex ratio of Shalgahi Sofla (107.4) lies approximately midway between the sex ratio in Bonvar Hossein (95.4) and that in Chogha Sorkh (122.0).

TABLE 25

Population of Shalgahi Sofla by Sex and Age
1973-74

Age Group	Male		Female		Total	
	No.	%	No.	%	No.	%
5	51	18.5	46	18.0	97	18.3
5 - 9	53	19.3	46	18.0	99	18.6
10 - 14	30	10.9	34	13.3	64	12.1
15 - 19	39	14.2	27	10.5	66	12.4
20 - 24	12	4.4	16	6.3	28	5.3
25 - 29	14	5.1	18	7.0	32	6.0
30 - 34	13	4.7	10	3.9	23	4.3
35 - 39	12	4.4	8	3.1	20	3.8
40 - 44	9	3.2	8	3.1	17	3.2
45 - 49	15	5.5	10	3.9	25	4.7
50 - 54	6	2.2	10	3.9	16	3.0
55 - 59	6	2.2	2	0.8	8	1.5
60 - 64	9	3.2	9	3.5	18	3.4
65 - 69	1	0.4	4	1.6	5	0.9
70	5	1.8	8	3.1	13	2.5
All Groups	275	100.0	256	100.0	531	100.0
%	51.8		48.2		100.0	

Source: Field studies

PLATE 4   Hand weeding sugar beet for agribusiness near Shush

TABLE 26

General Population Features of the Three Villages and Rural Dezful

Population Feature	Borvar Hossein 1973-74	Chogha Sorkh 1973-74	Shalgahi Sofla 1973-74	Three Villages a. 1973-74	Rural areas of Dezful Shahristan b.c.	
					1956 National census	1966 National census
Population (No.)	295	392	531	1,218	121,015	72,965
%	(100.0)	(100.0)	(100.0)	(100.0)	(100.0)	(100.0)
Male (No.)	144	216	275	635	56,491	38,214
%	(48.8)	(55.1)	(51.8)	(52.1)	(46.7)	(52.4)
Female (No.)	151	176	256	583	64,529	34,751
%	(51.2)	(44.9)	(48.2)	(47.9)	(53.3)	(47.6)
Sex Ratio	95.4	122.0	107.4	108.9	87.6	109.9
Fertility ratio	913	1,281	1,000	1,059		957
Emigrants 1969-74 (No.)	16	28	49	93		
% of current population	(5.4)	(7.1)	(9.2)	(7.6)		

Sources: a. Field studies

    b. General Statistical Department of the Ministry of the Interior, Gozaresh Mashruh Hozeh Sarshomary Dezful, Vol 19, Tehran, Iran 1959, p 1 (for the 1956 data) and Iranian Statistical Centre, Plan Organization National Census of Population and Housing November, 1966, Vol 77, Tehran, Iran 1968, op. cit., p 5.

Notes: c. The boundaries of the Dezful Census District (Statistical Region) in 1956 differ from those of 1966, see Table 17, note (e).

The combined general demographic data of the three villages is given in Table 26 along with the comparative figures for rural Dezful. It should be noted that the combined general demographic features of these three villages expressed as percentages, correspond very closely to those recorded for the rural areas of Dezful **Shahristan** in the 1966 census. The major difference is in fertility ratios which for the three villages is 1,059, noticeably higher than the corresponding figures of 957 for Dezful **Shahristan**. The fertility ratio for rural Iran as a whole in 1956 was calculated at 910 (11)and the corresponding ratio in 1966 was 922(12). The relatively high fertility ratio in the villages studied is evidence of a rapid rate of population growth which could provide a large potential labour force in the future for rural Dezful.

4.8   Household Composition in Three Dezfulli Villages

The **khanevar**, household, has been treated by demographers as the basic socio-economic unit, but it can be defined in a number of ways. The Dezfulli peasantry consider a **khanevar** as a number of persons who share the same food (**dest toi yek telit** – literally 'hands in the same bowl'). More generally a **khanevar** may be defined as one or more persons, usually related to each other, sharing the same house and kitchen where principal members often pool their income and expenditure. Thus, a **khanevar** is not quite the same as a **khanevadeh**, 'family': for a **khanevar**, apart from family members, can include blood relatives, hired labourers or even long-term guests. This is analogous to the conventional distinction made by western sociologists between a 'family' and a 'household', the latter being considered essentially as an economic unit. A family is defined as a domestic group consisting either of parents and children (nuclear) or additionally including one or more collateral or affinal relatives (extended). Incomplete (deficient) families are those lacking either husband or wife, and include single unmarried persons not attached to any household.

An analysis of the Second National Census Report undertaken by Jamshid Behnam revealed that in 1966 there were approximately five million households in Iran, of which 1.9 million were urban and the remainder rural. Of the urban households only 1.83 per cent included non-family members and for rural households the corresponding figure was 0.83(13) . In the three Dezfulli villages studied, only four (two per cent) of the total 199 households contain a non-relative member. Since the percentage of rural households with non-relative members is so very small, the distinction between **khanevar**, (household), and **khanevadeh** (family) is insignificant and household data will therefore be used to analyse the composition of peasant families in 1974.

(a) Bonvar Hossein

In Bonvar Hossein most landholding and landless peasant families are of the nuclear type - husband, wife and their unmarried children. Two of these families are childless, and in two other households polygamy is practised (each household head having two wives). Furthermore, the percentage of extended families among the landless peasants is considerably less than that for the landholding ones.

TABLE 27

Composition of Households in Bonvar Hossein
1973 - 74

Type of family	Households with land rights		Households landless		Total	
	No.	%	No.	%	No.	%
A. Nuclear	17	44.7	8	66.7	25	50.0
B. Extended	16	42.1	1	8.3	17	34.0
- Families include married children	(7)				(7)	
- Families include other relatives	(7)		(1)		(8)	
- Families include non-relatives	(2)				(2)	
C. Others, ie incomplete families	5	13.2	3	25.0	8	16.0
Total	38	100.0	12	100.0	50	100.0
%	76.0		24.0		100.0	

Source: Field studies

Note: The non-relative member in each of these households is a shepherd.

(b) Chogha Sorkh

The household composition in Chogha Sorkh is relatively similar to that in Bonvar Hossein. Over half of the families in Chogha Sorkh are of a nuclear type (polygamy is practised in only one of these households) and the majority of the extended families include one or more collateral relatives The one non-relative member of a peasant household is significantly considered by informants as a **kaniz**, maid servant. She receives no cash or kind payment for her services but is provided with food, board and clothing. Among the landholding households there are three fraternal families in which two brothers have jointly formed one household in which incomes are pooled and costs shared. Usually the older brother is considered the head of the household and assumes the responsibilities of the father in an extended family.

TABLE 28

Composition of Households in Chogha Sorkh
1973 - 74

Type of family	Household with land rights		Household landless		Total	
	No.	%	No.	%	No.	%
A. Nuclear	29	55.8	7	58.3	36	56.2
B. Extended	22	42.3	3	25.0	25	39.1
- Families include married children	(8)				(8)	
- Families include other relatives	(10)		(3)		(13)	
- Families include non-relatives	(1)				(1)	
- Fraternal joint families	(3)				(3)	
C. Others, ie incomplete families	1	1.9	2	16.7	3	4.7
Total	52	100.0	12	100.0	64	100.0
%	81.2		18.8		100.0	

Source: Field studies

Note: The non-relative member is a maid servant

(c) Shalgahi Sofla

In Shalgahi Sofla the percentage of households with a nuclear type of family (47 per cent) is relatively smaller than in either of the two other villages. One explanation for this is that the percentage of households with a tribal background in Shalgahi Sofla is relatively higher than in the two other villages (27.0 per cent as compared with ten per cent in Bonvar Hossein and 12.5 per cent in Chogha

Sorkh), and the extended family system is more prevalent among tribal than non-tribal peasants. This can be seen by comparing the household composition of extended families in the three villages. Nearly 49 per cent of the extended families in Shalgahi Sofla consist of households in which sons and their wives live in the father's household. The corresponding percentage in Bonvar Hossein is 41 per cent and in Chogha Sorkh 32 per cent.

Among the extended families in Shalgahi Sofla there is one household in which polygamy is practised and there are four fraternal families. The proportion of these fraternal families to the total number of extended families in Shalgahi Sofla is nearly the same as in Chogha Sorkh (11.4 per cent in the former as compared with 12.0 per cent in the latter).

TABLE 29

Composition of Households in Shalgahi Sofla
1973 - 74

Type of family	Households previously with land rights		Households landless		Total	
	No.	%	No.	%	No.	%
A. Nuclear	30	50.8	10	38.4	40	47.0
B. Extended	23	39.0	12	46.2	35	41.2
– Families include married children	(12)		(5)		(17)	
– Families include other relatives	(7)		(6)		(13)	
– Families include non-relatives	(1)				(1)	
– Fraternal joint families	(3)		(1)		(4)	
C. Others, ie incomplete families	6	10.2	4	15.4	10	11.8
Total	59	100.0	26	100.0	85	100.0
%	69.4		30.6		100.0	

Source: Field studies

Note: The non-relative member is a rent paying driver.

The combined household data of these three villages (Table 30) suggest certain features which may be general throughout rural Dezful.

The nuclear family with about four unmarried children is the dominant household type in the three villages. Behnam has suggested that 73.1 per cent of 2.1 million rural households were of the nuclear type with a number of unmarried children (14). This dominance of the nuclear family in the past decade is a major change from the traditional extended family. In the past the extended family was the basic social unit in Iran and "it gained its acceptance in a predominantly agrarian society and was later reinforced by Islamic beliefs and practices"(15). Its disappearance is no doubt due to factors such as mechanization which reduces the need for family labour and thus 'under employed' male members have gradually moved out to form separate household units.

The proportion of nuclear families among landless households in the villages of Bonvar Hossein and Chogha Sorkh is noticeably higher than that among landholding ones. Ajami's work in three Shiraz villages also underlines these differences in family pattern. His studies show that in 1966 90.0 per cent of landless households were of the nuclear type and only ten per cent were of the extended type, while among the farm operators' households, the corresponding figures were 33.3 per cent and 66.6 per cent respectively. Ajami maintains that the higher percentage of extended families among the farm operator households is a function of the economic demands of the households for farm hands to help the family with the cultivation and management of the fields (16). Further expansion of mechanized farming may reduce this difference between two categories of peasantry, and in the near future there may be fewer dissimilarities between the traditional landholding and landless peasants.

In comparing the household compositions of the three villages, there is little empirical evidence to suggest that current variations in household pattern are related to the particular farming system prevailing in each of these villages; there is also no indication that rural family changes have been caused solely by any of the agrarian reform programmes of the past two decades. To assess the impact of any of these programmes on household composition, one would need more comprehensive data on the family situation both before and after the agrarian reform. In any case, family and household are only one component of village structure. Above them is the superstructure, originally of landlord and today of local administration.

TABLE 30

Composition of Households in Bonvar Hossein, Chogha Sorkh and Shalgahi Sofla
1973 - 74

Type of family	Bonvar Hossein		Chogha Sorkh		Shalgahi Sofla		Three Villages	
	No.	%	No.	%	No.	%	No.	%
A. Nuclear (Total)	25	50.0	36	56.2	40	47.0	101	50.8
Households with land rights	(17)		(29)		(30)		(76)	
Households without land rights	(8)		(7)		(10)		(25)	
B. Extended (Total)	17	34.0	25	39.1	35	41.2	77	38.7
Households with land rights	(16)		(22)		(23)		(61)	
Households without land rights	(1)		(3)		(12)		(16)	
C. Others (Total)	8	16.0	3	4.7	10	11.8	21	10.5
Households with land rights	(5)		(1)		(6)		(12)	
Households without land rights	(3)		(2)		(4)		(9)	
Total	50	100.0	64	100.0	85	100.0	199	100.0

Source: Field studies

Chapter Notes

1. Gremliza, **op. cit.**, pp 18–27. There is no comparison with populations outside the Pilot area.

2. Ehlers and Goodell, **op. cit.**, pp 53–56. This is based on the records of the 1956 and 1966 national censuses.

3. Richard Moore, Khalil Asayesh and Joel Montague "Population and Family Planning in Iran", **The Middle East Journal**, Vol 28, No 4, 1974, p 396.

4. Ahmad Pehpour, "Description of the Social Groups in the Rural Areas of Iran", a paper presented in the Settlement Study Centre, Rehovol, Israel, May 1967, p 17.

5. H.T.Khazaneh, "Urbanization Process in Iran", in the proceeding of the **International Union for the Scientific Study of Population Sydney Conference,** (Sydney, Australia, 1967), p 752.

6. Moore, Asayesh and Montague, **op. cit.**, p 396.

7. Veenenbos, **op. cit.**, p 13.

8. General Statistical Department of the Ministry of Interior, **Gozaresh Mashruh-e Hozeh Sarshomary Dezful,** **op. cit.**, p h.

9   Iranian Statistical Centre, Plan Organization, **National Census of Population and Housing,** Vol 77, Dezful **Shahristan, op. cit.**, p 1.

10. The detailed statistical calculations and the fieldwork observations on which the following comments are based are given in Salmanzadeh C., **The Impact of Agrarian Reform Measures on Village Social Structure in Rural Dezful,** unpublished PhD , Reading, England, 1976, pp 308–314.

11. Ajami, "Social Classes, Family Demographic Characteristics and Mobility in Three Iranian Villages", **op. cit.**, p 67.

12. Ajami, **Shishdangi, op. cit.**, p 53.

13. Jamshid Behnam, **Sakht-hie Khanevadeh va Khishavandi dar Iran,** (Family and kinship structures in Iran) (Tehran, Iran: Kharazmi publishing Company, 1350/1972) p 12.

14. Behnam, **op. cit.**, p 13.

15. Ajami, "Social Classes, Family Demographic Characteristics and Mobility in Three Iranian Villages", **op. cit.**, p 68.

16. **Ibid.,**

PLATE 5   View of Dezful

5   VILLAGE AND FAMILY SOCIAL STRUCTURES
IN DEZFUL SHAHRISTAN

5.1   Introduction

Prior to the land reform programme of the 1960s, the traditional Dezfulli village had a clearly defined social structure
and hierarchy based on the traditional landlord-peasant sharecropper farming system (malik-o-raiyat). At present villages
are adjusting to the effects of the reforms and the consequent
changes in social structure.

5.2   Pre-Land Reform Social Structure

Up to 90 per cent of the rural population in the Dez Irrigation Project area before the 1960s land reform programme
lived as sharecropping peasants in about 180 villages, most
of which were 'owned' by influential local landlords to whom
the peasant tenants gave a share of their harvest. The
traditional village was socially and politically structured in
a rigid and formalized manner which maximized exploitation
by the landlord as is shown in Figure 11. The system survived because land in Dezful was relatively fertile, there was
abundant water and there had been a long history of sedentary
agriculture.

5.3   Village landlord

The role of malik-e deh, the village landowner, (1) and other
individuals in the village social structure depended on the
malik's background, (tribal or non-tribal), the size of his
landholding (the entire village or part), his residential status
(absentee or resident), and the nature of his administration
(personal management or rental to a third party). In villages
where the raiyata, (peasants) belonged to the same tribe as

FIGURE 11

A 'Typical' Pre-Land Reform Traditional Village Social Structure
in Rural Dezful

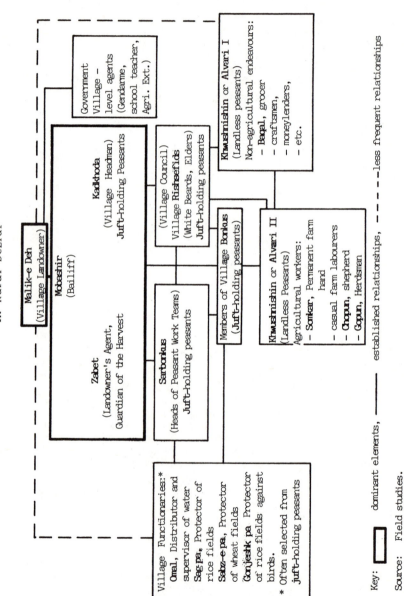

Malik-e Deh
(Village Landowner)

Mobashir
(Bailiff)

Government
Village –
level agents
(Gendarme,
school teacher,
Agri. Ext.)

Kadkhoda
(Village Headman)
Juft-holding Peasants

Zabet
(Landowner's Agent,
Guardian of the Harvest

(Village Council)
Village **Rishsefids**
(White Beards, Elders)
Juft-holding peasants

Khwushnishin or **Alvari I**
(Landless peasants)
Non-agricultural endeavours:
– **Baqal,** grocer
– craftsmen,
– moneylenders,
– etc.

Sarborkus
(Heads of Peasant Work Teams)
Juft-holding peasants

Members of Village **Bonkus**
(**Juft-**holding peasants)

Khwushnishin or **Alvari II**
(Landless Peasants)
Agricultural workers:
– **Sonkar,** Permanent farm
hand
– casual farm labourers
– **Chopun,** shepherd
– **Gopun,** Herdsman

Village Functionaries:*
Omal, Distributor and
supervisor of water
Sag-pa, Protector of
rice fields
Sabz-e-pa, Protector
of wheat fields
Gonjeshk-pa Protector
of rice fields against
birds.
* Often selected from
juft-holding peasants

Key: dominant elements, ———— established relationships, – – – –less frequent relationships

Source: Field studies.

their **malik**, organizational structures would be simpler
than in non-tribal counterparts. Tribal obligations to the
khan (chief) (also **malik-e deh**) rendered the functions of
zabet, landlord's harvest guard, unnecessary, and the
easier communication between **malik** and **raiyat** dispensed
with intermediaries such as a **mobashir** (bailiff). However,
tribal villages in rural Dezful were rare and the majority
of non-tribal villages were under **maliks** whose control rested
upon a rigid formalized social structure.

A few villages were owned by a single **malik**, but it was
common practice for most villages to be owned jointly. A
single **malik** could also have a share in a number of
villages on a **musha** (shared ownership) basis.

Although the majority were absentee, they normally lived
in nearby towns – Dezful, Andimeshk or Shush – and paid
frequent personal visits to their villages. A few resided
further afield in Tehran, Isfahan or Shiraz. Even these
maliks however, would visit their villages at least once
or twice annually. Amir Bahman Khan Bakhtiar, for example
a part-owner of Shalgahi Sofla, in the 1950s would travel
from Shiraz by private plane to visit his village. A few
maliks like Hadji Ali Kamali, part-owner of Qaleh Qazi still
lives in his village and used to exercise close and personal
supervision over the activities of his **raiyats** and thus did
not employ a **mobashir** or **zabet**. Village landowners would
either manage their property themselves, or lease the estate
to a third party for one year or more on a fixed cash
contract basis. If a village was entirely owned and
managed by a single **malik**, he would appoint the village
officials (**kadkhoda**, headman, **mobashir**, bailiff and **zabet**,
harvest guard); and, having decided which crops were to
be grown would pay his share of production costs. At
harvest time, he would receive his customary share of the
crop and pay his appointed agents for their services.

In cases of joint village ownership, not all **maliks** would
be individually represented at village level. The practice
was to choose one of the joint owners to represent the
interests of all the others, he would then act as sole **malik**.
However, production costs, payments to agents and the landowner's harvest share would be shared by the group in proportion to their individual shares. This procedure was
usually adopted to avoid conflict which might jeopardize
the **malik's** income because of the resulting confusion at
harvest time. In Kutian in 1960-61, for example, a dispute
between the joint owners (the closely related Qotb and Asaf
families) over who should act as representative **malik** enabled the peasants to avoid donating to them the landlord's
share of the harvest – an experience that persuaded the
joint owners of the advantages of solidarity! The managing
malik often undertook this role, simply for prestige, although
sometimes he received an extra harvest share in consequence.
When **maliks** leased their land to a third party the **mustajir**,
(lessee) would undertake managerial supervision of the
village and appoint his own agents, as if he were the real

malik. He would share production costs, collect the landlord's share of harvest, and make an agreed cash payment
to the malik's representative. Generally speaking, there
was a more 'cordial' relationship between malik and raiyat
when the village was controlled by an owner-manager than
when his function was taken on by a mustajir, probably
because the mustajir was often regarded as a get-rich-quick
opportunist.

The malik (as owner-manager or representative-manager)
had full control over village land allotment and production,
and controlled the raiyats themselves through his agents.
Although raiyats in rural Dezful were not usually badly
treated, they were considered as little more than 'subjects'
of their maliks. When a village was sold, for instance,
not only the land changed hands, but the peasant tenants
who cultivated it were also transferred to the new malik.
Indeed, Morio Ono considers the traditional village as not
merely a tract of land but also as a unit of management
which provided a fairly constant annual amount of rent
either in kind or in cash; thus the proprietorship of a deh,
(village) was separable from its managerial rights which
could be leased out to a third person(2). Field studies
suggest that some maliks considered their raiyats (especially
the good ones) among their assets. Soltan Hossein Khan
Rashidian, son of a former landowner of Chogha Sorkh
claimed that most maliks in rural Dezful valued a good
raiyat above fertile land and abundant water. "What could
a malik do with lots of land and water, but no one to
cultivate it for him?" Some maliks would even use financial
inducements to persuade a desirable peasant to come to his
village – a practice which used to be another source of
conflict among the local landowners. For some influential
maliks, possession of good raiyats meant prestige, while
for others numbers rather than quality mattered. Undesir-
able peasants could easily be expelled from the village and
involved the malik in no further obligation. There was,
after all, no such organization as a "farmers' union" to
support the peasant rights.

Basically, however, most Dezfulli landowners were primarily interested in the economic benefits of the malik-o-
raiyat system. Apart from the economic prerogative of the
harvest share from his raiyats there was also the social
prestige implicit in the malik's prerogative of enjoying the
respect and hospitality of his raiyat and on visits to the
village, he would expect to be entertained and feasted by
them. There were other practices which were expected by
some maliks, such as unpaid labour from the raiyats, for
cleaning the main irrigation ditches, or working on his
personal land. A few major maliks relied on raiyat support
in their disputes with other maliks. They would recruit
tofangchi (riflemen) from their raiyats and bring them to
town to fight on their behalf. Many peasant lives would
be lost in feuds of this kind.

Some landowners even required their raiyats to give them
gifts for 'permission to marry'. A group of village elders

would visit their **malik**, present him with a **kaleh qand** (sugar loaf), and assorted confectionary to 'sweeten his mouth', and ask him to authorize the marriage of a young villager. At first the **malik** would refuse his permission until the elders presented him with a 1,000 rials banknote ($14), whereupon he would reluctantly authorize the marriage.

On the other hand the **malik's** privileges were not without responsibilities which were often numerous and burdensome. His responsibilities fell into three categories: the provision of services directly related to farming, the provision of security and certain civil responsibilities.

His major agricultural responsibility was the general management of village farming. This involved: 'bringing water' to the village, participating in village decisions, sharing the risk of crop failure and providing the peasants with emergency credit. In cases of drought or pest damage, both **malik** and sharecropper suffered from reduced yields, and in times of famine the **malik** would even provide interest free loans.

The **malik** was also responsible for safeguarding village life and property. This was a vital consideration in most Dezful villages, where, in the past, attacks from tribal raiders from the Zagros mountains and the plains were common. Lack of security brought village farming to a total halt, as in 1948 when the population of Bonvar Hossein fled to nearby villages because of continuous harassment and raiding by nomadic tribesmen. The **malik** had to intervene with local tribal chiefs and establish a friendlier relationship before the villagers would return and resume normal life.

The **malik** had 'implicit ' civil obligations towards his peasants, he might or might not discharge. Most Dezfulli **maliks** however, would act as mediators between the villagers and government agencies. This involved, for example, defending peasants in the courts, mediating in disputes between the peasants and the gendarmerie, and seeking deferments or exemptions from military service. Some **maliks** according to Gholam Hossein Mostofi, a former major Dezfulli landowner, would also be involved in their peasants' family affairs. He might be required to contribute to wedding costs or to finance secondary education for promising village students. He might also pay for a peasant's medical treatment, and, occasionally, even mediate in marital conflicts, - usually by persuading the wife to return to her husband's household. This 'benevolent paternalism' caused a situation of **rodarbasi** (reticence) where the peasant would often hide his true feeling toward the **malik** showing deference and respect which enhanced the **malik's** superior social position and improved his control of village affairs.

These responsibilities were often too onerous for the average **malik** to cope with, especially if he had little local influence or lacked a strong personality. As a result many **maliks** leased their villages annually to more influential or more formidable **maliks** who were 'better suited' to use

their power and influence. Thus, out of the hundreds of
maliks in rural Dezful, only a few had the combination of
influence and power necessary to manage their own village
and to act as **mustajir**, (lease holders) in numerous other
villages as well. In fact, the whole of the region came
under the influence of a handful of influential **maliks**, who,
between them, regulated local life.

5.4 Agents and Officials

The absentee landlord had three village level agents to
safe-guard his interests. These were his **mobashir** (bailiff),
zabet (harvest controller) and **kadkhoda** (village headman).
The **mobashir** and **zabet** were not usually natives of the
village in which they operated, although the **kadkhoda** was.
The **mobashir** was the landowner's representative during
harvest division and was responsible together with the **zabet**
and **kadkhoda** for arranging the shipment of the landlord's
share to town. He usually only stayed in the village during
harvest time as he often held a similar post in other
villages controlled by the same **malik** or **mustajir**. His
services were paid for in cash.

The **zabet** protected the landlord's interests in the
village. At harvest time, he would make sure that the
peasants did not try to cheat the landlord by witholding
part of the crop or by wilfully neglecting the harvest.
In some villages there was a permanent **zabet** who was aided
when necessary by one or more seasonal **zabets**.

During the harvest, both **mobashir** and **zabet** would live
in **kopiter** or **toi zabeton**, a room adjacent to the threshing
floor, in order to guard the harvest. The **zabet** carried
a **mohr**, a large wooden stamp, embossed with the **malik's**
distinctive symbol which was used to 'seal' each individual
pile of threshed grain each evening so that the following
morning any grain removed from the pile would be noticed.
The **zabet** according to Gol Mohammad, a former **zabet** of
Chogha Sorkh could also punish any peasants (especially
the younger ones) who tried to cheat the **malik** or who failed
to perform his specific responsibilities (by delaying the
harvest for example). He had his own unique method of
punishment. On one occasion when Gol Mohammad caught
a woman stealing some sesame seeds from the undivided
harvest, he denounced her as a thief and made her stand
on a rooftop in full view of all the villagers. This action
caused the woman deep shame and embarrassment and acted
as a deterrent to others. The **zabet** would be paid by the
malik. In the case of Gol Mohammad his annual salary
was 100 **manns** of wheat and 100 **manns** of rice (amounting
to about 12,800 rials at 1957–58 farm prices) plus full board.

The position and responsibilities of **kadkhoda** (often also
called **kayid** or, in Arabic-speaking villages, **sheik** – as
is the **malik** there) were much more involved than those of
mobashir or **zabet**. He was customarilly 'employed' by the
landlord from amongst villagers with land rights to head

the village, to manage minor civil affairs and to serve
as an intermediary between peasants and **malik**. Since
1930, the **kadkhoda** has also acted as a medium of communication between government and the villagers. Thus for
example, "he assisted gendarmerie personnel in seeking
military conscripts and in collecting taxes"(3). Although
he was not, and still is not, a civil servant, he was
recognized by the State as the local official certifying
births, marriages and deaths, and often arbitrated in minor
disputes and crimes,(4) and as representative of village
interests to Government.

In spite of this triangular function, the **kadkhoda's** major
activities were to supervise the village economy in the
malik's interests and to entertain the landlord's guests
and visiting government agents. This customary practice,
according to Mash Parviz, a former **kadkhoda** of Shalgahi
Sofla was misused by some **maliks** to force an unwanted
kadkhoda to resign. So many guests were sent to the
village that the **kadkhoda** would be unable to meet the cost
of entertaining them all and would resign from his post.
The **malik** himself would retain his benevolent image and
avoid village censure since it would be assumed that the
kadkhoda had resigned of his own volition.

The 'basic salary' of the **kadkhoda** was one-tenth of the
malik's share of harvest. In addition the **malik** would grant
him one or more extra **jufts** in compensation for entertainment
costs. In some villages, peasants also contributed to the
kadkhoda's salary by providing a certain amount of free
labour on his land.

The **kadkhoda** usually had an 'office staff' - one or more
nockars (servants) and a **pakar** (footman - also known as
sahragard (fieldman) who was employed as the messenger.
His duties included making public announcements of the
kadkhoda's orders from the rooftop and also summoning
peasants whom the **kadkhoda** wished to see.

Proir to the 1950s, the only government agents operating
at the rural level were gendarmes, **mamor-e sabet** (regis-
trars), and in some villages a school teacher and an agricultural extension officer. The local head of the gendarmerie was, and still is, responsible for maintaining law and
order. The gendarmerie itself, however, was in the past
the tool of local politicians and landlords (5) and, considered
by many peasants as the 'Angel of Death'(6). The registrar
visited the village only infrequently and the school teacher
was usually non-resident returning to Dezful after daily
classes. The agricultural extension officer might or might
not be a resident of the village and his work was usually
severely hampered by the closed village community since
he had to work through the **malik** or his agents and was
thus dependent on their goodwill. Other government agents,
occasional visitors to the village if the **malik** approved,
included the Malaria Eradication Officer, health workers
and the veterinarian.

5.5   Village Functionaries

Village farming depended on a number of 'functionaries' who looked after the irrigation and guarded the fields against theft or damage. They were usually recruited from among the **juft**-holding peasants and were hired communally by the village.

The **omal-e chaltok** (rice irrigator) was of particular importance since rice was an economically important crop and the landlord's harvest share was high (50 per cent). His selection was a major concern for both landlord and **juft**-holders. He had to be familiar with the characteristics of each **chal** (field) in order to divide it into small uniformly watered plots which minimised seepage. The irrigator also had to be recognized communally as being impartial, fair and **khoda shons** (God fearing), so that he would provide an equal service for all. In many Dezfulli villages the post was 'hereditary'. In Bonvar Hossein, Mulla Hossein (a village elder) has been rice irrigator for the past five years and before him his late father held the same position. Traditionally, the village rice irrigator was appointed and paid by the **malik** in kind; either a fixed amount of rice (200 to 250 **manns** of rice per season) or a certain percentage of the landlord's harvest share (two to four per cent). He only dealt with the rice crop, other crops being irrigated by the individual farmers or, as often was the case, by each member of a **bonku** (work team) taking turns in irrigating the **bonku's** plots.

The fields were guarded by the **sabz-e pa**, (wheatfields guardian),**gonjeshk pa** (rice fields bird guardian), and **sag pa** (rice fields boar guardian). The **sabz-e pa** would be hired for one or two months when the wheat and barley fields were green and would prevent animals from being grazed there. The **gonjeshk pa**, who was usually a boy of about 15 or so, was hired for about one month in October to scare away sparrows and similar birds. The job of the **sag pa** however, was more involved and in rural Dezful it was recognized as an established profession(7). Wild boars caused extensive damage through trampling and flattening the crop and, to keep them off, the professionnal **sag pa** would use a rifle and ten or more trained dogs. (The dogs were worth the price of a milking cow - 7,000 rials or more). He would tour the rice fields with his dogs each night from about 7 pm to 6 am, from late September to early November. Field guardians were traditionally compensated by the peasant **juft**-holders and not by the landowners, and payment for their services was usually made in kind. They could also be reinforced by locals acting as **sho pa** (night watchmen) to protect the fields from theft or as **o pa**, to prevent anyone from diverting irrigation water before it reached the village land.

Villagers were able to perform these various additional tasks as functionaries and at the same time carry on with their own farming activities as **juft**-holders, because once they were employed they themselves became employers, hiring landless peasants from the village to undertake their agricultural duties, and income from their employment as village functionaries would be used to pay those whom they had in turn employed.

5.6 Peasant juft-holder and Landless Villager

The peasant **juft**-holders in rural Dezful would usually organize themselves in a number of **bonkus** (work teams). Each team would elect a **sarbonku** (leader) from among themselves, to represent the group interest in land allotment and various other farming operations.

Apart from the **bonku**, there also existed an informal **rishsefid** group (council of elders), usually composed of those peasant farmers with status, wealth and experience to command the respect necessary for village leadership (8). The council often included several **sarbonkus** or even an elderly **bonku** member but its influence was usually slight acting only as a liason between village and landlord. Another group, the **anjoman-e deh** (the village council), was introduced in 1952 as an 'official' group formalizing the council of elders to create interest in local government and to initiate community self-help projects.

Landless peasants **alvari** (Dezful) or **khwushnishin** (in Iran generally – the term means literally "dry settler") often constituted one third or more of the village and were not all directly engaged in agricultural activities. Those involved in agriculture included **somkar**, permanent farm labourer; **chopun**, shepherd; **gopun**, herdsman or casual farm labourer.

Traditionally, each **juft**-holding peasant would recruit a **somkar** to assist him with ploughing, harvesting and other work. The **somkar** and his family would join the farmer's household sharing meals with his employer and living in his compound. The **somkar's** wife would usually assist in the household chores. He was hired on an annual verbal contract basis and would begin work in August (after the rice transplanting) through to the following rice transplanting season (July to August). His salary was paid in kind at one-eighth of the farmer's harvest share. Some farmers would also hire part-time workers from among the landless peasants during wheat harvesting and rice transplanting – times of peak labour demand. A few peasants might also find employment as shepherds and herdsmen but the communal herdsman often had to be recruited from outside the village as no one from the village would be willing to undertake a job of such low status.

Landless peasants not employed in agriculture included the village **baqal** (grocer), **nozulkhor** (money lender who might also be a **juft**-holder) and craftsmen. Craftsmen were usually found in larger villages where their services were in more demand and included: **delavar** or **najar** (carpenter), **ahangar** (blacksmith), **nalband** (farrier), **joldoz** (saddler) and **moqani** (well digger). In smaller villages, such services were provided by craftsmen from the nearby town of Dezful. In larger villages there was also the **mullah** (religious leader). However, most villages in rural Dezful had neither **mullah** nor **mosque**. A travelling **mullah** visited the village during the month of Muharram to perform **rouzeh khwani**, a commemoration of the death of the Shia **Imams**, or on the death of prominent villagers.

5.7 Village Itinerants

The villages of rural Dezful were often visited by various itinerants, such as the **mullah**, who formed an integral part of peasant life. They included pedlars selling household goods, and **dalak** or **salmani**, itinerant barbers who also performed circumcisions.

The largest category of itinerants included 'social parasites', who depended on alms, from the **darvishs**, (devotees of the Imam Ali), **papeas** (devotees of Shahzadeh Ahmad) and **sayyids** with black or green turbans to signify their claim of direct descent from the Prophet Mohammad. Their visits were more frequent during harvesting when they would beg a few handfuls of grain from each peasant **juft**-holder. Landlords rarely, if ever, gave such alms, but the accumulated contributions from the villagers often exceeded the harvest share of an average sharecropper farming half a **juft**.

Another group were the **doanavices** – writers of 'secret prayers' – who practised faith and charm healing. Their most frequent customers were women who believed they could cure infertility, impotence and illness. Although few people were cured or even able to follow the complicated 'prescription', the reputation of the **doanavices** was high and they would visit a village year after year.

5.8 Post-Land Reform Social Structure

The main change has been the disappearance of the **malik** and his partial replacement by government agents and the village elders. The consequent changes are schematically shown in Figure 12. The landlord's interests in village affairs have been effectively removed along with his land, and even those few who have retained part of their holding have, nevertheless, lost their customary influence in village life if not the respect of the peasantry.

There have been other consequences too, particularly for the landowner's representatives. The **mobashir** and **zabet** have, of necessity, been forced to seek other employment, but the **kadkhoda** still continues although the remuneration originally supplied by the landowner has not been replaced by any other source. His position is in fact slowly being eroded and may well disappear in future.

During the last decade, government representation at

village level has increased and its activities have widened
to encompass many aspects of village affairs, government
agents having taken over some of the landlord's traditional
functions. The expanded and strengthened gendarmerie
(reflecting strong central government), has ensured local
security and various tribal groups who previously threatened
the peace and security of peasant cultivators are better
controlled. "The Gcvernment has effectively taken over
all rural pacification, so that even the catching of
cattle thieves has become an official job of the town gendarmerie, and the rural population is meant only to report
the trouble" (9).

However, other responsibilities have not been taken over
by government. Amongst them are emergency credit provisions, crop failure support and overall management of
village agriculture. In addition the personal rapport which
sometimes characterized the landlord-peasant relationship
has completely vanished. Nevertheless the village is no
longer a closed community, and government representatives
have found it easier to make contact, so that dialogue has
developed between peasant and urbanized representative.

The village elders on the other hand, have retained and
even consolidated their former position. Their increased
importance derives from the procedures used to redistribute
land rights. Only those peasants with cultivation rights
(nasaq-juft holders) were eligible but there were no written
records of individual villager status. Thus the land reform
office agent organized a meeting in each village where the
population elected four trustworthy men (moatamedin) as
village representatives in listing peasants with land rights.
The moatamedin (often the same rishsefid group) were individuals whose judgement was trusted and respected by the
majority of the villagers and they have continued to help
in settling minor disputes over village land rights.

In Bonvar Hossein, the moatamedin have not only assumed
some of the responsibilities of the official village council,
but have also taken over piecemeal some of the administrative and civil functions of the malik and kadkhoda. They
handle a broad spectrum of activities including mediating
in minor domestic disputes; settling bride price; witnessing
marriage, birth and death certificates; helping to obtain
military service exemption; hosting wedding and funeral
ceremonies; and organizing communal work, such as cleaning
irrigation ditches. They also manage the recently established sandoq-e omimi (general communal fund) financed
mainly by casual contributions from peasant households
together with rents from plots of village lands (30,000 rials
in 1973-74) rents from the village baqal (3,000 rials),
selling rice straw. The general fund is used to finance
the Muharram rouzeh khawani, commemoration of the death
of Imam Hossein, giving alms, helping widows or paying
for the village representative to attend government ceremonies
in Dezful. All these services are performed 'unofficially'
and with no recompense, except, apparently, for the respect
of the community.

FIGURE 12

A 'Typical' Post-Land Reform Traditional Village Social Structure
in Rural Dezful

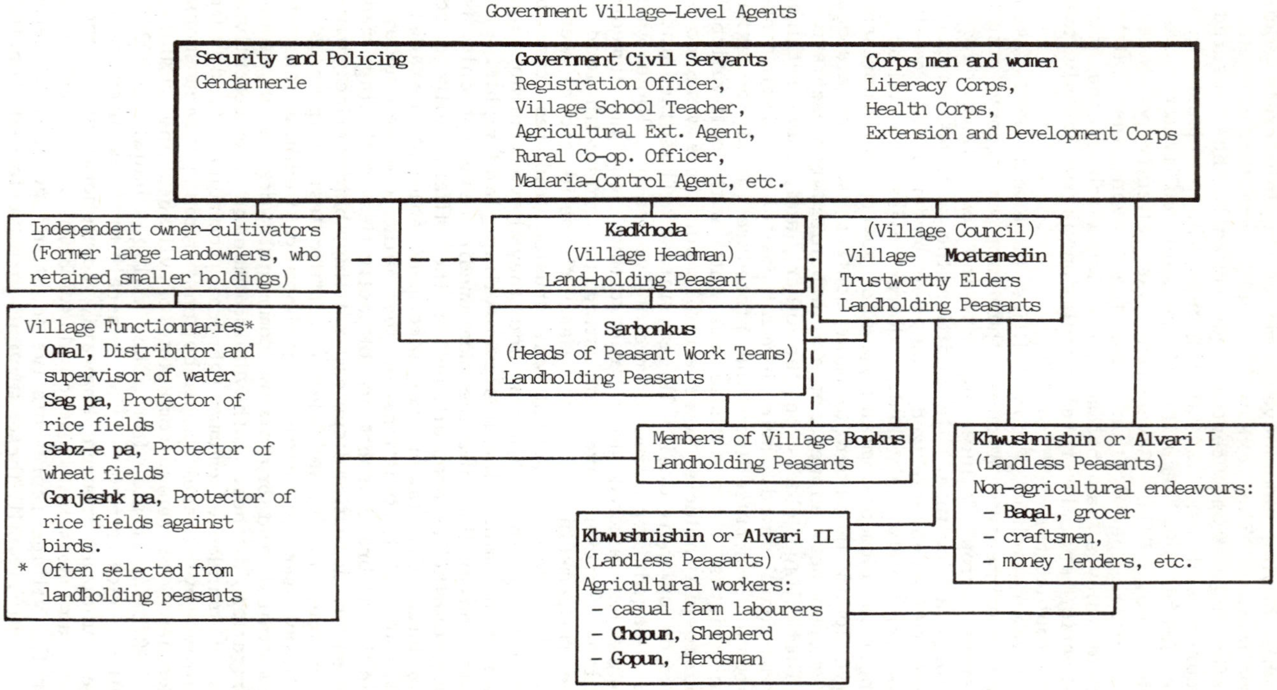

Government Village-Level Agents

Security and Policing
Gendarmerie

Government Civil Servants
Registration Officer,
Village School Teacher,
Agricultural Ext. Agent,
Rural Co-op. Officer,
Malaria-Control Agent, etc.

Corps men and women
Literacy Corps,
Health Corps,
Extension and Development Corps

Kadkhoda
(Village Headman)
Land-holding Peasant

Sarbonkus
(Heads of Peasant Work Teams)
Landholding Peasants

(Village Council)
Village **Moatamedin**
Trustworthy Elders
Landholding Peasants

Members of Village **Bonkus**
Landholding Peasants

Khwushnishin or **Alvari I**
(Landless Peasants)
Non-agricultural endeavours:
 - **Bapal**, grocer
 - craftsmen,
 - money lenders, etc.

Khwushnishin or **Alvari II**
(Landless Peasants)
Agricultural workers:
 - casual farm labourers
 - **Chopun**, Shepherd
 - **Gopun**, Herdsman

Independent owner-cultivators
(Former large landowners, who
retained smaller holdings)

Village Functionaries*
Omal, Distributor and
supervisor of water
Sag pa, Protector of
rice fields
Sabz-e pa, Protector of
wheat fields
Gonjeshk pa, Protector of
rice fields against
birds.
* Often selected from
landholding peasants

Key: ▢ dominant elements, ——— established relationship, — — — less frequent relationships

The various functionaries have retained their original functions in the villages which are still traditional, but they are now directly employed and responsible to the farmers and may even offer their services on a contract basis to independent owner-cultivators.

Peasants with land rights still cultivate their holdings through the **bonku**, though its structure and functions have been slightly modified. Those **khwushnishins** (landless peasants) who were previously employed as **somkars**, have become redundant because of gradual mechanization and the reduction in holding size. Casual farm employment (outside peak labour demand periods) has also been reduced. The **chopun** (shepherd) and the **gopun** (herdsman) still continue as do those **khwushnishins** who were engaged in non-agricultural pursuits although as roads and access to Dezful have improved the village **baqal** and craftsmen have diminished in importance. With the exception of the **mullah**, itinerant visits have become less frequent. Services are available in Dezful and the amount of alms given has fallen - so consequently have visits from 'social parasites'.

A Dezfulli village in a farm corporation bears more resemblance to a commercial agricultural organization than to a traditional peasant community. The farm corporation manager is quite different from the former landlord. He is a government employee, has a university degree and is mainly concerned with the technical and business side of agricultural production. His social status places him outside the village, and there is little rapport with the peasant shareholders. Few of the previous village **juft**-holders, now shareholders, except for members of the Executive Committee , are employed by the farm corporation and the majority have had to find employment outside the village. Those that are employed are mainly concerned for their individual well-being. Recently, an **anjoman-e vahid rustai** (unified rural council), has been established to replace the former individual village councils and to encourage 'community participation' in social and physical projects although it has, as yet, little effect.

In villages affected by the agribusinesses, the traditional socio-political structure has completely disintegrated. Villagers have sold their landrights to the government and await resettlement in the **shahraks**, the new resettlement centres. No recognizable socio-political structure has formed there so far and the inhabitants have not developed any sense of being members of a community. In fact, life in the **shahraks** is one of people sharing the same physical facilities without attempting to cultivate any genuine social relationship.

5.9 Social Stratification and Mobility

It is clear that traditional village life is hierarchically organized not only in Dezful but throughout Iran(10). Keddie divides adult male agriculturalists into two classes of non-

cultivators and cultivators, each of which is further divided
into several strata, listed in generally declining order of
prestige, of which between four and seven are found in
every village. She maintains that only part of those strata
covering absentee landlords or large-scale renters were
eliminated in villages affected by the land reform programme. "Below that, stratification remained, and in some
cases became more acute"(11).

Keddie's typology is not completely appropriate for the
traditional Dezfulli village and considerable variation existed
from one village to the next. In the three villages studied
in detail, at the top of the social structure was the place
of **malik**, followed by his agents and then the **juft**-holding
peasant cultivators. The latter class was further sub-
divided by factors such as age, experience and wealth,
rishsefid (village elders) being at the top followed by
village functionaries. Here the **omal-e chaltok** (rice irrigator) was the highest because of his economic importance.
After the functionaries came the **sarbonkus** (heads of the
work-team), and finally the 'ordinary' peasant **juft**-holders.
Among **juft**-holders there was further stratification in terms
of **juft** size and/or livestock ownership. Finally landless
peasants employed in agriculture were in a lower stratum
than those engaged in non-agricultural activities.

In the post-land reform years, apart from the obvious
changes involved in the departure of the **malik** and his
agents, the only other major alteration in hierarchical
structure has been the replacement of **rishsefid** by the **moatamedin**. The stratification of the other inhabitants has
remained unchanged, except for the **somkar**, who has joined
the casual labour group.

Smith indicates that before land reform in rural Iran
'social mobility was almost impossible. Those at the top
justified their position by pointing to customary practice'
(12). In the post-reform years, social mobility in the rural
areas has been based on criteria such as position, achievement and education rather than on birth and family ties (13).

In rural Dezful, there is no tangible evidence of a rigid
caste or closed class system, and social mobility is usually
possible. Nevertheless, various indirect restrictions on
social mobility do exist. For instance before giving his
daughter in marriage, a peasant owning one **juft** or more
might make the stipulation that she should not be required
to do any work outside of her husband's house. This would
effectively prevent her marriage into an inferior stratum
where, because of economic necessity, wives, as well as
mature daughters, would be required to work in the fields
alongside the men during rice transplanting. In this way,
marriages involving vertical movement between strata are
discouraged and villagers tended to marry within their own
stratum.

There are also isolated cases of 'residential segregation'.
In Bonvar Hossein the **gopun's** (herdsman) household is
practically isolated from the rest of the community. Although
a commune village employee and given a room for himself

and his family, he is not expected to participate in village affairs nor is there social interaction between him and the other villagers.   He may only attend a wedding or funeral but must sit near the door with the children, where he is ignored.   His low status and social isolation is apparently due to his association with cows, considered in Dezful as being second only to donkeys in lack of intelligence and general stupidity.   The word **gaave** (cow) is commonly used as an insult, and the stigma connected to association with cows is such that no villager would ever consider working as a **gopun**, even though his annual salary exceeds the average peasant income.   The **gopun**, therefore, had to be recruited from the nearby Bakhtiari tribe where no such stigma exists.

Sheep, on the other hand, are esteemed, probably because of the peasants' tribal origins as nomadic shepherds, and shepherds are not despised today.   A village sheep owner expressed this attitude by saying "If I had a **dokhtar-e karr-o-shall** (blind and paralysed daughter) I would not give her to the son of a herdsman even though he may be rich.   But if I had a beautiful daughter, I would be happy to give her in marriage to a shepherd, for even though he might not be wealthy, he is certain to be intelligent".

5.10   Village Stability

In pre-land reform years, an atmosphere of mistrust and suspicion characterized the relationship between the **malik** and **raiyat**.   The peasantry used all means at its disposal to retain as large a share of the harvest as possible while the landowner attempted to frustrate this and to maximize **his** share.   This open expression of mistrust was an integral part of the traditional **malik-o-raiyat** sharecropping system. Ono observed in 1967 that "it is never taken as degrading of his character for one **malik** to openly speak of his bad faith in his own **raiyat**.   Similarly, it is regarded as natural for the **raiyats** to express their dissatisfaction openly to third persons(14).Hanessian commented:

> "There is a wide gulf between the peasant and his landlord.   In no sense is there an attitude of co-operation or the sensation of being engaged in a mutual or co-operative enterprise.   The situation is normally one of mutual suspicion..   The landlord regards the peasant as the lowest form of unskilled labour whose sole function is to provide him with his profits, and who will, if treated with kindness, simply take advantage of the relationship and cheat the landlord.   Corresponding to this attitude is the highly conservative nature of the peasant, who resists stubbornly any effort to change his ancient habit of living or of tilling the land.   To him the landlord is a distant figure - one to be feared and who is

usually   unapproachable   except   through   his
agents" (15).

Nevertheless, the village functioned as a relatively stable
community.   The landlord's representatives would seldom
allow any conflict to develop which could hinder **juft**-holder
production thus indirectly affecting the landowner's harvest
share.   Since the land reform, however, the disappearance
of the landowner's controlling hand means that minor fric-
tion can develop into major conflicts involving several
villagers.   During the 1974 harvest in Bonvar Hossein, for
example, one farmer wanted to harvest his wheat early but
damaged his neighbour's crop in doing so,   There was an
argument, a fierce dispute and then a fight.   Only mediation
by some elders prevented a wider village conflict - a conflict which participants believed, could never have occurred
in pre-reform times.

In fact villagers have not yet been able to organize
effective management of their own affairs.   Other aspects
of the problems resulting from changed conditions after
the land reforms, are demonstrated by reactions in Bonvar
Hossein to the new DIP water delivery system.   The irrigation scheme lay-out involves metering at the head gate to
each 100 hectare plot, a system more compatible with large-
scale farming than with the numerous widely scattered small
plots characteristic of peasant cultivation. Accurate metering
is very difficult in measuring discharged water in the latter
case and the DIP water authority has decided to use the
village as its metering unit rather than individual peasants.
The Authority has in consequence asked the villagers to
select a representative to sign the necessary documents,
but no one in the village wants to do this.   The reason
is that 'when a man takes the responsibility of representing
his entire village in signing the water documents, he is
taking a big risk.   There is a chance that some villagers
will refuse to pay on time and since nowadays there is no-
body in the village to make these people pay their water
debts, the representative will get into trouble.   The water
authority will pressurize him to make the payment or go
to jail -'who wants to go to jail'!

As a result the Authority has compromised - they accepted
five village representatives, each man 'signing' (thumbing)
the documents on behalf of a small group of blood relatives
and close friends.

These local attitudes underline the current political instability in Bonvar Hossein and by implication the other
remaining traditional villages in the DIP area.   The **kadkhoda** now, since he is unpaid, has failed to take his post
as village representative to government seriously and,
consequently losing village support, has left the village
in a state of **bisarparasty**, ('headlessness').   The village
council has no administrative authority, so the only alternatives are government agents of a few **moatamedin**.   The
former are 'outsiders' and often unwilling to become
seriously involved in the villagers' domestic problems, while

the informal group of **moatamedin** has no official sanction to substitute for the **kadkhoda**. The current leadership vacuum may only be filled when the remaining traditional villages are resettled in the new **shahraks**, or included in the **hozeh omran rustai** (rural polarization programme).

5.11   Structural Change and Decision Making

Before land reform took place, Dezful peasant society was a close community with little or no outside influence, authoritarian in structure and dominated by the presence of the landlord. Although the landlord could intervene directly or indirectly through his agents at any level of the traditional community, the peasant could never make a direct approach to his landlord – the only avenue being through the **kadkhoda**. Landlord–peasant relationships were based on a one-way vertical structure, in which the landlord was completely dominant and discussion or confrontation between peasant and landlord was unheard of.

All major decisions on the choice of crops or number of **chals** to be cultivated were the landlord's alone, a situation which has produced a peasantry incapable of any major decisions, lacking confidence to make any significant innovation. The peasant agricultural ideology is, in consequence, corporate, little depending on the security of the **bonku**. **Bonku** members were virtually powerless to make any major decision affecting the community as a whole since this power was delegated to the traditional village elite – the elders. Even this elite had little influence on farming using its influence instead in domestic and inheritance disputes. This elite which did not impinge on the landlord's authority, divided its allegiance between the peasantry and the landlord, and acted as a link designed to avoid conflict and promote compromise between the two.

Since the early fifties a new political elite, effective at village level has appeared. It includes, in addition to the gendarmerie, the schoolmaster, extension agent and health officer (Malaria Eradication Programme). Indeed, it is more a collection of disparate individuals than a united cohesive elite, each member having specific interests in the village. Only the extension agent with an interest in changing farming practices threatened the traditional village decision-making process and interfered with the landlord's traditional prerogative. Indeed he was resented by both landlord, who saw him as undermining his authority, and peasant who was reluctant to endorse and apply his suggestions without the landlord's approval. Such approval was seldom given so the extension agent was rarely effective in improving traditional farming methods and the peasantry's ability to innovate and accept innovation was severely inhibited.

The post-land reform exclusion of the landowner as the major village decision maker created a gap in the decision-making structure which the peasants themselves were expected

to fill.   However, their traditional exclusion has left them
with little aptitude to fulfil these functions themselves.
Decision-making is now a long drawn-out process, requiring
unanimity rather than majority decision to end it, and
incapable of rapid response to emergencies.

One of the reasons for this is that although the land
reforms have physically replaced the landlord by the peasant
himself, the latter has not been able to empathise with the
farmer's original role in decision-making.   Instead, peasant
aspirations were limited to an emulation of the village
kadkhoda, whose activities had been observed daily and
who, as the landlord's agent was considered to be a petty
tyrant.   The individual peasant is now concerned primarily
in maintaining his self-esteem by demonstrating his individual right of decision – usually by rejecting the wishes
of his peers.   As a peasant in Bonvar Hossein said, 'I
cannot be a landlord, but I can be a **kadkhoda**'.   Although
decision-making is often a fruitless process, most peasants
eventually accede to the arguments and opinions of the
traditional elite.

The political elites have become more numerous and important partly as a result of government policies, and partly
because of the landlord's disappearance.   The inherent
conservatism of the landlord is no longer an obstacle to
change and innovation, but this is offset by the peasant's
own conservatism and intransigence.   Only if the political
elite are more compatible with village life – integrating
local peasants **into** the elite structure as government agents
– and if the traditional elite is encouraged as a centre for
decision-making in the village – enabling majority decisions
to be made rapidly in the general interest – will the
peasantry become more receptive to new ideas.

Nevertheless, even if this be done, major problems will
still reside in the peasant's own perception of his universe
and his place within it – a perception that will be governed
by traditional ideas of family.

5.12   Family and Individual

The typical Dezfulli peasant family is patriarchal – the
father rules the household and makes the decisions; the
wife's opinion is unimportant for her activity is confined
to household tasks, housekeeping and assisting in agriculture
at times of peak labour demand.   In 1972 it was noted that :

> " When such processes, as decision-making were
> examined, rural parents demonstrated definite
> patriarchal authority patterns.   Among urban
> families, movement towards egalitarian patterns
> was found but a definite patriarchal orientation
> was still present among the majority of urban
> parents under study.   Wives usually accepted
> the male's role as the decision-maker for the
> family"(16).

However, some Dezfulli peasants have recently adopted a more egalitarian approach, particularly those who are less tradition-bound. The husband might consult his wife on, say, new investments, pilgrimages to Mashad or marriage partners for daughter or son. This could well be partly due to increasing contacts with urban society. Improvements in the mass media - such as the availability of television in villages supplied with electricity - has played an important part here.

However, sons and daughters are still excluded from any major family decision, especially if they are young and unmarried. The daughter's place is at home, close to her mother, where she learns how to perform housekeeoing chores and is prepared for marriage at a very early age and soon learns that "they hold a very unimportant position in the family and that they must marry and have children, especially male offspring, if they are to achieve any degree of influence in the household and in the village among the other women" (17).

Peasant preference for male rather than female offspring is mainly based on a belief that sons are economic 'assets' while daughters are economic 'liabilities'. This view is often reflected in the names given to younger daughters. It is not uncommon in families with three or four daughters for some to be named **'Basi'** (from **doktar bas** - literally 'sufficient daughters') or **Nakhasteh** (unwanted). Converselv, boys' names are often explicit statements of thanks to God for a son - **'Khoda Rahm'**, (God's mercy) or **'Khoda Resan'** (God-given).

Boys in consequence have considerable freedom and enjoy household privileges denied to girls, but learn early on to obey their father's decisions, a custom which extends into adulthood and after marriage.

As Figure 13 shows, the male life-cycle in Dezful is strictly segmented by age. In childhood discipline is strict and the father demands complete obedience, for the child's individuality is largely ignored. At about seven years old, when the child is ready for school he already understands **adab** - politeness and respect for one's elders. At school itself, education is a process of reiterating, without necessarily understanding, information dispensed by the teacher. There is no dialogue, either at school or in the home for the child is excluded from even passive participation in family and community affairs. Until 15 years old, his life is directed by adult male authority - father, grandfather or any village elder. At adolescence the youth, as he now becomes, may attend informal village discussion where his passive presence is tolerated.

Passage to 'manhood' is marked by a beard and fully recognized upon marriage. However, the young man must still defer to his elders, despite marriage, since he will still live in his father's house. His whole livelihood is often dependent on his father to whose authority he must submit. On the father's death authority usually passes to the eldest son and, the male hierarchic structure still

FIGURE 13

A Dezfulli Male Peasant 'Life Cycle'

Age, Year	The Stages of Life of a Male	Event
80+		
70	**Pir–e Mard**	
60	(Old Man)	End of active
50	**Mard–e Mosen**	participation
40	(Aged Man)	in village decisions
38		
36	**Aqal–e Mard**	
34	('Mature Man or Middle–Aged)	
32		
30		Beginning of
28		active parti-
26		cipation in the village
24	**Mard–e Javan**	decisions
22	(Young Man)	
20		Marriage (Active parti-
18		cipation in family decisions
16	**No–Javan** (Adolescent)	
14		Puberty
12		(Regular religious
10	**Pesar** or	prctices
9	**Guak** (Dezfulli) (Boy or Lad)	required)
8		
7		Beginning of
6		schooling
5	**Bacheh** or **Kudak**	
4	(Child)	
3		Circumcision
2	**Bacheh–e Kuchulu**	
1	(Little Child)	
Birth	**No–zad** or **Tefle** (Infant or Baby)	

Source: Field studies

prevails within the family. Contrary to Islamic inheritance law the sons receive equal shares of the patrimony, while daughters receive nothing or are bought out. This is done to prevent inherited or acquired land rights from disruption by a daughter marrying outside the village.

The eldest son may receive a larger share of the inheritance because, Robert Alberts suggests, the eldest son succeeds as head of the **khanevar** and must pay for the burial. He also needs additional finance as the new head of the extended family(18).

The sons, usually those who inherit land rights, join the **bonku** for seasonal land assignment, as very junior members, but their status within the family and village now is a reflection of their proven capabilities as well as their age. From early middle age through to middle age (from 30 to 60 or so) the peasant has a voice in the community that increases as he grows older, until in late middle age he achieves the status of village elder. Thereafter he gradually withdraws from active decision-making, though he is still the head until his death.

In brief, all authority stems from the patriarchal family structure: admission into family and community decision-making is strictly governed by **adab**, age and ability.

5.13   A Marriage

Marriage is the basis of the family and is regarded as the ceremonial initiation to full manhood and more active participation in community affairs. In Iran generally, marriage is characterized by its universality, its occurrence at an early age, and its connection with polygamy and endogamy(19). Universality is demonstrated by census data. In the 1956 census, 68.5 per cent of all males and 71.4 per cent of all females, 15 years and older were married - in rural areas the figures were even higher at 70.9 per cent for men and 73.3 per cent for women. The corresponding figures in the 1966 census (68.4 per cent and 74.1 per cent respectively) showed that marriage had become an even more universal institution and in rural areas around Tehran a staggering 96.7 per cent of men aged 44 years and 99.5 per cent of women were married(20). Similar patterns exist in rural Dezful as Table 31 shows. In rural Dezful, girls tend to marry at a younger age than the boys and the figures also suggest that widowers were more likely to re-marry than widows and that women were longer-lived than men.

Until recently it was usual for a girl to be betrothed at birth and married at puberty (10 - 13 years). Payman's study on this tendency to early marriage indicates that (at the national level). In 1966 the national statistics for early marriage showed 2.7 per cent of girls in the 10 - 14 age group and 50.1 per cent in the 15 - 19 age group were married. The corresponding figure for men was 0.1 per

TABLE 31

Marital Status of Age Group of 15 and over
in Selected Dezful Villages, 1973-74

Population	Bonvar Hossein		Chogha Sorkh		Shalgahi Sofla		Three Villages	
	Male	Female	Male	Female	Male	Female	Male	Female
15 and over (total)	81	75	105	89	141	130	327	294
(%)	100.0	100.0	100.0	100.0	100.0	100.0	100.0	100.0
Married (No.)	56	64	84	73	113	112	235	249
Married (% of total)	69.1	85.3	80.0	82.0	80.1	86.2	77.4	84.7
Not married (No.)	25	11	21	16	28	18	74	45
Not married (% of total)	30.9	14.7	20.0	18.0	19.9	13.8	22.6	15.3
Not married Single	(21)	(5)	(19)	(3)	(27)	(4)	(67)	(12)
Not married Divorced		(3)	(2)		(1)	(2)	(7)	(5)
Not married Widow/Widower	(4)	(3)		(13)		(12)		(28)

Source: Field studies

cent in the 10 - 14 age group and 6.3 per cent in the 15 - 19 group(21). In Dezful early marriage was much more common among girls than boys. Four of 82 girls (4.9 per cent) and none of the boys in the 10 - 14 age group were married in the three field study villages. More significantly 50 of 62 (80.6 per cent) of girls in the 15 - 19 age group but only 17 of 84 (20.2 per cent) of the boys were married - a female:male ratio of 1:40.

The reasons for this are economic, social, political and traditional. Patriarchal poverty encourages early marriage of girls and rural or tribal **patterns of cohesion** reinforce the practice, as does the generalized male preference for a younger spouse.

Although monogamy is the most prevalent form of marriage polygamy is still practised among certain groups. Traditionally it was frequent in urban circumstances, although usually confined to bigamy. In the three field study villages polygamy was limited to four households - two per cent of the total 199 households. Its low incidence generally is related to the prescriptions of equal treatment governing polygamy under Islamic law and to the economic burdens involved.

The 1967 Protection Law (Civil), further restricted the practice of polygamy by requiring that the husband should obtain the permission of the first wife before acquiring a second one outlawing temporary marriages and restricting the husband's divorce rights(22). Most Dezfulli peasants however, have no knowledge of the civil law governing divorce, and the two divorces which have taken place in Bonvar Hossein recently for example, have in conformity with strict Muslim law been by pronouncement of the divorce by the husband.

Moezi indicates that endogamy is relatively high in rural and tribal areas and the Fertility Sample Survey of 1965-66 in rural areas of Tehran Shahristan revealed that 32.9 per cent of marriages were between relatives(23). The analysis of marriage and kin relationship in the three field study villages (Table 32) shows that one in every four marriages has been between related, partners.

Patri-parallel first-cousin marriage has not only been popular in rural Dezful, but it is a preferred form amongst most traditional Iranian families. There are a number of socio-economic reasons for this practice, but in Dezful the major consideration is one of perpetuating alliance patterns for work and social reasons. Although it is accepted that patri-parallel first-cousin marriage might be genetically unsound, it maintains close ties between related families, traditionally necessary for agricultural activities such as pooling labour during wheat harvesting and rice transplanting. It also eases the process of bride selection since all parties already know each other and negotiations over the bride-price are usually conducted in a more amicable manner. Marriage with non-related partners is rare traditionally, it may split a village land holding, if a husband from another village claims his wife's inherited share of

TABLE 32

Marriage Patterns and Kin Relationships

Degree of Relationship	Bonvar Hossein						Chogha Sorkh						Shalgahi Sofla						Three Villages					
	With Land Rights		Landless		Total		With Land Rights		Landless		Total		With Land Rights		Landless		Total		With Land Rights		Landless		Total	
	No	%	No	%	No	%	No	%	No	%	No	%	No	%	No	%	No	%	No	%	No	%	No	%
A. Marriage with relatives	14	30.4	1	11.1	15	27.3	21	32.8	3	30.0	24	32.4	13	18.6	4	17.4	17	18.3	49	26.7	7	19.0	56	25.2
Paternal First Cousins	(9)				(9)		(5)		(3)		(8)		(4)		(4)		(8)		(18)		(7)		(25)	
Maternal First Cousins	(2)				(2)		(3)				(3)		(4)				(4)		(9)				(9)	
Distant Relatives	(3)		(1)		(4)		(13)				(13)		(5)				(5)		(22)				(22)	
B. Marriage with non-kin	32	69.6	8	88.2	40	72.7	43	67.2	7	70.0	50	67.6	57	81.4	19	82.6	76	81.7	132	73.3	34	80.9	166	74.8
Total	46	100.0	9	100.0	55	100.0	64	100.0	10	100.0	74	100.0	70	100.0	23	100.0	93	100.0	180	100.0	42	100.0	222	100.0

Source: Field studies

the village land.   This land-based factor in marriage re-
inforces the kinship link as is shown by the fact that
marriages between kin groups are less common among the
landless peasants than those with land rights.   In the three
field study villages 19 per cent of the landless married
peasants are related to their spouses while the corresponding
figure for peasants with land rights is 26.7 per cent.

5.14   The 'Family Protection Scheme'

In many Dezfulli villages the primary patri-lineal function
is the provision of a kind of accident insurance to its
members.   This 'insurance scheme' is often referred to by
local peasants as the **khin-o-cho**, (the Lur call it **jersh**
and Arabic speakers use the term **fasel**) – khin, blood and
cho, club.   'Active membership' is restricted to those males
who can fight – usually the male members of the lineage
families between the ages of 18 and 60.   However, membership is voluntary and involves a corporate unity and
corporate liability.   Each member represents the whole lineage and the lineage represents each member.   A member's
conflict with another individual or another lineage involves
the whole of his lineage.
The **khin-o-cho** is an old tribal institution shared by the
families with a common ancestry and has come to replace
the protection and mediation offered by the landlord to his
peasants in pre-reform years.   It can be invoked in case
of accidents, to settle informal disputes or, more formally
for cases of murder, adultery, theft or to secure a member's
release from imprisonment.   The "Scheme" is put into operation automatically when one of these situations occurs and
offers a protection independent of judgement or guilt.   Its
main function is to achieve a solution or settlement, not
by replacing more formal legal processes but by minimising
their consequences.   This may involve, for example,
obtaining a written declaration of forgiveness from the
complainant family or lineage which is accepted by the Court
as mitigation.   Here the "Scheme's" first task is to collect
a financial subscription from each member.   This is done
by the local lineage representatives amongst the members
scattered in various villages, each subscription being determined by the total sum required – itself a function of the
seriousness of the accident or crime.
A meeting is then arranged between the elders of the
lineage and the other party involved where the settlement
is lengthily negotiated.   Arrangements are often also made
to cement future good relations and to create a blood tie
by offering a bride usually to the son or brother of the
victim, or to the victim himself if he be still alive and
single.   Otherwise a sum equivalent to a 'brideprice' (about
30,000 rials) must be given in addition to whatever compensation has been agreed.   The amount given in compensation
varies.   For example, death due to a car accident, it might
be between 100,000 and 200,000 rials, while for murder it

would be double this amount. For adultery, the amount is the highest of all and often no satisfactory compensation can be agreed, so a feud develops.

In April 1974, for example, the driver of the pick-up truck of Zavieh Hamodi was involved in an accident which led to the death of an individual and, consequently, imprisonment of the driver. A sum of 250,000 rials ($3,571) was immediately collected by his lineage (each active member contributing 300 rials ($4.30). This money was presented to the family of the victim as the **pil-e khin**, (blood money) and in return, a written declaration of forgiveness was received. This statement was used in court to reduce the sentence.

The **khin-o-cho** can also act as a stimulus to personal conflict or feud where one or both of the combatants has the assurance of the backing of the whole of the lineage to settle a problem by violence if necessary.

5.15   Deviations from Traditional Life Style

Changes in family structure and function cannot solely be imputed to the impact of agrarian reform, for they are the result of interaction between an infinite number of factors. However, changes in life style of the sons of the traditional elite demonstrate the sort of deviance from traditional life that has appeared increasingly frequently during post-reform years. This means in essence that younger villagers pattern their lives on a more 'urban style', relying less on mutual kin help and more on individualism.

Smith also refers to the family transformation at the national level and maintains that

" Many Iranians are in midst of a transitional stage , as they lessen their reliance on the extended family structure and begin to establish new relationships within the nuclear family unit. The desire for independence is reflected in the creation of nuclear family households separated from the father's residence, the weakening of parental authority, the determination of young men and women to gain a voice in the selection of marriage partners, the increased tension among family members, and a disregard for the obligations toward the wider group of kinsmen. Men seeking employment have migrated to the towns and cities, often leaving their family behind, and women have begun to venture outside the confines of the kin groupings. After the introduction of military conscription in 1925, family life was disrupted; the exposure of young men to modern ideas and practices added to their discontentment with rural living conditions".
(24)

The peasant's increasing contact with the urban sector

(a consequence of infra-structural development) seems to play a much greater role in influencing family change than water and land reform do, alone.   However, the role of agrarian reform has been to act as a catalyst which has helped to facilitate far-reaching social change beyond the sphere of agriculture. This reaction, which agrarian reform programmes may have helped to initiate, is still continuing and further changes seem likely before a new stability is achieved in Iran. (25)

Chapter Notes

1. In rural Iran, the Farsi term **malik**, landowner, is often used interchangeably with **arbab**, landlord. However, the Dezfulli peasant used to refer to his landlord as **aqa**, sir, if he happened to be a **sayyid**, descendant of Prophet Mohammad; **khan**, (a title given to a tribal chief), if he had a tribal background; and **sheik**, equivalent to the **khan** title in the Arabic speaking villages.

2. Morio Ono "On socio-economic structure of Iranian villages, with special reference to deh", **Development Economics**, Vol 5, No 3, 1967, p 453.

3. Smith **et al., op. cit.,** p 117.

4. George J. Jennings "Economy and Integration in Changing Iranian Villages", **Proceedings of the Minnesota Academy of Science,** Vol 28, 1960, p 116.

5. Smith **et al., op. cit.,** p 117.

6. Paul Vieille, "La Societe Rurale et le Developpement agricole du Khouzistan", (Rural Society and Agricultural Development in Khuzestan), **Annales Economies Societes Civilisations,** Vol 27, No 2, 1972, p 89.

7. Lorimer, **op. cit.,** p 488.

8. William Green Miller, "Geographical Review, Hasseinabad: A Persian village", **The Middle East Journal,** Vol 18, No 14, 1964, p 489.

9. Grace Goodell,"Some aspects of village social structure and family life in northern Khuzestan",A paper presented in the International Conference on Social Sciences and Problems of Development, Persepolis (Shiraz), Iran, 1974, p 13.

10. Nikki R. Keddie, "The Iranian Village before and after Land Reform", **Journal of Contemporary History,** Vol 3, No 3, 1968, pp 69–91.

    Nikki R. Keddie, "Stratification, social control and capitalism in Iranian villages before and after land reform", in Richard Antoun and Iliya Harik (eds.) **Rural Politics and Social Change in the Middle East,** (Bloomington, Indiana, USA: Indiana University Press, 1972), pp 364–402.

11. Ibid., p 381.

12. Smith **et al., op. cit.,** p 116.

13. Ibid., p 106.

14. Ono, **op. cit.,** p 452.

15.   John Hanessian Jr., **Yasouf-Abad, An Iranian Village**, (Southwest Asia Series, Vol 12, No 4), (USA: American Universities Field Staff Inc., 1963), p 6.

16.   Jacquiline Rudoph Touba, "The Family and Social Development", a paper presented in the International Conference on Social Sciences and Problems of Development, Persepolis (Shiraz), Iran, June 1-4, 1974, p9.

17.   Emilio G. Collado III, "Cultural Change and Economic Development in Rural Iran - a study of modernisation in the Village of Mamazan", (Unpublished Senior Honours Thesis, Harvard University, Cambridge, Mass., USA, 1965), p 49.

18.   Robert Charles Alberts, "Social Structure and Cultural Change in an Iranian Village", (Unpublished PhD Dissertation, University of Wisconsin, Madison, Wisconsin, USA, 1963), p 560.

19.   Asdollah Moezi, "Marital Characteristics in Iran", in the proceeding of the **International Union for the Scientific Study of Population Sydney Conference**, (Sydney, Australia, 1967), p 976.

      Habibullah Payman, **Tahavol va Vaz-e Zanashuie dar Iran** (Change and situation of marriage in Iran), (Tehran, Iran, Tehran University Institute of Social Research, 1970), pp 14-33.

20.   Moezi, **op. cit.**, p 977.

21.   Payman, **op. cit.**, pp 19-32.

22.   Smith **et al., op. cit.**, p 138.

23.   Moezi, **op. cit.**, p 981.

24.   Smith **et al., op. cit.**, p 132.

25.   These words were written before the February 1979 Iranian Revolution.

PLATE 6   Cotton picking in project area

6 THE TRADITIONAL RURAL ECONOMY
AND AGRICULTURAL CYCLE
IN DEZFUL SHAHRISTAN

6.1 Introduction

One aspect of peasant life that has been fundamentally affected by land reform has been the local rural economy. In traditional rural Dezful, the economy was based on crop and livestock farming through sharecropping techniques. The Dez Irrigation Project covers about 167,000 hectares which, before the 1960s, contained a gross cultivation area of nearly 120,000 hectares (71.9 per cent of the total). Approximately 11,200 hectares (ten per cent) of the gross cultivation area was occupied by the village housing, threshing grounds and access roads leaving about 108,800 hectares as the net farming area for the dominant share-cropping pattern. Farming techniques were of two types:

1. **zerat-e dym**, (dry farming), crops were rain-fed only,
2. **zerat-e abi**, (irrigated farming), moisture requirements were supplemented as necessary by irrigation.

The non-irrigated farming areas, about 23,700 net hectares (21.8 per cent) - were limited to districts too far away from the main source of irrigation water, as in the vicinity of Chogha Mish, or on elevated high ground, where irrigation was impractical as around Koluli Kaja. Table 33 shows how the cultivable land was divided between dry and irrigated farming on the one hand and between sharecroppers and owner-cultivators on the other. Most of the non-share-cropping cultivation was concentrated in dry farming districts. Throughout most of the non-peasant farming areas mechanized tillage equipment was only introduced in the late 1940s.

In addition to crop farming, the major activity was and still is intensive market gardening, run on a commercial basis, on some 1,800 hectares to the southeast of Dezful,

TABLE 33

The Distribution of Dry and Irrigated Farming Areas
in the Dez Project Area, 1957-58.

Type of Farming	Method of Land Exploitation	Farmland with Sharecropping			Farmland without Sharecropping			Total Net Farmland		
		Hectarage (Net)	Vertically %	Horizontally %	Hectarage (Net)	Vertically %	Horizontally %	Hectarage (Net)	Vertically %	Horizontally %
Dry Farming		10,900	12.0	46.0	12,800	72.7	54.0	23,700	21.8	100.0
Irriagted Farming		80,300	88.0	94.4	4,800	27.3	5.6	85,100	78.2	100.0
Total Net Farmland		91,200	100.0	83.8	17,600	100.0	16.2	108,800	100.0	100.0

Source: Adapted from:

Nederlandsche Heidemaatschappij "Report on the Dez Irrigation Project, Supplement No 1"
June 1959, (unpublished), pp III-1 to III-8.

(at Qumish Hadjian and Qumish Mumeuan) and irrigated by
qanats. Otherwise vegetables were rarely grown except on
personal one-tenth hectare plots in the villages for domestic
consumption. Vegetables were discouraged because they
needed a disproportionate amount of water and the landlord's
harvest share was proportionally low (one-third rather than
a half as with the sesame crop).
     Citrus fruits are still grown in the Dezful area, but land
for fruit trees was rarely assigned to peasants since this
could establish **haq-e risheh**, (root rights) for the peasant
and the landlord might lose his rights. Instead, landlords
cultivated citrus orchards themselves, leasing them to local
gardeners with market connections when the fruit ripened.

6.2 Crop Farming

     Traditionally, dry farming gave a single winter cereal
crop, while irrigated farming provided double cropping,
cereals in winter and rice and sesame in summer.
     Crop choice was very limited and dictated by the land-
lord's requirements. For him, the main crops had to be
non-perishable so that his harvest share could be stored.
Thus wheat and barley were the main winter crops, and
rice and sesame the major summer ones. Marketing such
produce was easy. Price fluctuations for wheat and rice
were usually small ($\pm$ ten per cent) and both are traditional
staples in Iran. Wheat was often sold to the government,
and rice and sesame were sold to local merchants or **haq-
ol-amalkars**, dealers who worked on a commission basis.
Grain is also easier to police and divide at harvest time
since cereal harvests could be completed at one time unlike,
say, cotton, which requires several periodic harvestings.
Barley was used for the landlord's horses and mules.
     Crop rotation, in the dry farming zones was based on
a two-year cycle and on a three-year cycle in the irrigated
districts. This meant that in dry farming areas 50-60 per
cent of the cultivable land was sown with wheat and barley
and the remaining 40-50 per cent would be left fallow.
The cultivated and fallowed areas would be reversed the
following year. In summer, all land would remain idle.
In the irrigated districts, a more complex pattern of rotation
was used and it is illustrated in Figure 14. The land that
had been fallowed for a year and used only for grazing
after the rice harvest - the **kortech** - was considered more
fertile than the other areas under cereals. The stove was
left to decompose on the surface, for "the decomposition of
the rice stoves seems to be of great importance to the soil,
as it is commonly said that the first wheat crop gives the
highest yields". On the other hand, the cultivation of
cereals following a rice crop improved the soil structure
which as a result of the puddling and the long anaerobic
conditions had become very dense, and "during the first
and second cropping seasons, structures improved again
gradually till about normal"(1).

TABLE 34

Estimated Areas of Traditional Winter and Summer Crops,
The Dez Project Area, 1957-58.

Crop Type and Method of Exploitation	Dry Farming			Irrigated Farming			Total		
	Ha.	Vertical %	Horizontal	Ha.	Vertical %	Horizontal	Ha.	Vertical %	Horizontal
WINTER CROPPING									
Wheat	11,100	46.8	18.5	48,900	57.5	81.5	60,000	55.1	100.0
Sharecropping	(5,100)	(21.5)	(9.8)	(47,200)	(55.5)	(90.2)	(52,300)	(48.1)	(100.0)
Non-Sharecropping	(6,000)	(25.3)	(77.9)	(1,700)	(2.0)	(22.1)	(7,700)	(7.0)	(100.0)
Barley	3,700	15.6	19.9	14,900	17.5	80.1	18,600	17.1	100.0
Sharecropping	(1,700)	(7.2)	(10.6)	(14,400)	(16.9)	(89.4)	(16,100)	(14.8)	(100.0)
Non-Sharecropping	(2,000)	(8.4)	(80.0)	(500)	(0.6)	(20.0)	(2,500)	(2.3)	(100.0)
Broad Beans	-	-	-	1,400	1.6	100.0	1,400	1.3	100.0
Sharecropping	-	-	-	(1,300)	(1.5)	(100.0)	(1,300)	(1.2)	(100.0)
Non-Sharecropping	-	-	-	(100)	(0.1)	(100.0)	(100)	(0.1)	(100.0)
Vegetables	-	-	-	400	0.5	100.0	400	0.4	100.0
Sharecropping	-	-	-	-	-	-	-	-	-
Non-Sharecropping	-	-	-	(400)	(0.5)	(100.0)	(400)	(0.4)	(100.0)
Gardens	-	-	-	200	0.2	100.0	200	0.2	100.0
Sharecropping	-	-	-	-	-	-	-	-	-
Non-Sharecropping	-	-	-	200	(0.2)	(100.0)	200	(0.2)	(100.0)
Fallow Land	8,900	37.6	31.6	19,300	22.7	68.4	28,200	25.9	100.0
Sharecropping	(4,100)	(17.3)	(19.1)	(17,400)	(20.4)	(80.9)	(21,500)	(19.8)	(100.0)
Non-Sharecropping	(4,800)	(20.3)	(71.6)	(1,900)	(2.3)	(28.4)	(6,700)	(6.1)	(100.0)
Amount of Net Farm Land	23,700	100.0	21.8	85,100	100.0	78.2	108,800	100.0	100.0
SUMMER CROPPING									
Rice	-	-	-	11,300	13.3	100.0	11,300	10.4	100.0
Sharecropping	-	-	-	(10,900)	(12.8)	(100.0)	(10,900)	(10.0)	(100.0)
Non-Sharecropping	-	-	-	(400)	(0.5)	(100.0)	(400)	(0.4)	(100.0)
Sesame	-	-	-	5,300	6.2	100.0	5,300	4.8	100.0
Sharecropping	-	-	-	(5,100)	(6.0)	(100.0)	(5,100)	(4.6)	(100.0)
Non-Sharecropping	-	-	-	(200)	(0.2)	(100.0)	(200)	(0.2)	(100.0)
Vegetables (including Pulses)	-	-	-	1,500	1.8	100.0	1,500	1.4	100.0
Sharecropping	-	-	-	(800)	(0.9)	(100.0)	(800)	(0.7)	(100.0)
Non-Sharecropping	-	-	-	(700)	(0.9)	(100.0)	(700)	(0.7)	(100.0)
Gardens	-	-	-	200	0.2	100.0	200	0.2	100.0
Sharecropping	-	-	-	-	-	-	-	-	-
Non-Sharecropping	-	-	-	200	(0.2)	(100.0)	200	(0.2)	(100.0)
Fallow Land	23,700	100.0	26.2	66,800	78.5	73.8	90,500	83.2	100.0
Sharecropping	(10,900)	(46.0)	(14.7)	(63,500)	(74.6)	(85.3)	(74,400)	(68.4)	(100.0)
Non-Sharecropping	(12,800)	(54.0)	(79.5)	(3,300)	(3.9)	(20.5)	(16,100)	(14.8)	(100.0)

Source: Adapted from : Nederlandsche Heidemaatschappij, "Report on the Dez Irrigation Project, Supplement No.1" June 1959, (Unpublished), pp III-16. III-7.

FIGURE 14

The Traditional Pattern of Crop Rotation in
the Irrigated Areas of the Dez Project

Year	Season			
1	Winter	CEREALS	CEREALS	FALLOW
	Summer	RICE	FALLOW	FALLOW
2	Winter	FALLOW	CEREALS	CEREALS
	Summer	FALLOW	RICE	FALLOW
3	Winter	CEREALS	FALLOW	CEREALS
	Summer	FALLOW	FALLOW	RICE
4	Winter	CEREALS	CEREALS	FALLOW
	Summer	RICE	FALLOW	FALLOW

The areas traditionally used for different crops cannot be easily established as they varied annually, depending on factors such as availability of water and machinery available for tillage and harvesting. However, Heidemy estimated the hectarage of major crops in its 1957/58 survey for the original DIP area. Their data, amended for the current project area is given in Table 34. Table 35, which bases its figures on average yields and market values provides a basis, in conjunction with Table 34, for estimates of total production and crop values for that year, as proposed in Tables 36 and 37. In Table 37, it has been assumed that total annual gross value per hectare was 3,700 rials (as opposed to 4,990 rials in the Dez Pilot area). Cropping patterns and gross annual value in terms of farming method used are shown diagrammatically in Figures 15 and 16. These detailed figures clearly demonstrate the importance of wheat - 50 per cent of the total sharecropper's harvest and 40 per cent of the non-sharecropper's harvest. Rice, almost entirely a sharecropper's product, is a quarter of the total, and vegetable production generates nearly 40 per cent of annual gross value for non-sharecropping. However, arable farming is only part of traditional agricultural activity in Dezful.

TABLE 35

a

Average Yields of Major Crops (in Kg/Ha) and
Approximate Farm Prices (in Rials/Ton), 1957-58 [b]

Produce	Yield			
	Dry Farming	Irrigated Farming	Approximate Weighted Area	Price
Wheat	600	660	650	5,300
Barley	650	710	700	3,300
Broad Beans (Dried)	–	900	900	5,400
Rice	–	1,600	1,600	5,300
Sesame	–	220	220	10,300
Winter Vegetables	–	15,000	15,000	1,100
Summer Vegetables	–	8,000	8,000	2,000
Gardens (Citrus Fruits)	–	5,000	5,000	7,000

Sources; a. Adapted from:
DIP, "Review of Progress in the DPIP Agriculture",
op. cit., p 2.

b. Adapted from:
DIP, "Agriculture and Irrigated Report to IBRD",
op. cit., p 6.

TABLE 36

Crop Production Estimates,
The Dez Production Area, 1957-58.
(Area in Hectares, Production in Tons)

Kind of Crops	Sharecropping		Non-Sharecropping		Total
	Amount	%	Amount	%	Amount
Wheat Hectarage	52,300		7,700		60,000
Production	33,995	87.2	5,005	12.8	39,000
Barley Hectarage	16,100		2,500		18,600
Production	11,270	86.6	1,750	13.4	13,020
Broad Beans Hectarage	1,300		100		1,400
Production	1,170	92.9	90	7.1	1,260
Rice Hectarage	10,900		400		11,300
Production	17,440	96.5	640	3.5	18,080
Sesame Hectarage	5,100		200		5,300
Production	1,122	96.2	44	3.8	1,166
Winter Vegetables Hectarage	–	–	400		400
Production	–	–	6,000	100.0	6,000
Summer Vegetables Hectarage	800		700		1,500
Production	6,400	53.3	5,600	46.7	12,000
Gardens Hectarage	–	–	200		200
Production	–	–	1,000	100.0	1,000

Note: Production estimates are based on crop areas given in Table 34
and weighted average yields presented in Table 35.

TABLE 37

Approximate Gross Value of Crop Production, The Dez Project Area, 1957-58 [a]
(Production in Tons, Value in Thousand Rials)

Crops	Sharecropping			Non-Sharecropping			Total	
	Amount	% Vertically	% Horizontally	Amount	% Vertically	% Horizontally	Amount	% Vertically
Wheat (Production)	33,995			5,005			39,000	
Value	180,173	52.9	87.2	26,527	43.2	12.8	206,700	51.4
Barley (Production)	11,270			1,750			13,020	
Value	37,191	10.9	86.6	5,775	9.4	13.4	42,966	10.7
Broad Beans (Production)	1,170			90			1,260	
Value	6,318	1.9	92.9	486	0.8	7.1	6,804	1.7
Rice (Production)	17,440			640			18,080	
Value	92,432	27.1	96.5	3,392	5.5	3.5	95,824	23.9
Sesame (Production)	1,122			44			1,166	
Value	11,557	3.4	96.2	453	0.7	3.8	12,010	3.0
Winter Vegetables (Production)	–			6,000			6,000	
Value	–	–	–	6,600	10.8	100.0	6,600	1.6
Summer Vegetables (Production)	6,400			5,600			12,000	
Value	12,800	3.8	53.3	11,200	18.2	46.7	24,000	6.0
Garden (Production)	–			1,000			1,000	
Value	–	–	–	7,000	11.4	100.0	7,000	1.7
Total Gross Value	340,471		84.7	61,433		15.3	401,904	100.0

Note: a. Crop value estimates are based on crop production records given in Table 36 and farm prices presented in Table 35.
See also the diagrammatic representation of these data in Figure 15.

FIGURE 15

Cropping pattern by farming method

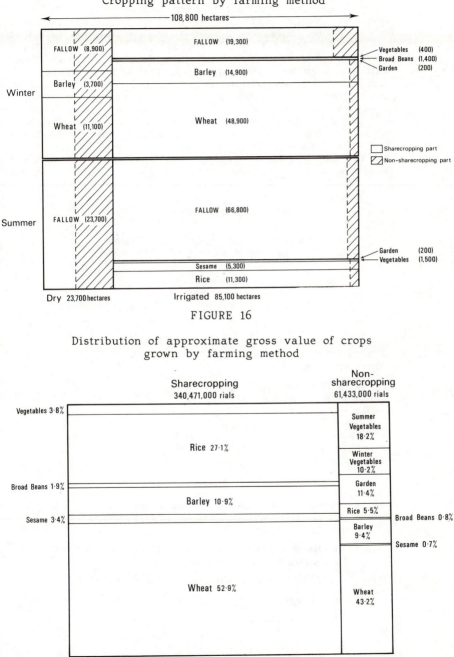

FIGURE 16

Distribution of approximate gross value of crops
grown by farming method

Total estimated gross value of crops 401,904,000 rials

6.3   Stock Raising

Stock raising (particularly sheep) was prevalent in Dezful
especially amongst peasants with nomadic tribal backgrounds.
It was limited only by the 1962 Law for Nationalization of
Forests and Pastures which reduced the available natural
pasture. Villages of Bakhtiari (Chogha Mish) or Lur stock,
(Chichali Sagvand) frequently held flocks of 1,000 or more
sheep, but for non-tribal sharecroppers, livestock breeding
was limited to a few sheep and cattle, mostly for domestic
consumption rather than the market. This lack of interest
was probably due to the peasants' lack of protection from
sporadic village raids by nomads and to the landowner's
dislike of stock-raising from which he would receive no
benefit and which he feared would adversely affect the
peasant's activity in arable farming and thus his harvest
share.

TABLE 38

Estimates of Livestock Population in
the Dez Project Area, 1957-58.

Animal	Estimated Number	
	Total	Per juft [a.]
Draft and Transport Animals [b]	19,100	3.2
Production Animals	110,600	18.6
Water Buffalo - old [c.]	(3,000)	(0.5)
Water Buffalo - young [d]	(1,200)	(0.2)
Cows and Heifers	(10,000)	(1.6)
Calves	(6,000)	(1.0)
Sheep and Goats	(60,000)	(10.0)
Lambs and Kids	(30,000)	(5.0)
Poultry	100,000	16.8

Source: Adapted from Nederlandsche Heidemaatschappij, "Report on the Dez
          Irrigation Project, Supplement No 1, June 1959 (Unpublished)
          pp III - 8 to III - 9.

Notes: a.   The total number of **jufts** in the DIP area, as reported by the
               Dezful Land Reform Office in 1962 was 5,963.

          b.   Including oxen, donkeys, mules and horses.

          c.   3 years

          d.   3 years

Nevertheless, the total amount of stock raising, in Dezful, was considerable. Heidemy's 1957-58 agricultural survey reported on the farm animal population for the original DIP area, which contained 6,750 **jufts**. Table 38 shows the 1957-58 farm animal totals in the present DIP area (with only 5,963 **jufts**) and the average number per **juft**. In reality, there was considerable variation in livestock distribution among the peasant **juft**-holders. At that time, most water buffalo were concentrated in about 40 'dairies' some with as many as 500 animals. These dairies lay close to Dezful and were operated by Arabic-speaking buffalo herdsmen, locally called **torfia**. In fact buffalo breeding is generally the prerogative of Arabic-speaking tribal peasants in Iran.

TABLE 39

Average Livestock Production in Kg/Head and
Approximate Prices in Rials/Kg, 1957-58.

Product	Production per head [a]	Price [b]
Milk [c]		10
Buffaloes	800.0	
Cows	200.0	
Ewes and Goats	15.0	
Meat [d]		32
Buffaloes – old	167.0	
Buffaloes – young	75.0	
Cows and Heifers	80.0	
Calves	50.0	
Sheep and Goats	20.0	
Lambs and Kids	9.0	
Chickens	0.8	
Eggs [e]		38
Layers	2.0	
Wool and Hairs		56
Sheep	1.1	
Goats	0.8	

Sources: a. Observations in Bonvar Hossein and other traditional villages.
          b. Nederlandsche Heidemaatschappij, "Report on the Dez Irrigation Project, Supplement No.1", June 1959 (Unpublished), p IV - 20.

Notes: c. Buffaloes milked about 100 days, giving 8.0 kg of milk each per day; cows 150 days, 1.4 kg each per day; and ewes and she-goats 150 days, 0.1 kg each per day.
          d. Meat production expressed on basis of dressed weights.
          e. Average 50 eggs per layer per year; 25 eggs weighed approximately one kg; and farm price for eggs 1.5 rials each.

          No reasonable records could be secured on the economic value of hides and skins. Animal dung is used as fertilizer for vegetable crops or dried for cooking fuel.

TABLE 40

Estimated Gross Value of Livestock Products,
The DIP Area, 1957–58.

Product	No of Animals [a]		Production [b]		Gross Value [c]		
	Total No	Average per Juft	Total Ton	Per Kg.	Total '000 Rials	Per Juft Rials	%
Milk			4,820	808	48,200	8,080	62.9
Buffaloes	2,700	0.5	(2,160)				
Cows	9,300	1.6	(1,860)				
Ewes and Goats	53,300	8.9	(800)				
Meat			560	94	17,920	3,000	23.4
Buffaloes – old	130	0.2	(22)				
Buffaloes – young	880		(66)				
Cows and Heifers	450	0.3	(35)				
Calves	1,320		(66)				
Sheep and Goats	14,800	2.5	(296)				
Lambs and Kids	4,400	0.7	(40)				
Chickens	44,000	7.4	(35)				
Eggs							
Layers	90,000	15.1	180	30	6,840	1,150	9.0
Wool and Hairs			65	11	3,640	610	4.7
Sheep	54,300	9.1	(60)				
Goats	5,700	1.0	(5)				
Total					76,600	12,840	100.0

Sources: a. Adapted from the following: – Nederlandsche Heidemaatschappij "Report on the Dez Irrigation Project, Supplement No 1", June 1959 (Unpublished), p III – 9 and – FAO Report to the Government of Iran on the Development of Land Water Resources in Khuzestan, FAO Report No 553, Rome, Italy, FAO 1956, p 347.

b. Production estimates are based on average yield given in Table 39.

c. Livestock values are based on farm prices presented in Table 39.

TABLE 41

Estimates of Produce Gross Value for the DIP Area
including Gross Product Value per **Juft** and
per Hectare, 1957–58.

Product	Total Gross Value [a]		Gross Value/hectare	
	Rials '000	US Dollar equivalent ($=75 rials)	Rials	US Dollar equivalent ($=75 rials)
Total Agricultural Products	478,504	6,380,053	4,400 [b]	60
Livestock Products	76,600	1,021,333	–	–
Crop Products (108,800 net hectares)	401,904	5,358,720	3,694 [c]	49
Non-peasant farming (17,600 net hectares)	61,433	819,107	3,490	47
Sharecropping (91,200 net hectares)	340,471	4,539,613	3,733	50
– A Dry Farming **Juft** (crops only) (30 net hectares)	55	733	1,833	24
– A Dry Farming **Juft** (30 ha crops and livestock)	68	907	2,267	30
– An Irrigated Farming **Juft** (crops only, 14.3 net ha)	57	760	3,986	53
– An Irrigated Farming **Juft** (14.3 ha crops and livestock)	70	933	4,894	65

Notes: a. Total value of agricultural products at 1957–58 farm prices.

b. As compared to 5,500 rials per net hectare, in the Dez Pilot area in the same year, reported in "Basic Legal Documents, Dez Irrigation Pilot Project", p 34.

c. As compared to 4,790 rials per net hectare, in the Dez Pilot area in the same year, reported in: DIP, "Agriculture and Irrigation Report to IBRD", **op. cit.**, p 6.

6.4   Peasant and Landlord Incomes

Average yield and livestock farm prices are given in Table 39, and Table 40 shows the approximate amount of   livestock products and their estimated gross value in 1957–58.   It provides a composite picture of total agricultural income in rural Dezful based on the figures given in Tables 33–39, and a basis from which the individual incomes in 1957–58 of peasant sharecroppers and landlords can be calculated. This can be done by making use of the traditional harvest shares taken by the landlord and peasant for various crops as shown in Table 41.   From this it can be seen that the gross return per hectare for a **juft** varies widely.   A single-cropped dry-farming **juft** produced an average gross return

TABLE 42

Estimated Sharecropping Produce Gross Value for Peasants and Landowners from the DIP Area (91,200 hectares), 1957-58.

Kind of Crop	Total Production				Landowner's Traditional % of harvest		Landowner's Share				Peasant's Share			
	Amount Ton	Gross Value Rials '000	% Vert	Horiz	Dry Farm.	Irri-gatn.	Amount Ton	Gross Value Rials '000	% Vert	Horiz	Amount Ton	Gross Value Rials '000	% Vert	Horiz
Wheat	33,995	180,173	52.9	100.0	10	16	5,290.3	28,039	30.8	15.6	28,704.7	152,134	61.0	84.4
Barley	11,270	37,191	10.9	100.0	10	16	1,746.3	5,763	6.3	15.5	9,523.7	31,428	12.6	84.5
Broad Beans	1,170	6,318	1.9	100.0		16	187.2	1,011	1.1	16.0	982.8	5,307	2.1	84.0
Rice	17,440	92,432	27.1	100.0		50	8,720.0	46,216	50.7	50.0	8,720.0	46,216	18.6	50.0
Sesame	1,122	11,557	3.4	100.0		50	561.0	5,778	6.4	50.0	561.0	5,779	2.3	50.0
Summer Vegs.	6,400	12,800	3.8	100.0		33	2,136.0	4,272	4.7	33.3	4,264.0	8,528	3.4	66.7
Total		340,471	100.0	100.0				91,079	100.0	26.8		249,392	100.0	73.2

of under 2,000 rials (including livestock products) compared
to a gross return of nearly 5,000 rials for an irrigated juft
of approximately half its size. For the juft-holder, however,
the differences were not very great because of the differences
in size between dry farming and irrigated jufts. Here the
presence or absence of livestock played a major role. The
gross returns for landowners on the one hand and for the
peasantry on the other are given in Table 42.

Average production values per hectare amounted to 3,733
rials, from which the landowner's share in 1957-58 was
around 1,000 rials and the peasant's 2,734 rials. Many
local Dezfulli landowners had other sources of income, such
as vegetable and fruit wholesale trading and preaching in
religious ceremonies. In the public sector, some held
positions such as a secondary school teacher in Dezful or
an assistant local banker. The landowner's income from
agriculture, was in any case, not limited to participation
in sharecropping as many were themselves cultivators, or
leased land. The landowners' shares from sharecropping
and non-sharecropping cultivation are listed in Table 43.
The gross average valuue per net hectare in non-sharecropping cultivation amounted to 3,490 rials and included
a 362 rial income from citrus growing.

The landowners' net income was considerably reduced by
physical and administrative costs of 55.9 million rials, as
shown in Table 44 so that the net return would fall from
the gross value of 91.1 million rials to 35.2 million rials,
a return of 386 rials ($5.2) per farming hectare from share-
cropping. However, this small return was unimportant for
many local landowners who were as interested in social
prestige as in economic benefits associated with land
ownership.

Peasant net income is difficult to assess as input, such
as family labour, cannot be quantified, and part of the
output - wheat and rice - was used for domestic consumption. Instead the net income of an average juft in the
irrigated districts of the DIP ai :a, will be used to indicate
income levels. Such a calculation involves several assump-
tions and generalizations, such as the following:-

i. Average juft size at 14.3 hectares in the DIP area
    (12 hectares in the Pilot area where cultivation was
    more intensive) was calculated by dividing the net
    irrigated farming area under sharecropping by the
    total number of jufts in 1957-58.

ii. The juft cropping pattern, assumed to be represen-
    tative, comprises winter cropping of 58.8 per cent
    (8.4 ha) wheat, 17.9 per cent (2.6 ha) barley, 1.6
    per cent (0.2 ha) broad beans, and summer cropping
    of 13.6 per cent (2.0 ha) rice, 6.3 per cent (0.9 ha)
    sesame, and 1.0 per cent (0.1 ha) vegetables.

iii. Seven persons (farmer plus six household members)
     form the 'average juft'.

iv. The total production and the gross value of livestock

TABLE 43

Estimate of Landowner's Gross Income from Sharecropping and Non-Sharecropping Operations in the Dez Project Area, 1957-58.

Source	From Sharecropping				From Non-Sharecropping				Total			
	Amount	Gross Value	%		Amount	Gross Value	%		Amount	Gross Value	%	
	Ton	Rials '000	Vert.	Horiz.	Ton	Rials '000	Vert.	Horiz.	Ton	Rials '000	Vert.	Horiz.
Wheat	5,290.3	28,039	30.8	51.4	5,005.0	26,527	43.2	48.6	10,295.3	54,566	35.8	100.0
Barley	1,746.3	5,763	6.3	49.9	1,750.0	5,775	9.4	50.1	3,496.3	11,538	7.6	100.0
Broad Beans	187.2	1,011	1.1	67.5	90.0	486	0.8	32.5	277.2	1,497	1.0	100.0
Rice	8,720.0	46,216	50.7	93.2	640.0	3,392	5.5	6.8	9,360.0	49,608	32.5	100.0
Sesame	561.0	5,778	6.4	92.7	44.0	453	0.7	7.3	605.0	6,231	4.1	100.0
Winter Vegetables	–	–	–	–	6,000.0	6,600	10.8	100.0	6,000.0	6,600	4.3	100.0
Summer Vegetables	2,136.0	4,272	4.7	27.6	5,600.0	11,200	18.2	73.4	7,736.0	15,472	10.1	100.0
Gardens	–	–	–	–	1,000.0	7,000	11.4	100.0	1,000.0	7,000	4.6	100.0
Total	–	91,079	100.0	59.7	–	61,433	100.0	40.3 [a]	–	152,512	100.0	100.0

a. Gross income from the non-sharecropping sector of 17,600 hectares:: $\frac{61,433,000}{17,600}$ = 3,490 rials/hectare (including

incomes from the fruit (citrus) growing sector of 17,400 hectares: $\frac{54,433,000}{17,400}$ = 3,128 rials/hectare gross income, excluding orchards).

were derived from Table 40, so that livestock production was assumed to be reserved to **juft**-holders only.

TABLE 44

Estimate of Landowner's Major Expenditures

Item	Expenditures	
	Amount Million Rials	% of Total
Maintenance of irrigation system and cost of water distribution	30.0	53.7
Payments to the Village Headman	9.1	16.3
Payments for Management	10.0	17.9
Payments to the Village Development (5% of gross revenue) Fund	4.6	8.2
Taxes (6% of net income)	2.2	3.9
Total	55.9	100.0

Source: Adapted from:
Nederlandsche Heidemaatschappij "Report on the Dez Irrigation Project Supplement No 1", June 1959 (Unpublished), p III-21.

Total **juft** production and consumption for an average irrigated **juft** in 1957/58 is shown in Table 45. Cash income was derived mainly from the sale of products surplus to direct domestic consumption – 40 per cent of the wheat, 90 per cent of the rice and 50 per cent of livestock products – and amounted to an average of 26,557 rials ($354). The Heidemy report showed that for 6,750 dry and irrigated **jufts** within the original Dez Project, the cash income per **juft** was about 20,600 rials in 1957-58(2). Annual payments and household expenditures for the average **juft**, of around 19,600 rials, as shown in Table 46 would only leave 7,000 rials available for improvement on the farm or in the house. Figure 17 summarizes the division of total production value between landowners and peasantry, while Figure 18 summarizes the peasant household economy.

With the advent of land reform, many factors governing income have changed. However, various aspects of pre-land reform social and economic organization have persisted in

TABLE 45

Estimated Farm Production and Consumption of
an Average Irrigated **Juft**

Product	Area Summer and Winter Crops Ha.	Production Gross Yield Kg/Ha	Total Kg.	Gross Value Farm Price Rials/Kg.	Total Rials	Landlord's Share of Harvest Amount Kg.	Value Rials
A. Crop Products							
Wheat	8.4	660	5,544	5.3	29,383	887	4,701
Barley	2.6	710	1,846	3.3	6,092	295	974
Broad Beans (dried)	0.2	900	180	5.4	972	29	157
Rice	2.0	1,600	3,200	5.3	16,960	1,600	8,480
Sesame	0.9	220	198	10.3	2,040	99	1,020
Summer Vegetables	0.1	8,000	800	2.0	1,600	264	528
Total	11.2 S 3.0 W	–	–	–	57,047	–	15,860
B. Livestock products							
Milk	–	–	808	10.0	8,080	–	–
Meat	–	–	94	32.0	3,008	–	–
Eggs	–	–	30	38.0	1,140	–	–
Wool	–	–	11	56.0	616	–	–
Total	–	–	–	–	12,844	–	–
Grand Total	11.2 S 3.0 W	–	–	–	69,891	–	15,860

Product	Peasant's Share of harvest Amount Kg.	Value Rials	Food Amount Kg.	Value Rials	Feed Amount Kg.	Value Rials	Seeds Amount Kg.	Value Rials	Total Amount Kg.	Value Rials	Balance above subsistence Amount Kg.	Value Rials
A. Crop Products												
Wheat	4,657	24,682	1,600	8,450	–	–	1,050	5,565	2,650	14,045	2,007	10,637
Barley	1,551	5,118	–	–	1,226	4,046	325	1,072	1,551	5,118	–	–
Broad Beans (dried)	151	815	127	686	–	–	24	130	151	815	–	–
Rice	1,600	8,480	30	159	–	–	120	636	150	795	1,450	7,685
Sesame	99	1,020	–	–	–	–	9	93	9	93	90	927
Summer Vegetables	536	1,072	90	180	–	–	–	–	90	180	446	892
Total	–	41,187	–	9.505	–	4,046	–	7,496	–	21,046	–	20,141
B. Livestock Products												
Milk	808	8,080	444	4,440	–	–	–	–	444	4,440	364	3,640
Meat	94	3,008	36	1,152	–	–	–	–	36	1,152	58	1,856
Eggs	30	1,140	22	836	–	–	–	–	22	836	8	304
Wool	11	616	–	–	–	–	–	–	–	–	11	616
Total	–	12,844	–	6,428	–	–	–	–	–	6,428	–	6,416
Grand Total	–	54,031	–	15,933	–	4,046	–	7,496	–	27,474	–	26,557 Cash Income

FIGURE 17

Sources of income from crops for landowners and peasants

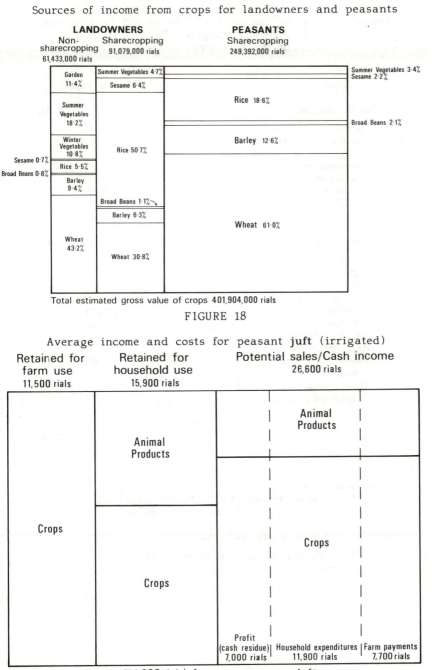

Total estimated gross value of crops 401,904,000 rials

FIGURE 18

Average income and costs for peasant **juft** (irrigated)

Total gross income (54,000 rials) from an average *Juft*

TABLE 46

Annual Farm Cash Payments and Household Expenditures,
for the Average Irrigated Farming **Juft**,
in the DIP Area, 1957–58.

Items		Payments, Rials
A. Cash Farming Payments		7,700
Permanent Farm Hands [a]		4,000
Temporary Farm Labourers [b]		1,000
Village Officials (eg. Waterman, Watchman etc.)		700
Farm Implements (Purchase and Repairs)		1,000
Miscellaneous Payments (Debts etc.)		1,000
B. Household Expenditure		11,900
Food Stuffs		4,200
Sugar	(1,800)	
Tea	(800)	
Cooking Oil and other food items	(1,600)	
Clothing		3,500
Utilities (Kerosene)		600
Household Utensils		200
House Repair and Building		1,000
Feasts		1,000
Transportation		400
Miscellaneous (Medical Fees, Bathkeeper, Barber etc)		1,000
Total		19,600

Source: Adapted from:
Nederlandsche Heidemaatschappij, "Report on the Dez Irrigation
Project Supplement No 1", June 1959 (Unpublished) p III – 21.

Notes: a. The payments were usually made in kind

b. Estimated labour costs during wheat harvesting, rice
transplanting etc.

villages which still follow traditional agricultural practices. In discussing the rural economic organization of post land reform, rural Dezful, the traditional village of Bonvar Hossein will be taken as an archetype, typical of traditional villages throughout the Dez Irrigation Project area.

6.5 Village Crop Production

Cropping patterns and the kinds of crops grown have not changed radically in post-land reform years – wheat still dominates as the main winter crop as does rice in summer. The comparative data on crops before and after land reform are shown in Tables 47 and 48. Table 47 includes data from Shalgahi Sofla and Chogha Sorkh to indicate local variations as well.

It is clear from Table 48 that there have been six changes in village land use and crop types.

1. Juft-holders have leased out about 70 hectares (17.3 per cent) of their 'surplus' land for 30,000 rials, to a private cultivator. The rent goes into the village general fund.

2. Each farmer now has a fixed domestic garden plot of about a quarter of a hectare around the village perimeter for onions, garlic and vegetables.

3. Sesame has been replaced by summer pulse crops which require less labour input and are better suited to soil as nitrogen fixers. Mung beans, for instance, also constitute one of the peasants' food staples.

4. Since 1968 Berseem clover has been planted in the rice carts immediately after paddy harvest as a fodder crop. This practice has been one of the few achievements of the DIP Village Production Service Programme.

5. Rice cultivation is only half that of ten years earlier (48 hectares as compared to 92 hectares), because of restriction in water availability and the introduction of water charges.

6. The wheat crop hectarage has increased by almost 50 per cent over the past ten years, probably because irrigation was unnecessary and the market was stable.

Increases in rice and wheat yields by 1973/74 are mainly due to the use of chemical fertilizer, rather than improvements in agronomical practices. In 1958-59 no fertilizer was used in Bonvar Hossein, but by 1973-74 it was used on almost every crop – 100 kilograms per hectare for wheat, nearly 200 kilograms per hectare for rice – as a result of the Khuzestan Fertilizer Testing and Promotion Programme.

The financial position of the peasantry in the post-land reform can be derived from a consideration of the 1973/74 production figures and market values. These are listed in Table 49 for Bonvar Hossein jufts, together with estimates of domestic consumption and surplus production for sale. Comparable data for 1958/59 is given in Table 45.

TABLE 47

The Cropping Hectarage of Bonvar Hossein, Shalgahi Sofla and Chogha Sorkh, 1963-64

Cropping	Bonvar Hossein		Shalgahi Sofla		Chogha Sorkh		3 Villages (average)
	Ha.	%	Ha	%	Ha.	%	%
A. WINTER CROPPING							
Wheat	166	28.0	302	45.9	380	62.0	45.2
Barley	30	5.1	128	19.5	62	10.1	11.6
Broad Beans	4	0.7	8	1.2	7	1.1	1.0
Vegetables	3	0.5	3 c	0.5	6	1.0	0.7
Garden	2	0.3	11	1.7	5	0.8	0.9
Other crops a	8	1.5	13	2.0	22	3.6	2.4
Fallow	380 b	63.9	192	29.2	131	21.4	38.2
Net Farmland	593	100.0	657	100.0	613	100.0	100.0
B. SUMMER CROPPING							
Rice	91	15.3	101	15.4	105	17.2	16.0
Sesame	41	6.9	-	-	32	5.2	4.0
Pulses	30	5.1	-	-	42	6.9	4.0
Vegetables	8	1.3	10	1.5	4	0.6	1.1
Garden	2	0.3	11	1.7	5	0.8	1.0
Fallow	421	71.0	535	81.4	425	69.3	73.9

Source: Dez Irrigation Project "Winter and Summer Crops Survey Record", 1967, (Unpublished).

a. These included crops such as onions, garlic etc. and in the case of Chogha Sorkh, a part of this land was utilized for growing Berseem.

b. In Bonvar Hossein over 150 hectares of the village farm lands were not cultivated in addition to the area under the annual fallow.

c. Nearly five hectares of the village gardens belonged to the peasants.

TABLE 48

Bonvar Hossein Winter and Summer Crops
1963-64 and 1973-74.

Cropping	1963 – 64 [a]		1973 – 74 [b]		Change
	Ha.	%	Ha.	%	Ha
A. WINTER CROPPING					
Crops	213	35.9	303	51.1	+ 90
Wheat	(166)		(235)		
Barley	(30)		(30)		
Broad Beans.	(4)		(10)		
Vegetables	(3)		(6)		
Garden	(2)		(2)		
Other crop [c]	(8)		(20)		
Land Leased [d]			70	11.8	+ 70
Fallowed (seasonal and permanent)	380	64.1	220	37.1	–160
Total	593	100.0	593	100.0	
B. SUMMER CROPPING					
crops	173	29.2	98	16.5	– 75
Rice (including the nursery)	(92)		(48)		
Sesame	(41)		(0)		
Pulses	(30)		(40)		
Vegetables	(8)		(8)		
Garden	(2)		(2)		
Fallowed (seasonal and permanent)	420	70.8	495	83.5	+ 75

Sources: a. Data reported in Dez Irrigation Project "Winter and Summer Crops Survey Record", 1967, (Unpublished)

b. Field studies

Notes   c. In 1973-74 cropping, this constituted Berseem Clover and in 1963-64 this included onions, garlic etc.

d. Land leased to a private cultivator and not farmed by the peasants.

TABLE 49

Crop Production Gross Value and Usage per Juft,
Bonvar Hossein, 1973-74.

Product	Area Summer and Winter Ha.	Production Gross yield kg/ha	Production Total kg	Gross Value Farm[a] Price rials/kg	Gross Value Total '000	Share of Harvest Used on the Farm — Food[b] Amount kg	Food[b] Value rials '000	Feed Amount kg	Feed Value rials '000	Seeds Amount kg	Seeds Value rials '000	Total Amount kg	Total Value rials '000	Balance above Subsistence Amount kg	Balance above Subsistence Value rials '000
Wheat (grain)	9.6	716	6,880	10.0	68.8	1,800	18.0	-	-	800	8.0	2,600	26.0	4,280	42.8
Wheat (straw)		800	960	10.0	9.0	-	-	-	-	-	-	-	-	-	9.0
Barley	1.2	800	960	10.0	9.6	-	-	800	8.0	160	1.6	960	9.6	-	-
Berseem (green)	0.5	8,000	4,000	3.0	12.0	-	-	4,000	12.0	-	-	4,000	12.0	-	-
Broad Beans (fresh)	0.4	2,500	1,000	5.0	5.0	200[c]	1.0	-	-	(20)	-	200	1.0	800	4.0
Rice	1.6	1,800	2,800	20.0	56.0	700	14.0	-	-	80	1.6	780	15.6	2,020	40.4
Mung Beans (dried)	0.8	1,000	800	15.0	12.0	100	1.5	-	-	20	0.3	120	1.8	680	10.2
Green Beans (fresh)	0.8	2,000	1,600	6.0	9.6	100[d]	0.6	-	-	(20)	-	100	0.6	1,500	9.0
Total	S.11.7 W. 3.2	-	-	-	182.0	-	35.1	-	20.0	-	11.5	-	66.6	-	115.4

Source: Field studies

Notes: a. Farm gate prices
         b. Approximate rates of food consumption (0.6 kg wheat and 0.2 kg rice per adult member per day, per household of eight adults (equivalent)
         c. Including seed stock
         d. Including seed stock.

There has clearly been a considerable increase in gross production values of from 57,047 rials (1958–59) to 182,000 rials (1973–74) – more than a 200 per cent increase – mainly due to sharp increases in farm prices (wheat up from 5.3 rials per kilogram in 1958 to 10.1 rials in 1974, and rice from 10 rials to 20 rials per kilogram). In fact, there has been almost 100 per cent increase in 15 years – mainly since 1972. The increase in prices is due in part to the increased **per capita** income in Iran since 1973. This has risen from 8,000 rials ($110) in 1958 (3) – to $435 in 1971 and to an estimated $1,274 in 1975 (4) , and has ultimately increased demand on a domestic food supply that could not cope, so prices have risen. The government's farm price support scheme has guaranteed farmers prices above the old market price and thus contributed towards the general increase in farm prices.

Peasant crop production involves considerable expenditure. This totals 44,400 rials per **juft**, as shown in Table 50, and must be added to the annual 14,600 rials payment for land to give total production costs of 59,000 rials. Thus 56,400 rials are left as cash income.

6.6 Stock Raising Production

Stock raising in Bonvar Hossein is not as economically important as crop farming. Most households keep a few head of cattle and sheep, and raise a few chickens, to produce milk, meat and eggs for domestic consumption. Occasionally, some of these products are bartered locally or sold in Dezful. Table 51 shows details of livestock in the village in 1973/74, together with comparable 1973/74 figures for Shuhan and general 1958/59 Dez Irrigation Project area **juft** figures. Shuhan, which is an Arabic–speaking tribal village has a much greater emphasis on livestock – a remnant, perhaps, of nomadic origins. It is noticeable that the number of work and transport animals in Bonvar Hossein, especially oxen, has decreased considerably since the adoption of mechanized ploughing and threshing in 1968. The village cattle produce an estimated 40 tons of milk per annum (100 cows @ 400 kg/head). Milk productivity is very low because of endemic disease and poor sanitary conditions. Most milk produced is consumed in the households, in the form of yoghurt. Raw milk is used mainly by mothers with breast feeding infants, and by children or sick members of the household. Selling 'surplus milk' has been limited to a few households. The practice started in 1971 when the new road was constructed, and these few have been selling a part of the milk which, prior to 1971, was consumed by the households. The care, feeding and grazing of cattle, as well as other farm animals, have not changed in traditional villages. Customarily, each village hires a **gopun** (herdsman) for grazing all the village cattle communally.

Goodell, reporting on the relationship between sheep

TABLE 50

Crop Production Costs per Juft, Bonvar Hossein, 1973–74.

Crop	Ploughing Costs (Tractor)		Seeds Purchased		Transplanting Labour Costs		Fertilizer		Irrigator		Watchman		Harvesting (Labour Costs)		Threshing (Tractor)		Total Rials
	Kind Kg	Rials	Kind Kg	Rials	Kind Kg	Rials	Kg	Rials	Kind Kg	Rials	Kind Kg	Rials	Kind Kg	Rials	Kind Kg	Rials	
Wheat and Barley (10.8 ha)	400 (wheat)	4,250					700	7,000			32	340	-	6,800 [a]	120 wheat	1,280	19,670
Berseem (0.5 ha)			6	200			12	120									320
Broad Beans (0.4 ha)			40	800			40	400									1,200
Rice (1.6 ha)	80 (rice)	1,600			542	11,040 [b]	300	3,000	24 wheat 80 rice	1,900	24	480			40	800	18,820
Mung Beans (0.8 ha)		800								400						200	1,400
Green Beans		900	40	1,200			50	500						400			3,000
Total	-	7,550	-	2,200	-	11,040	-	11,020		2,300		820	-	7,200	-	2,280	44,410
Payments for land/juft																	14,600
Grand total																	59,010

Source: Field studies

Notes:　a. Wages for 3.4 farm labourers for 10 days @ 200 rials per day

b. Wages for:　1.7 men transplanters @ 30 manns of rice @ 1600/mann　=8,160
　　　　　　　　0.9 women transplanters @ 20 manns of rice　　　　　　=2,880
　　　　　　　　　　　　　　　　　　　　　　　　　　　　　　　　11,040

TABLE 51

Livestock Population in Bonvar Hossein,
Shuhan and the DIP Area.

Number / Kind of Animal	Bonvar Hossein a. 1973-74 Total	Per house-hold = 50	Per Juft = 24.5	Shuhan 1972-73 b. Total	Per house-hold = 39	Per Juft = 24.5	DIP c. 1957-58 Per Juft = 5963
Work & Transport Animals	30	0.6	1.2	34	0.9	1.4	3.2
Production Animals	665	13.3	27.1	1,446	37.1	56.0	18.6
Cows and Heifers	(140)	(2.8)	(5.7)	(350)	(9.0)	(14.3)	(1.6)
Calves	(25)	(0.5)	(1.0)	(50)	(1.3)	(2.0)	(1.0)
Water Buffaloes (young and old)	(-)	(-)	(-)	(34)	(0.9)	(1.4)	(0.7)
Sheep and Goats	(350)	(7.0)	(14.3)	(712)	(18.3)	(29.1)	(10.0)
Lambs and Kids	(150)	(3.0)	(6.1)	(300)	(7.7)	(12.2)	(5.0)
Poultry	550	11.0	22.4	600	15.4	24.5	16.8

Sources: a. Field studies
          b. Adapted from:
             Ehlers & Goodell, "Traditionelle und Moderne Formen der Landwirtschaft
             in Iran", Marburger Geographische Schriften, Heft 64, Marburg FRG
             1975, Chart 8.
          c. Adapted from:
             Nederlandsche Heidemaatschappij, "Report on the Dez Irrigation Pro-
             ject, Supplement No 1", June 1959 (Unpublished), pp III-8 to III-9.

ownership and economic status, states that in Shuhan in
1972/73 "all the wealthier men in the village have sheep
and that, further, all the wealthier men acquired their
substantial (or differential) wealth through sheep ... Until
quite recently the traditional road to prosperity was through
sheep and water buffalo.   Both produce quick returns,
especially sheep, although agriculture may begin to do so
now that the landlord does not take his share'(5). In Bonvar
Hossein because of the lack of available natural pasture
villagers invest their surplus cash in urban land or houses.
The number of sheep in the village has fallen recently.
No communal shepherd is normally hired for sheep , as for
cattle, and not all sheep are put into one flock. Normally,
a village has several small flocks, each major sheep owner
forming his own individual flock, and smaller owners pooling
their animals to form flocks of 100 or more.
    Traditionally, chickens were raised for domestic con-
sumption or sale and for use as formal gifts or bribes and

for formal hospitality.

In rural Dezful, as well as in other parts of Iran the peasant has been the main national poultry producer until 20 years ago, although he would rarely use poultry in his own household. Chickens were killed for the purposes mentioned above, particularly for hospitality to the landlord or his representatives. Some landlords also demanded, in addition to their customary harvest share, two chickens per **juft** as **morg-e shab-e aid**, (the chicken for the new year).

These traditional patterns of behaviour have now fallen off. Poultry are raised in the traditional way - left to forage for themselves. Although improved breeds - Rhode Island Reds and Leghorns - have been imported since the 1950s, peasants have rejected them. Their experience has proved that **morg-e frangi,** ('foreign hens') are extremely susceptible to disease to which the local breeds are immune and thus they cannot be raised without the provision of vaccination and adequate feeding arrangements. The village poultry population fluctuates because of disease and domestic requirements, but in 1974 each household had some ten laying hens and broilers (20 per **juft**). The egg production is very low - 70 eggs per hen per annum - all but 17 per cent of which is consumed domestically.

Stock raising activities provide products which are mainly used domestically - only a small portion is marketed. Table 52 gives details of production, value and use of these products. The gross value of livestock products per **juft** at 1974 farm prices amounted to 37,400 rials ($535). The **juft** membership (estimated eight adults) consumed a quantity equivalent to 28,450 rials ($407) so that the residual surplus value is 8,950 rials ($128).

6.7   Peasant Cash Income and Household Expenditure

Bonvar Hossein has a semi-subsistence economy, - major food staples are produced and consumed domestically the surplus being sold and the remaining profit used to purchase limited quantities of supplementary food. Table 53 shows average cash purchases per **juft** in 1973/1974 and should be compared with Table 46 which is based on the 1958/59 Heidemy survey of the Dez Irrigation Project. The discrepancies between the two sets of data arise from an unrepresentative conservatism in the Heidemy estimates of **per capita** food consumption and expenditure (6). Another source of discrepancy is probably related to the improvement in peasant finances as well as to Heidemy's general underestimate of average household expenditure.

The recent Goodell report on the neighbouring village of Shuhan seems to be more in line with Bonvar Hossein. In 1972-72 the average Shuhan household, "consisting of 4 - 7 adult consumers and 3 - 4 children or more, needs to purchase only five major food staples: about 20 kilos of sugar a month, 15 kilos of cooking oil, 1 - 4 kilos of tea, 6 - 10 kilos of meat (highly variable - it may drop to 2

TABLE 52

Livestock Production and Consumption per Juft
Bonvar Hossein, 1973–74.

Product	No of Stock	Production Annual per head kg	Production Total kg	Gross Value Price Rials /kg	Gross Value Total Rials	Used on Farm Amount kg	Used on Farm Value Rials	Balance above Subsistence Amount kg	Balance above Subsistence Value Rials
Milk			1,690	15	25,350	1,190	17,850	500	7,500
Cow	4	400	(1,600)						
Ewe	6	15	(90)						
Meat									
Sheep & Goats	3	15	45	160	7,200	45	7,200	–	· –
Chickens	10	1	10	140	1,400	10	1,400	–	–
Eggs	10	3	30	80	2,400	25	2,000	5	400
Wool and Hairs	7	1	7	150	1,050	–	–	7	1,050
Total	–	–	–	–	37,400	–	28,450	–	8,950

Source: Field studies.

TABLE 53

Household Expenditure Estimates per Juft,
Bonvar Hossein, 1973–74.

Item	Quantity[a] kg	Price[b] Rials/kg	Value Rials
A. Foodstuff			23,400
Sugar	200	30	(6,000)
Tea	20	200	(4,000)
Cooking Oil	110	70	(7,700)
Meat	30	160	(4,800)
Vegetables and Pulses	80	10	(800)
Salt and Spices			(100)
B. Clothing			5,000
C. Utilities (Kerosene and Gas)			1,000
D. Household Goods			1,000
E. House (Maintenance and Building)			1,500
F. Feasts			1,500
G. Transportation (to and from Dezful)			2,000
H. Miscellaneous (Medical fees etc.)			2,000
Total	–	–	37,400

Source: Field studies
Notes: a. Household equivalent to eight adults
         b. Dezful retail prices.

- 3 kilos in some families) and 5 - 10 kilos of chick peas,
potatoes and tomatoes"(7).
    Another element which has changed considerably is trans-
port. The increase by 1974 over the 1958 figure is mainly
due to more frequent journeys to Dezful and Shush on the
new road system.
    In Bonvar Hossein the costs of 'supplementary food items',
transportation and other household goods, amounting to
37,400 rials on average per **juft**, would normally reduce
the farm net income by more than half. The average
peasant's net income (above subsistence) of 62,900 rials
per average **juft** of 16.5 hectares consists of 56,400 rials
income from crop growing and 6,500 rials from stock raising.
By 1974 net farm income had risen to 3,812 rials ($54) per
net hectare or 7,860 rials ($112) per adult as compared with
1958 figures of 1,320 rials ($17.6) per hectare or 2,690 rials
($36) per adult.   This radical change in farm income is
primarily related to the sharp price increases.   The list
of farm prices in Table 54 shows that prices of major farm
products have increased by between 50 and 368 per cent
during the past 15 years.   If the 1973-74 net farm income
were to be calculated on 1957-58 farm prices, the net farm
income per hectare and per adult would decrease to 1,410
rials ($19) and 2,900 ($39) respectively – figures not substantially higher then in pre-land reform years (see Table
55).   For many peasant farmers in Bonvar Hossein the net
farm income is in any case considerably lowered by debt.
    Quite apart from the lack of any significant change in
that income in a traditional village such as Bonvar Hossein,
the organization of work has also remained substantially
the same.   This persistence of the traditional system has
occurred despite the disappearance of the landlord and is
symbolized by the **juft**.

6.8   Jufts and Cultivation Rights

    The basic agricultural activities in Bonvar Hossein have
centred around crop production and in many respects, since
the village was unaffected by farm corporation on agribusiness schemes, techniques have changed little since pre-
land reform days.   The major change, both socially and
economically, has been the disappearance of the landowner.
In these respects, Bonvar Hossein is again an archetype
of the organization of labour and land distribution in arable
farming in Dezful.   Before land reform in the 1960s and
farm mechanization in the 1950s, the land was worked for
the landowner on a sharecropping basis.   This minimized
risk and expenditure for the landowner and provided work
and livelihood for the landless peasants.
    Nevertheless, not all peasants benefited because, to become
a sharecropper he had to acquire the use of a pair of oxen
(for ploughing), two donkeys or a mule (harvest transport),
a plough and tools.   He also needed al least two permanent
workers, himself and a helper – (either a **somkar**, a hired

TABLE 54

Farm Gate Prices for Crop and Livestock Products and Supply and Services

Item	1957–58 Rials	1973–74 Rials	Price Increase Amount Rials	%
CROP PRODUCE (Per kg)				
Wheat	5.3	10.0	4.7	88.7
Barley	3.3	10.0	6.7	203.0
Broad Beans (fresh)		5.0		
Broad Beans (dried)	5.3			
Rice (husked)	10.0	20.0	10.0	100.0
Sesame	10.3			
Mung Beans (dried)		15.0		
Green Beans (fresh)		6.0		
LIVESTOCK PRODUCTS (kg)				
Milk	15.0	10.0	5.0	50.0
Meat	32.0	150.0	118.0	368.7
Eggs	38.0	80.0	42.0	110.5
Wool	56.0	150.0	94.0	167.9
FARM SUPPLY				
Fertilizer (kg)	11.0	10.0	1.0	10.0
Water Charges (m^3/sec) [a]	0.0	0.2		
SERVICES Crop Growing per **Juft** [b]				
Winter Grain Ploughing (Tractor)	2,250.0	4,250.0	2,000.0	88.7
Sabz–e pa (Wheatfield Watchman)	1,800.0	340.0	1,640.0	88.7
Grain Harvesting (Labour)	3,400.0	6,800.0	3,400.0	100.0
Grain Threshing (Tractor)	680.0	1,280.0	6,000.0	88.7
Rice Ploughing (Tractor)	800.0	1,600.0	800.0	100.0
Transplanting (Labour)	5,500.0	11,000.0	5,500.0	100.0
Rice Omal, Irrigator	950.0	1,900.0	950.0	100.0
Sag pa and **Gonjeshk pa** (Ricefield Protectors)	240.0	480.0	240.0	100.0
Rice Threshing (Tractor)	400.0	800.0	400.0	100.0
SERVICES Stock Raising				
Gopun, Herdsman (head of cattle/year)	120.0	500.0	380.0	316.7
Chopun, Shepherd, (flock /year)	15,000.0	32,000.0	17,000.0	141.7

Source: Field studies

Notes: a. Water charges were not implemented in 1973–74.

b. Most services were paid for in kind, but here are converted to their equivalent monetary value.

TABLE 55

Estimates of Production Costs and Returns per Juft Bonvar Hossein 1973-74, and the DIP area in 1957-58.

Costs and Returns	Bonvar Hossein 1973-74 [a] per juft				DIP 1957-58 [b] per juft	
	at 1973-74 prices		at 1957-58 prices		at 1957-58 prices	
	Rials	$[c]	Rials	$[d]	Rials	$
CROP FARMING						
Gross Value of the total Crop Products	182,000	2,600	92,000	1,227	57,047	761
Gross Value of the Produce Consumed	66,600	951	33,300	444	21,046	281
Gross Value of the Landlord's Harvest Share	–	–	–	–	15,860	212
Gross Value of the Crop above Subsistence	115,400	1,649	55,700	743	20,141	269
Production Costs	44,400	634	22,200	296	7,700	103
Payment for the Land	14,600	209	14,600	195	–	–
Net Income from Crop Farming	**56,400**	806	**18,900**	252	**12,441**	166
STOCK RAISING						
Gross Value of the total Livestock Products	37,400	534	20,192	269	12,844	171
Gross Value of the Produce Consumed	28,400	408	14,612	195	6,428	86
Gross Value of the Products above Subsistence	9,000	129	5,580	74	6,416	86
Production Costs (Herdsman's wage) [e]	2,500	36	1,240	17		
Net Income from Stock Raising	**6,500**	93	**4,340**	58	**6,416**	86
TOTAL FARM NET INCOME	**62,900**	899	**23,240**	310	**18,857**	251
Household Expenditure	37,400	534	18,700	249	11,900	159
CASH AVAILABLE	**25,500**	364	**4,540**	61	**6,957**	93

Source: Field studies

Notes: a. The average size of **juft** of Bonvar Hossein 16.5 hectares and eight adults attached to each **juft**.
  b. The average size of **juft** of DIP 14.3 hectares and seven adults attached to the average **juft**.
  c. The rate of exchange in 1973-74 was 70 rials to a dollar.
  d. The rate of exchange in 1957-58 was 75 rials to a dollar.
  e. The costs of herdsmen of 1957-58 were included in the Crop Production Costs.

labourer, or unpaid family member) - plus adequate seasonal labour for harvesting and transplanting.

The landowner wanted efficient cultivation of his land for maximum return - and, if suitably equipped peasants were unobtainable, he would provide credit to likely starters for animals and implements, to be repaid over a period of years. A qualified peasant was assigned a **juft**, in reality the right to cultivate village land as a sharecropper. The word means 'pair' and may refer to the pair of oxen traditionally used for ploughing. Thus the word is applied to the amount of land that a pair of oxen can cultivate (8). Elsewhere in Iran words such as **khish** (Khuzestan: dry farming area) or **zorij** (Khorasan) are used for the same purpose and during the land reform period the term **nasaq** (cultivation rights) was used. Traditionally, the irrigated **juft** was half the area of a dry-farming **juft** (30 hectares) because the latter was used for one crop a year only whereas the former provided two. In fact the pre-land reform irrigated **juft** ranged from 9.7 to 16.6 net hectares, an average of 14.3 hectares) including fallow land (9). Quite apart from farming type, other factors affected **juft** size - such as landowner holding size, availability of labour and land fertility. There was no lower limit to the size of a **juft** as in theory, at least, the landowner's holding was infinitely divisible and no qualified peasant farmers were refused. There was however, an upper limit - the maximum area that a sharecropper could cultivate during a single season. On average an Iranian peasant farmer with a pair of oxen is said to have been able to plough about 2,000 square metres per eight-hour working day (10). In rural Dezful, a peasant could plough and sow between three to five **manns**, (24 to 40 kilograms) of wheat or barley in a day (equivalent to an area of 2,500 - 4,000 square metres) (11) - a great contrast to a tractor ploughing ten hectares a day.

The ploughing period for winter cereals is from the beginning of November until early December. Thus a peasant with an ox-drawn plough could plough nine hectares, which when fallow land is added gives an average **juft** size of some 14.5 hectares. Although in dry farming areas the **juft**-holder was permanently assigned to specific fields, this was not the case in irrigated areas. Instead the **juft**-holder had the right to share cultivable village land with all other **juft**-holders. **Jufts** were not equally distributed among the peasants - although most held one **juft** each, many held less than one **juft**, probably through inheritance division while the more prosperous held two or more.

The number of **jufts** in Bonvar Hossein has fluctuated over the past 40 years from eight to 30. Just before the 1962 Land Reform Law, there were 24.5 **jufts** an average size of 16.5 hectares each. The total hectarage in Bonvar Hossein is 593 hectares of which nearly one-third is of relatively poor quality and permanently fallow. Only about 400 hectares is actually cultivable. Land was granted only to **juft**-holders in proportion to the number of **jufts** held.

The number of **jufts** has since remained unchanged, although the number of cultivators has increased through inheritance. In 1974, 38 of 50 households in Bonvar Hossein held land shares, the rest being landless peasants. Now the average holding is 0.6 **jufts**, equivalent to ten hectares and details of the distribution are given in Table 56 together with comparable data for the neighbouring village of Shuhan.

TABLE 56

Distribution of **Jufts** among the households of
Bonvar Hossein and Shuhan, 1973–74.

Household	Bonvar	Hossein [a]		Shuhan [b]	
Size of	Household		Juft	Household		Juft
Holding	No	%	No	No	%	No
Four jufts				1	2.6	4
Three jufts				1	2.6	3
Two jufts	1[c]	2.0	2	–		–
One juft	8	16.0	8	12	30.8	12
Half a juft	29	58.0	14.5	11	28.2	5.5
Landless	12	24.0	–	14	35.8	–
Total	50	100.0	24.5	39	100.0	24.5

Sources: a. Field studies
b. Eckart Ehlers and Grace Goodell, **Traditionelle und Moderne Formen der Landwirtschaft in Iran** (Traditional and Modern Forms of Agriculture in Iran) (Marburg, Germany: Marburger Geographische Schriften, 1975), pp 246–248.

Note: c. The four sons of the former **kadkhoda**, recently divided their father's two **jufts** among themselves, each taking half a **juft**. This makes the total number of **juft**-holders 41 and not 39 as it appears above.

6.9 Juft Distribution

Cultivable land in any village varies in fertility and topography so, to make the land allotted to each **juft**-holder as uniform as possible, the total cultivable area was divided into **chals**, (literally meaning 'pits') – fields – such that within each **chal** fertility and topography were uniform though adjacent **chals** might differ in fertility, topography and size (see Table 57).
The local measurement of **chal** size was made in **manns**, where one **mann** of land was the area which could be sown with one **mann** or eight kilograms of wheat. Although a weight unit (a **mann** = eight kilograms) it was also used

TABLE 57

The Size and the Allotment of **Chals** (Fields) in
Bonvar Hossein Village, 1973–74.

Series	Chal Name	Chal Size		No. of Allotments		Remarks
		Mann	Appr. Ha	Winter Crops	Summer Crops	
1.	Horeh	200	16	–		Fallowed
2.	Zir-e Chapak	100	8	2W		
3.	Sorkheh	300	24	3W	7R	½ chal used for rice
4.	Poshte Jub	200	16	3W		
5.	Sar-e Galal	100	8	3B		
6.	Poshte Kharman	100	8	3W	7R	
7.	Chal-e Aqa Kap	100	8	2W	4R	½ chal used for rice
8.	Dareh Varun (Dareh Zeinal Abadin)	100	8	3W	5RN	
9.	Sar Barik	300	24	–		Fallowed
10.	Khoft-e Meli Kube	60	5	–		Fallowed
11.	Zire Ab Bareh	100	8	1W		
12.	Poshte Jub, Zir Ab Shur	200	16	2W		
13.	Poshtak Khir Ali	30	3	2BB		
14.	Chah Mohammad	80	6	1W		
15.	Konar Shir Koshteh	100	8	1W		
16.	A-Hamzeh	30	3	1W		
17.	Belan	40	3	–		Fallowed
18.	Chal-e Chiti Pain	150	12	1W		
19.	Korteh Ku	70	6	1W		
20.	Chal-e Konar	70	6	1W		
21.	Chal-e Merah	100	8	1W		
22.	Chal-e Zargarha	60	5	–		Fallowed
23.	Deymak Kalbi	100	8	6BB		
24.	Hadji Mohammad	200	16	2B	5G	½ chal used for green beans
25.	Hadji Mehdi	30	3	leased out		
26.	Jai Baq-e Shir	100	8	leased out		
27.	Bil Kan	40	3	leased out		
28.	Jai Baq-e Lutieh (Jai Baq-e Asiaban)	40	3	leased out		
29.	Chal-e Chin (Hossein Mobar)	100	8	leased out		
30.	Dar Asiab Kohneh	30	3	leased out		
31.	Tatameh Hateh (I)	30	3	leased out		
32.	Zaheri Sar-e Rah-e Shuhan	300	24	leased out		
33.	Tatameh Hateh (II)	100	8	leased out		
34.	Zardeh	100	8	leased out		
35.	Konar Siah	100	8	2W	3M	
36.	Samte Joy Bala Raheh Zaheri	40	3	1B		
37.	Mashdi Mohammad (Hadji Mohammad)	100	8	3W		
38.	Khar Kee	30	3	2B	3R	
39.	Keshmashi	30	3	1W	3R	
40.	Aqa Lutfullah	40	3	1W		
41.	Chiti Bala	100	8	1W	5M	
42.	Poshtak Chiti	40	3	1W	1R	
43.	Bala Baq	100	8	3W		
44.	Baq-e Qadim (Poshtak Bala Baq)	100	8	1W	5R	
45.	Jai Masha	30	3	1W	1G	
46.	Meri Jie	40	3	1W	1G	
47.	Chal Namat	30	3	1W	1M	
48.	Turka Kul	100	8	–		Fallowed
49.	Poshtak-e Sare Rah Shuhan (Poshtak-e Zir Takhomdan)	30	3	1W		
50.	Doloran Payen	400	32	4W	1M	1/20 used for mung beans
					4G	4/20 used for green beans.

Key:

  Winter Crops: W = Wheat,   B = Barley,   BB = Broad Beans

  Summer Crops: R = Rice,   RN = Rice Nursery,   M = Mung Beans,   G = Green Beans.

Source: Field studies.

TABLE 58

Allocation of Chals for Major Crops,
Bonvar Hossein, 1973-74.

| Chal usage | No of Chals | | Cultivation Area | | | | No of Strips | | Average sized Strip |
	Chals Used	Chals Equivalent	Village Total Mann	Ha App	%	Per juft ha	Per juft	Village Total	sq m. app.
WINTER CROPPING									
Wheat	28	28.0	2,940	235	58.0	9.6	47	1,150	2,000
Barley	4	4.0	370	30	7.4	1.2	8	196	1,530
Broad Beans	2	2.0	130	10	2.5	0.4	8	196	510
Land leased (ie not cultivated by the juft-holders)	10	10.0	870	70	17.3	2.8	–	–	–
Fallowed	6	6.0	760	60	14.8	2.4	–	–	–
Total	–	50.0	5,070	405[a]	100.0	16.4	–	–	–
SUMMER CROPPING									
Rice (Nursery Area)	1	1.0	100	8	2.0	0.3	5	122	650
Rice (Paddy Area)	7 [b]	6.0	500	40	9.9	1.6	30	735	550
Mung Beans	4 [c]	3.1	250	20	4.9	0.8	10	245	816
Green Beans	4 [c]	2.7	250	20	4.9	0.8	11	270	740
Fallowed	39	37.2	3,970	317	78.3	12.9	–	–	–

Source: Field studies

Notes: a. Excluding the permanent fallowed land amounting to over 150 hectares, the peasants' vegetable plots, the two-hectare garden (belonging to one of the former landowners) and 20 hectares under Berseem clover (rice-carts from the previous summer crop).

b. Three whole chals plus half a chal.

c. Two whole chals plus half a chal, and 4/20 chal.

as land unit in the sense given above, wheat being used as the standard, whatever crop is involved in practice. Each season, apart from fallow **chals**, each **chal** was divided amongst all the **juft**-holders who would thus have land of equal fertility. In addition, the allocation of **chals** was changed seasonally, ensuring that all took turns at using plots of different quality.

Land allocation was not made by individual peasant **juft**-holder choice, nor by allotment by the actual landowner. The landowner was also anxious to see plots rotated amongst **juft**-holders, to avoid peasants establishing **haq-e risheh** or permanent rights to specific plots – a real problem in the early 20th century. Instead a system of lotteries was used. The lottery – **tir-o-qoreh** – was held twice a year and even today, although the landowner has gone, the same system is still used.

Lottery techniques varied from one village to the next, but it was always impartial and mutually acceptable to all **juft**-holders. Before the lottery, the peasants would team up into **bonkus** and each **bonku** would elect a representative or **sar bonku** to participate in the draw. A specific **chal**, was then divided between the **bonkus** in a single draw, or if large, in several draws, to provide plots of equal size. Each **bonku** then decided to cultivate its plot jointly or to subdivide it further between **bonku** members by another lottery draw.

The end result was that a **juft**-holder was allocated a number of small and scattered plots each season. The situation is illustrated in Table 57 for Bonvar Hossein during 1973-74 where 34 of the 50 **chals** were distributed during the winter and 16 during the summer.

This traditional allotment system divided Bonvar Hossein's land into more than a thousand seasonal plots, each **juft**-holder receiving 50 to 60 small and scattered strips. The actual cropping pattern is shown in Table 58. On average each **juft**-holder had 47 plots (2,000 square metres each) under wheat, eight strips (1,500 square metres each) under barley, and eight strips (510 square metres each) under broad beans. There were 30 plots of 650 square metres each for rice during the summer. The resulting plots were so numerous that it was impossible to remember the location of all of them and signs had to be used to identify them. Even so some peasants would unintentionally harvest the wrong plots.

Although the allotment system was just and democratic, it was agronomically unsound, discouraging investment in long-term land improvement. Nor was it conducive to soil conservation since plots manured to increase fertility would not be reallotted to the same **juft**-holder in the following lottery and the excessive land parcellation decreased efficiency and hindered mechanization.

6.10   Work Organizations - Bonku and Quora

In many parts of rural Iran, the traditions of several peasants with cultivation rights working the land as a unit still persists.   The membership of the unit, or work team (boneh) was voluntary(12) ,and its leadership - responsible for allocating individual responsibilities - was elective. All farming expenses and crop yields were shared by members in proportion to individual land holdings.

In traditional rural Dezful a similar type of group existed- the bonku - but its purpose was to facilitate the land allocation lottery between juft-holders each winter.   The number of jufts in each bonku had to be equal, so that equal sized plots could be assigned.   If there were 21 jufts in a village the juft-holders might group themselves into three bonkus, each with seven jufts or into seven bonkus, each with three jufts.   As a rule, the size of bonku in the villages with numerous jufts was larger than that of villages with fewer jufts.

The bonku allowed farmers who trusted each other to be hombar, to be neighbours, thus avoiding conflicts consequent on cultivating numerous individual plots.   Sometimes members of a bonku would decide on joint cultivation, locally referred to as az tokhm sharik ('sharing the seeds') - thus acting like a boneh.

Bonku membership was also voluntary and members could move from one bonku to another before the annual lottery. Membership was usually based on friendship, trust and family ties.   The sarbonku , who actually participated in the draw, would also be in cnarge of collecting dues for the village, 'functionaries', and would organize his group for communal village work.

Until 1972 - 73 Bonvar Hossein farmers were organized in six bonkus (four jufts per bonku), but thereafter they have organized smaller, two juft-bonkus.   Bonku membership varied from two to four (averaging 3.3), probably half the membership of the original four-juft bonku.   Within each bonku, farmers with half a juft each usually join together and farm their plot as a unit, while a farmer with one juft in the same bonku would farm independently.   The resulting unit of production is locally known as a quora - a term that covers both the land unit (one juft) and the farming operations on it.   If shared the quora is treated like a boneh, with shared expenses and yields.

The main reason for shared quora is that some of the farming tasks require five or six men and to hire labour is uneconomical for small plot holders - so instead labour is pooled between several plot holders.   The grain harvest exemplifies this, requiring five or six men - at least four men cutting (using hand sickles), and one (usually a boy) transporting the harvest to the threshing floor although four men are needed to load the donkey or mule with cut sheaves.

In Bonvar Hossein and, most probably, in other villages which have remained traditional, the recent tendency for small bonkus is said locally to be because it is 'easier

to get along with fewer people'. There are certainly other
factors. Demand for village communal labour has fallen
with the introduction of the irrigation scheme and as other
changes have occurred in agriculture. Thus the impetus
for larger groupings has vanished. Also in the current
social instability in village life since the landlords have
vanished, peasants try to reduce their contacts with untrust-
worthy villagers by participating in small groups.

Membership composition of the **bonkus** in Bonvar Hossein
is shown in Table 59 and demonstrates how friendship,
rather than kinship, is the basis of **bonku**. The main
reason for this is that one would feel 'freer' to work out
cultivation costs and harvest division than with relatives,
as one would often have **rodarbasi** (reticence). Familial
ties and deferential roles lead to a reluctance for involvement in economic transactions with close relatives. However,
there is also an increased tendency amongst villagers to
develop relationships with economic benefits. Peasants are
becoming more rational farmers, perhaps because of new
facilities, bringing the peasant closer to market and the
market economy.

6.11   Labour Requirements for Traditional Farming

In Bonvar Hossein, each **juft**-holding peasant used to
employ a permanent **somkar** (farm hand). Since tractor
ploughing started in 1970, however, **somkars** have become
redundant and tasks they once performed are undertaken
either by the farmer, by temporary labourers or through
communal hiring for the village. For wheat harvesting and
for rice transplanting – the two most labour intensive tasks
– special arrangements are made by each **juft**-holder.

The wheat harvesting in rural Dezful begins in early May
and lasts for two weeks. Although time is a crucial factor
in the harvest and hired combine harvesters have been
locally available since 1964, they cannot be used because
of the excessive land parcellation and scattered plots. The
only alternative is manual reaping using hand sickles.
On average, 5.8 men per **juft** are needed – 2.4 men unpaid
family labour and 3.4 hired labourers (**barzegars**) at a daily
wage of 200 rials (as compared to the average daily wage
of the Haft Tappeh cane harvester of 231 rials). In addition
the labourers are provided with free meals and lodging (30
rials per day per person). The total cost of hired labour
is thus, 7,400 rials per **juft**. Table 60 shows the harvest
labour requirements of the 12 **bonkus** and 25 **quora** of Bonvar
Hossein.

The daily harvest is brought to the threshing floor (where
each farmer has a specific spot – also determined by the
drawing of lots) and is accumulated until all of the farmers
have finished their job. Threshing now is done by hired
tractors (cost – 15 **manns** per **juft** – equivalent to 1,275 rials)
driving over the stalks with a roller rather than the pre-
1971 system involving three to four cattle and donkeys.

TABLE 59

The **Bonku** Composition in Bonvar Hossein, 1973–74.

Bonku No	Juft Composition of Bonku		Nos of Farmers	Relations Among Members
	Half a Juft Nos	One Juft Nos		
1	2	1	3	2 brothers and unrelated friend (2 brothers ½ **juft** each shared)
2	2	1	3	2 patri-cousins and a friend (2 cousins, ½ **juft** each, shared)
3	4		4	3 patri-cousins and a friend (formed two separate units)
4	4		4	2 patri-cousins + uncle + friend (2 cousins worked as a unit, the other two also formed a unit)
5	2	1	3	3 friends (2 friends, ½ **juft** each, shared)
6		2 [a]	2	2 friends (each worked individually)
7		2	2	2 friends (each worked individually)
8	2	1	3	3 friends (2 friends, ½ **juft** each, shared)
9	2	1	3	2 brothers and a friend (2 brothers, ½ **juft** each, shared)
10	4		4	4 friends (each 2 shared)
11	4		4	2 brothers + 2 friends (2 brothers shared, 2 friends shared)
12	5 [b]		5	5 unrelated friends (each 2 shared, the 5th one worked separately).
Total	31	9	40	

Source: Field studies

Notes: a. One of the members of this **bonku** actually owned ½ **juft** and in addition to his own share, rented ½ **juft** from another farmer who wished not to cultivate.

b. The only group with more than 2 **jufts** (2.5 **jufts**). This was to accommodate the extra ½ **juft**, existed above the 24 **jufts**, distributed into 12 **bonku**.

The threshed grain is innovated by wind separation and no labour is hired. Women work only on the threshing floor, cleaning the ground and sieving the grain.

In general, rice cultivation is more labour intensive than that of winter wheat and barley. Since 1970 the ploughing of rice nurseries and paddy fields has been done by hired tractors at a cost of ten **manns**, or 1,600 rials per **juft**. The nursery sowing is performed by the farmer, while the irrigation requires the skill of an **omal-e chaltuk**, the special rice irrigator. Peak labour need occurs during transplanting, usually commencing in late July and lasting for one month. Each **juft** requires at least a six-person team. Usually, the farmer organizes the work and maintains the dykes around the paddies. At least three **tolak zans** plant the seedlings brought to tnem from the nursery up to two kilometres away by a **tokh kash**, (young son of a farmer). The labour requirement of the 12 Bonvar Hossein **bonkus** is shown in Table 61. At least one of the immediate members of the farmer's household works amongst the trans-planters watching the hired labourers and trying to speed up the work. In case of neglect on the part of the hired labourers the family representative would report to the farmer who in turn would give the appropriate warning. Generally, as shown in Table 62, the ratio of family helpers to hired labourers is about three to two.

Hired labourers are either from the village, or from one of the nearby dry-farming villages inhabited by Chananeh Arabic-speaking peasants. In 1974 a representative from Bonvar Hossein contacted a **sheikh** of the nearby dry-farming village to secure the service of 22 men and 18 women trans-planters. The **sheikh** recruited the required number and brought them to Bonvar Hossein where each **juft**-holder selected his labourers. They were paid 30 **manns** (240 kilo-grams) of rice (6,000 rials) per man and 20 **manns** (160 kilograms), (4,000 rials) per woman. Men worked from 6 am to 12 noon and 3 to 5 pm, while women worked only in the morning. Unlike the housing arrangements for the wheat harvesters (who are provided with board and lodging in the farmer's household), transplanters are provided with reeds to make their own shelters near the threshing ground. They live in isolation and are rarely invited into the villagers' homes. The Arabic-speaking peasants are pre-ferred to Bakhtiari or Lur (used in the wheat harvest) as they can better tolerate the prolonged and intensive summer heat, and will accept lower rates of pay.

The rice crop is harvested in early November and the operation is performed manually, using sickles. The labour requirement for the work is usually limited to the household helpers and occasionally one or two labourers are hired for ten days. Threshing is done by hiring tractors and no winnowing is required.

TABLE 60

Labour Requirement During Harvest,
Bonvar Hossein, 1973-74.

Bonku	Quora	Juft Comp.		Family Labour	Hired Labour			Total Labour
		½ Juft No.	1 Juft No.	Family Labour	Local	Outside	Total	Total Labour
1	1A	2		3	2	1	3	6
	1B		1	3	–	3	3	6
2	2A		1	1	–	4	4	5
	2B	2	–	2	–	4	4	6
3	3A	2	–	3	–	2	2	5
	3B	2		2	1	2	3	5
4	4A	2	–	2	–	4	4	6
	4B	2	–	3	1	2	3	6
5	5A	2	–	4	–	2	2	6
	5B		1	1	1	3	4	5
6	6A [a]		1	1	1	5	6	7
	6B [b]		1	0	1	5	6	6
7	7A		1	2	3	2	5	7
	7B		1	4	–	2	2	6
8	8A		1	3	–	3	3	6
	8B	2		2	1	3	4	6
9	9A	2		2	1	3	4	6
	9B		1	3	1	1	2	5
10	10A	2		3	1	3	3	6
	10B	2		2	–	3	3	5
11	11A	2		2	1	3	4	6
	11B	2		3	2	1	3	6
12	12A	2		4	–	2	2	6
	12B	2		3	1	2	3	6
	12C [c]	1		1	2	–	2	3
Total				59	19	65	84	143 [d]
% of total				41.2	13.3	45.5		100.0

Source: Field studies

Notes: a.   The cultivator himself owned ½ juft, and in addition rented ½ juft.
         b.   The juft held by a widow.
         c.   The only Quora with ½ Juft
         d.   The number of man days per juft amounted to $\frac{1430}{24.5}$ = 60 days.

TABLE 61

Labour Requirement of 12 **Bonkus** during Rice Transplanting,
Bonvar Hossein, 1973-74.

Bonku	Quora	Juft composition of Bonku ½ juft No.	1 juft No.	Family Labour Male	Female	Total	Hired Labour Local Male	Female	Total	Arab Male	Female	Total	Total Labour Male	Female	Total
1	1A	2		2	3	5	2	–	2	–	–	–	4	3	7
	1B		1	2	–	2	–	–	–	2	2	4	4	2	6
2	2A		1	1	2	3	–	–	–	4	–	4	5	2	7
	2B	2		2	1	3	–	–	–	2	2	4	4	3	7
3	3A	2		3	1	4	–	1	1	1	–	1	4	2	6
	3B	2		2	–	2	1	–	1	1	2	3	4	2	6
4	4A	2		5	1	6	–	–	–	–	–	–	5	1	6
	4B	2		5	–	5	1	–	1	–	–	–	6	–	6
5	5A	2		4	1	5	–	–	–	–	1	1	4	2	6
	5B		1	1	1	2	1	–	1	1	2	3	3	3	6
6	6A [a]		1	1	–	1	1	–	1	2	2	4	4	2	6
	6B [b]		1	–	2	2	2	2	4	–	–	–	2	4	6
7	7A		1	2	–	2	3	–	3	2	1	3	7	1	8
	7B		1	4	1	5	–	–	–	1	–	1	5	1	6
8	8A		1	3	–	3	–	–	–	1	2	3	4	2	6
	8B	2		2	1	3	1	–	1	1	1	2	4	2	6
9	9A	2		2	3	5	2	–	2	–	–	–	4	3	7
	9B		1	3	1	4	1	–	1	1	2	3	5	3	8
10	10A	2		3	1	4	1	–	1	1	–	1	5	1	6
	10B	2		2	–	2	2	2	4	–	–	–	4	2	6
11	11A	2		2	2	4	1	–	1	1	–	1	4	2	6
	11B	2		5	1	6	–	–	–	–	–	–	5	1	6
12	12A	2		4	1	5	–	–	–	1	1	2	5	2	7
	12B	2		5	1	6	–	–	–	–	–	–	5	1	6
	12C [c]	1		1	1	2	2	–	2	–	–	–	3	1	4
Total				66	25	91	21	5	26	22	18	40	109	48 [d]	157 [e]
% of total						58.0			16.6			25.4			100.0

Source: Field studies

Notes: a. The cultivator himself owned ½ **juft**, and in addition rented ½ **juft**.

b. The **juft** held by a widow.

c. The only **quora** with ½ **juft**.

d. Women worked morning shifts only (five hours a day or 2/3 of an eight hour man-day) A total for transplanting equivalent to $(48 \times \frac{2}{3} \times 16)$ 506 man-days

e. Total man-days amounted to 2250 or near 90 man-days per **juft**.

TABLE 62

Labour Composition, Rice Transplanting,
Bonvar Hossein, 1973–74.

Type of Labour	Male		Female		Both Sexes	
	No	%	No	%	No	%
Family (unpaid)	66	60.0	25	52.1	91	58.0
Hired	43	39.4	23	47.9	66	42.0
Local	(21)	(19.2)	(5)	(10.4)	(26)	(16.6)
Arab	(22)	(20.2)	(18)	(37.5)	(40)	(25.4)
Total	109	100.0	48	100.0	157	100.0
% of Total	69.4		30.6		100.0	

Source: Field studies

Chapter Notes

1. Veenenbos, op. cit., p 63.

2   Nederlandsche Heidemaatschappij "Report on the Dez
    Irrigation Project,Supplement No 1", op. cit.,
    pp III-18 to III-20.

3. D & R, The Unified Development of the Natural Resour-
    ces of the Khuzestan Region, op. cit., p 3.

4. Kayhan Havai, 3.12.53/22.2.1975.

5. Ehlers and Goodell, op. cit., p 274.

6. Nederlandsche Heidemaatschappij "Report on the Dez
    Irigation Project, Supplement No 1", op. cit.

7. Ehlers and Goodell, op. cit., p 254.

8. Lambton, The Persian Land Reform 1962-1966, op. cit.,
    p 7.

9. Nederlandsche Heidemaatschappij, "Report on the Dez
    Irrigation Project, Supplement No 1". op. cit., pp III-13.

10. Mansur Attai, Zaraat (Agronomy) (Tehran, Iran:
    University of Tehran, 1345/1966), p 180.

11. In some of the dry-farming villages, eg. Chogha Mish
    (C-19), each juft holder was assigned to a specific
    field area permanently.

12. Javad Safi-nezhad, Boneh, (Tehran, Iran, University of
    Tehran, 1351/1972).

PLATE 7   Cleaning irrigation ditch near Safiabad

7. CHANGES IN RURAL ECONOMY AND AGRICULTURAL ACTIVITY IN DEZFUL SHAHRISTAN

7.1 Introduction

Although agriculture in Dezful has undergone major changes because of land and water reform programmes, there have been other causes as well. Most of these have been exogenous (governmental), but there have been several significant endogenous innovations(1). They have not only altered village cropping patterns but they have also affected other aspects of agrarian structures.

7.2 Changes in the Agricultural Pattern

The cropping pattern of rural Dezful has undergone considerable changes over the centuries. The main crops in ancient times were wheat and barley. During the Middle Ages rice, cotton, fruit and particularly sugar cane were cultivated and silk worms were introduced(2). In the more recent past, the traditional farming in rural Dezful has been dominated by wheat and barley as the main winter crops, and rice and sesame as the major summer crops. Other more recent field crops include broad beans in winter and black-eye beans (cow peas) and **maash**, mung beans or chickling vetch in summer.

Recently certain important field crops have lost their pre-eminence either because of government restrictions or for economic reasons. The opium poppy used to be grown in some of the villages, but in 1955 its cultivation was banned (3). In the early 1970s the restriction was lifted for farm corporations, but cultivation for pharmaceutical uses was closely supervised by the Ministry of Co-operation and Rural Affairs. Cotton cannot now be grown successfully because of an endemic pest, the spiney boll weevil. In 1974 however, some agribusinesses in the area tried again, using large amounts of pesticide - but local farmers cannot afford this.

Indigo (**vasmeh**), production, a Dezful speciality, has gradually disappeared since 1945 because of competition from synthetic dyes and has been replaced by newer crops, ie. green beans.

Dezful has always been renowned for its rich gardens. Khuzestan, particularly Dezful, was praised by Arab mediaeval writers for its rich variety of orchard products – plums, pears, melons, pomegranates, olives and citrus fruit(4).   Layard's observations in the middle of the past century confirm the mediaeval picture (5),   and in the recent past there was at least one **baq** (garden) belonging to the landlord in nearly every irrigated village.

Since land reform the number of orchards in the area has increased and 50 citrus groves alone have been established close to Dezful since 1973.   This has been due in part to the scarcity of privately owned agricultural land after land reform, and the introduction of agribusiness and farm corporation schemes.   Land prices have risen from 8,000 rials per hectare in 1957-58 to 20,000 rials per hectare in 1961-62 and to 200,000 – 500,000 rials per hectare in 1973-74 – a level that has made intensive land use essential. Iran-America, one of the agribusinesses in the area, also planted over 500 hectares of citrus, persuading local entrepreneurs to follow suit.   Increases in citrus fruit prices provided an added incentive.

Many of these new gardens have been created by former landowners on land excluded from the land reform programme. Unlike the traditional Dezfulli 'baq', where there was overcrowding of fruit trees, timber and evergreens, these new orchards used improved horticultural techniques with row planting and appropriate spacing for mechanical cultivation. The owners took an active part in the planning, establishing and management of their own gardens – a practice which was rare before the 1960s land distribution programme. The gross annual income per hectare from some of the new citrus orchards in the mid 1970s was as high as 200,000 rials ($2,860) (nearly 20 times the average per hectare gross income from crop farming in Bonvar Hossein).

People with urban backgrounds and in non-agricultural professions, are also taking an interest in garden cultivation with the result that land prices have increased still further. A garden which was valued at 100,000 – 200,000 rials in the early 1970s was priced ten times as much three or four years later and the urban investors were more concerned to benefit from the increase in land value rather than from fruit yield.

A side effect has been closer contact between the elite urban class, and rural inhabitants which may have caused greater imitation of urban life styles by younger villagers. The gardens also provided employment and many peasants were hired as permanent gardeners or temporary harvesters.

Vegetable market gardens (**muassiseh sabzikari**) have also increased.   In addition to traditional vegetables like onions, leeks, parsley and lettuce, they also grow melons, egg plants and cucumbers.   A significant innovation was the 1960s introduction by agricultural engineers of a new variety of water melon, locally known as 'handevaneh-e mohandesi', ('engineering water melons'), - the imported Charleston Grade variety. Most of the vegetable gardens have been concentrated in 1,800 hectares of land to the south-east of Dezful at Qumish Hadjian and Qumish Mumenan. Some of the 20 gardens there were privately owned farms and a few on leased land and large amounts of produce are exported throughout Iran. Local villagers, especially those affected by the agribusinesses and farm corporations, often found employment in the labour-intensive market gardens.

Livestock raising has been adversely affected recently and in the post-land reform period there has been a gradual decrease. This gradual decline is due in the main to restrictions on natural pasture use rather than to land reform.

Originally villages with large flocks could obtain a grazing permit from the local office of the Ministry of Finance for natural pastures on payment of a nominal levy ('haq-e alaf cher'). Since the 1962 nationalization of pasture and forest, the local Forestry Office issues the grazing permits free of charge. However they are difficult to obtain because of lack of proper records as to a flock's 'original' stock breeders, and grazing is only allowed for five months (November to March) each year. In addition, conservation measures have closed many pastures and elsewhere only a limited number of animals (one sheep per two hectares) are allowed(6).

Private grazing land has also become scarcer. Traditionally, uncultivated village land was used by many stock breeders on an annual verbal authorization from the land owner. At the end of the grazing season, one or two lambs (bareh tarofi) would be presented as an expression of gratitude but not as a levy. Agribusinesses and farm corporations have restricted free grazing. Although they may have allowed grazing, they charged an unacceptable 'grazing fee'. The only alternative is a western style feed-lot arrangement which itself is too expensive. As a result many local stock raisers have taken up other professions. Dezful, once a livestock exporting centre, now needs imported meat for domestic consumption(7).

7.3   Mechanization

Mechanized tillage first appeared in Iran some 40 years ago. Before this agricultural mechanization had consisted of water pumps on farms supplying water from nearby rivers or wells. In 1930 the Faculty of Agriculture of Tehran University "bought the first tractor, in connection with the first sugar-beet cultivation, and this was the beginning of farm motorization and mechanization" of Iran(8). Progress in farm mechanization was slow until immediately after the War, when Iran began to import tractors. Imports ceased in 1967 when a government-sponsored tractor manufacturing plant in Tabriz began to assemble Rumanian Universal tractors as a first stage to manufacturing different types of farm machinery for Iranian agriculture. Between 1969 and 1973, the plant marketed 25,000 tractors (9) - over 80 per cent of Iran's estimated 30,000 tractors at that time. Until 1967 only a few wealthy private operators and "farmers in the development areas such as Qazvin and Khuzestan development projects having access to a subsidized contract service" (10) mechanized their farms. However, thereafter the Ministry of Agriculture sold Universal tractors at cost on easy instalment terms through its provincial and local offices. Many peasant farmers throughout Iran have been buying them (often on a joint ownership basis) for personal use or to lease them to other cultivators. Greater emphasis will have to be placed on farm mechanization since Iran's average horsepower per hectare in 1975 was only 0.2 - one-tenth of that in Western Europe. The number of tractors was expected to rise to 60,000 by 1978 and to 200,000 by 1980.

Mechanization in Dezful differs from the national pattern. It is believed to have started in 1946 when Mahmood Naseri and Morteza Khonsari bought a tractor and a combine to cultivate their leased land (10,000 hectares)(11). Other major landowners then slowly followed suit and in 1950 Taymour Dinarvand, the **Kadkhoda** of the large village of Amaleh Taymour bought a tractor to cultivate his share of land; he also operated a small scale rental service for other cultivators in neighbouring villages. In the early 1950s the Agricultural Bank of Iran, in order to facilitate farm mechanization, provided easy loan terms and by 1957-58 there were 66 tractors and 33 combines in the DIP area (12)- one tractor for every three villages and one combine for every six. However, many were inoperative because of a lack of spare parts and inadequate local repair facilities. Users were not aware of the problems associated with mechanized agriculture and net returns per hectare were often very low, sometimes even a loss (13). Nevertheless by 1957-58, nearly 10,500 hectares of dry farming land to the north of Dezful (50 per cent of all non-irrigated land in the DIP area) were tilled mechanically (14).

The consequences of tractor use were significant. Large tracts of land formerly left fallow were cultivated either by landlords or entrepreneurs who leased fallow land. In addition, cultivation in some areas became more intensive and land was often used annually without the traditional winter fallowing. More significantly, increasing use of tractors meant a reduction in areas allocated to tenants as landlords became owner-cultivators. After 1962 the DIP Village Production Service intensified these changes. However, the major shift to mechanized cultivation started, as elsewhere, in 1967, when the government began selling Universal tractors and easy credit was made available.

Some peasants then began to invest in tractors as they used to in sheep. These tractors were not only used in the owner's villages, but were rented on contract to other villages. **Somkars** and **rabanis** (permanent farm hands), whose main responsibilities were ploughing and threshing, were made redundant by contract tractor ploughing and threshing.

The availability of a combine rental service after 1963 has allowed landowners to overcome their caution about expanding winter grain cultivation beyond their own ability to harvest the crop. The large landowners had been reluctant to invest in combine harvesters as their use would be limited to one month per year. In 1963-64 however, a local producer acquired the services of a combine owner in Kirmanshah (a town about 300 kilometres north west of Dezful) for his wheat harvest since the Dezful harvest in mid June was one month earlier than the harvest in Kirmanshah with its cooler climate. Since this successful experiment an increasing number of combine owners from Kirmanshah, Hamadan, Bijar and Shiraz arrive in Dezful in early May to offer their services to the local grain producers. Hiring charges vary according to hectarage and estimated yield per hectare, and are levied at the end of the harvest as an agreed percentage of the crop. In 1973-74, the rate in irrigated areas was ten per cent and in dry farming areas 15 per cent. The machine works ten to 16 hours a day and the operator carries sufficient small parts with him to avoid any delay in repairing. A driver (often a part-owner himself) and an assistant driver (mechanic) are attached to each unit, and during the harvest season both live on the job.

It is difficult to establish the real effects of mechanism in Dezful since the DIP and government mechanization programmes overlapped. In any case, the beneficial effects of large scale mechanization may well have been nullified by the traditional parcellation of land which has minimized the benefit of economies of scale.

7.4 Changes Involving Large-Scale Farming

The landlord-peasant sharecropping system was almost universal in rural Dezful until the late 1940s when minor but significant changes began to appear. The first was a change in land exploitation, with import of foreign labour and the second was to be the irrigation of **khaliseh** land.

In 1947 Mahmood Naseri (later to become Minister of Agriculture) and Morteza Khonsari leased 10,000 hectares from the Mafi family, major land holders at Hosseinabad in the Shush region, for large-scale farming experiment in the area. Irrigation improvements increased the cultivable proportion of this land and the first tractor and combine harvester in the Dezful area was bought. Nevertheless, the bulk of the land was still cultivated manually by local and Isfahani peasants. However, these peasants were **not** sharecroppers. Instead they paid **mushakerat** (a fixed amount in kind) as rent. Thus the lease holders avoided the risk of crop failure and the peasants could maximize their benefit should the harvest be good.

The Hosseinabad farm was also the first in Dezful to employ the Isfahani migrant peasants on growing **sayfi** (summer vegetable crops) from 1948-49. In fact, a large

part of the Hosseinabad farm was used for **sayfi** crops –
cucumber, water melon and cantaloup – and in 1949–50 the
gross **sayfi** return was 8,000,000 rials ($106,670) – a con-
siderable increase over the traditional summer crop income
(15). The high income encourages the newly established
Southern Agricultural Company (operating land watered by
the River Ojirub) and other large private producers to take
advantage of the skill of Isfahani peasant farmers in
increasing their revenue from land.

By 1957–58 when Heidemy surveyed the area, the original
leased land area had shrunk to 3,000 hectares and was
known as the Shush Modern Farm (16), because large portions
of the original area had been sold to the government for
the Haft Tappeh sugar cane plantation.   Since then it has
been split into two farms.

In 1935 the Iranian government decided to develop barren
khaliseh land by "the transfer of land to individuals or
companies who were prepared to irrigate land by means of
pumps.   The size of the holdings was limited to two and
a half times the area which could be irrigated by the pump
the holder undertook to install.   The holdings were to
become the private property of the holders, but the transfer
of the land during the first three years required the sanction of the Ministry of Finance" (17).

The Compagnie Agricole du Sud (Southern Agricultural
Company) was formed in 1948 to take advantage of this
incentive (18), as a joint venture by nine large bazaar merchants in Ahwaz with an initial capital of 200,000,000 rials
($2,666,700).   The Company received land in three different
areas between Ahwaz and Shush – 20,000 hectares in Abdul-
khan, some 30 kilometres from Ahwaz; 23,000 hectares in
Qumat, near the southern boundary of the DIP; and 7,550
hectares in the vicinity of Haft Tappeh, between the Shureh
and Ojirub rivers.

In the Haft Tappeh region, the Company began to build
a dam on the River Ojirub – most probably the first private
dam in Iran – at a cost of 70,000,000 rials ($933,340).
The associated irrigation network with a main irrigation
channel which was 14 kilometres long, four metres deep,
varying in width from eight to 16 metres, covered most of
the area which was sub-let to local and Isfahani peasants
on a **mushakerat** basis.   Some land was cultivated with
mechanized tillage and hired labour.   The land reform
caused 3,000 hectares to be distributed to the peasants,
leaving the Company with a 2,500 hectare 'mechanized farm'
and revenue from the sale of water from their irrigation
system.

Other landowners have reacted to land reform in various
ways, choosing between seeking incomes outside agriculture
or concentrating skill and resources on their reduced land
holdings, either by creating citrus groves or more intensive
farming.

7.5   Isfahani Migrant Peasants in Dezful

Isfahani farmers are generally acknowledged to be skilful frugal cultivators and, perhaps because of Isfahan's traditional stability and agricultural efficiency, rarely encountered elsewhere. However, cultivable land and water is at a premium with average holdings of only five hectares which are thus intensively and efficiently exploited. Typically half would be under wheat (to provide the staple for the peasant diet) and the other half would be under **kharboozeh** (Persian melon) – a product for which Isfahan is renowned.

Some 25 years ago, a major farm operator in the Shush region approached a **barfurush** or **maydandar** (fruit and vegetable wholesaler) in Ahwaz, himself from Isfahan, and asked him to negotiate for Isfahani peasants to cultivate his summer crop. The **barfurush** contacted peasants in his home area where they decided to move to Dezful temporarily since their own crop could be left to their families from late December to late July, only the June wheat harvest would be missed. Interested peasants were given an advance for family maintenance during their absence. The experiment was highly successful and was repeated. Today Isfahani peasant recruitment is a recognized procedure among major Khuzestani landowners since the migrant peasants' efficiency has increased awareness of the potential of the land and a corresponding and unexpected increase in its value.

The procedure of recruiting Isfahani peasants has now become 'institutionalized' by the introduction of a tenant contractor and formal written agreements. The contractor contacts the landowner in September to establish the amount of land and water available. Agreement is reached on the proportions given over to different **sayfi** crops. Usually on a 50 hectare farm, 40 hectares are allocated for growing water melons, eight for cucumber and egg plants and one or two hectares for tomatoes. A written contract is drawn up stating the amount of land and water to be released and the percentages that each is to receive from the crop sales (30 per cent for the landowner and 70 per cent for the contractor). There are also details of sharing the fertilizer and pesticide costs. All other incidental costs are borne by the contractor – ploughing, ditching, improving soil structure, water diversion materials, (rice straw), and manure. Seeds are provided by the contractor but charged to peasant workers.

The contractor goes to Isfahan (usually to his own village) recruits a work team of 12 to 15 men for each 50 hectares allotted to him. The organization of a typical Isfahani **boneh** (work team) is shown in Figure 19.

Usually the **boneh** members receive 50 per cent of the crop sales, the landowner 30 per cent and the contractor the remaining 20 per cent. The contractor gets 20 per cent because he must cover all incidental costs and the **boneh** members' advances of 10,000 to 15,000 rials each, and is

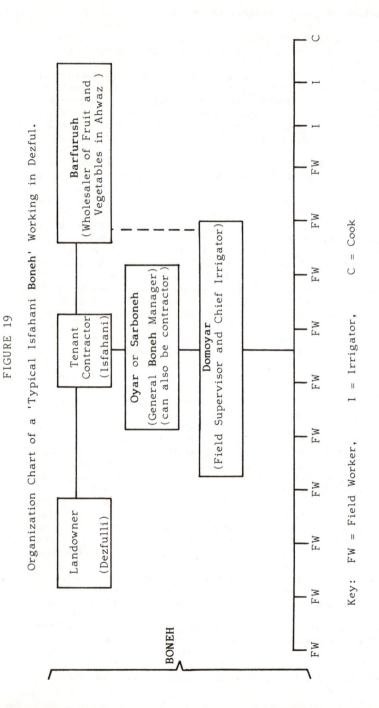

FIGURE 19

Organization Chart of a 'Typical Isfahani **Boneh**' Working in Dezful.

Key: FW = Field Worker,   I = Irrigator,   C = Cook

Source: Field studies

responsible for marketing the crop. Each individual **boneh** member has an equal share, the manager and the field supervisor take three and two per cent respectively off the top for their extra responsibilities.

Organizational discussions are carried out in Isfahan before departure so that work can start immediately on arrival at Dezful. Once there, a shelter and a rudimentary oven and stove for the kitchen are erected. The field workers work 12 hours a day, seven days a week under the direction of the **domoyar** (field supervisor) on planting, weeding and harvesting, and during their seven month stay, each is allowed one weeks holiday in Isfahan. The two irrigators irrigate individual plots, while the **domoyar** is also responsible for dividing water between the various crops. The **oyar** or **sarboneh**, often a close relative of the contractor, is responsible for arranging food supplies and the general direction of work as the contractor's representative. During the harvest he is particularly busy with produce transport to Ahwaz and to the market outlet arranged by the contractor with a **barfurush**. The **oyar** receives a quadruplicate receipt in return: one for the landowner, one for the contractor, one for himself and one for the **domoyar**. In this way, everyone concerned knows exactly how much revenue the crops have yielded and payment is made to all parties at the end of the season in the **barfurush's** office.

In 1972-73 one Isfahani **boneh** (with 15 members) cultivating 50 hectares in Necheychir had a gross income of about 1,600,000 rials to 32,000 rials ($457) per hectare. This is more than double the average per hectare gross income (11,030 rials - $153) from both winter and summer crops grown in Bonvar Hossein in 1973-74. An Isfahani **boneh** member returned home with 50,000 rials, comparable to the 54,280 rials earned by a **juft**-holder in Bonvar Hossein in summer 1973-74 - except that for the Isfahani, his earnings were a **supplement** to his income from his own land.

The same discrepancies exist between Isfahani migrants growing **sayfijat** at Hamidiyyeh and local Arabic-speaking peasants. The reason is the native inhabitants' lack of experience of farming **sayfi**, instead concentrating on wheat and barley. "According to the estimate of some inhabitants the revenue of Arabs from ten acres does not exceed 10,000 rials ($143). Therefore the difference between the income of an average Isfahani or Yazdi family and the income of an average Arab family is enormous" (19).

The Isfahani migrants success is due to their innate skill and systematic organization. They are aware of their reputation and somewhat arrogantly regard Dezfulli workers as their inferiors. Recently some locals have been able to join Isfahani **bonehs**, but because of their lack of experience in **sayfikari** they receive one tenth less than the regular Isfahani **boneh** members. The other cause for the migrants' success is their effective marketing to **barfurushes** (wholesalers) in Ahwaz rather than middlemen in nearby Dezful or Shushtar.

Indeed the success of Isfahani **boneh** system could be

applied to local cultivation - both peasant and landowner.
This non-directed or immanent change has occurred without
external official interference, and no attempt has been made
to incorporate the system into a development plan.   Its
potential in the transformation of traditional Dezfulli extensive farming to a more intensive and systematic market
gardening system is yet to be appreciated by modern
national agricultural planners.

7.6   Rural Employment and Unemployment

In addition to changes in agricultural techniques, there
have also been significant changes in the past two decades
in employment and employment opportunities.
Before the agrarian reforms of the 1960s, the bulk of the
peasant labour force was self-employed in traditional extensive agriculture and employment opportunities in the industrial and service sectors were practically non-existent.   This
has now changed, wage-earning employment has become more
available because of the reforms and the new large-scale
farm corporations and agribusiness enterprises.   The employment picture can best be seen by considering the villages
of Bonvar Hossein, Chogha Sorkh and Shalgahi Sofla, each
of which represents a distinctive type of farming;   Bonvar
Hossein still with traditional methods;   Chogha Sorkh under
a farm corporation scheme, and Shalgahi Sofla affected by
agribusinesses.
In rural Dezful it is difficult to be accurate about the
state of rural employment because of difficulties in distingui-
shing between permanent and absentee household members
and in establishing an individual's true age so that he/she
can be classified accurately as economically active or
inactive.
In general the age distribution of active individuals in
rural Dezful relates to traditions of agricultural activities
rather than to the Ministry of Labour formula of 12 to 64
years or to the conventional International Labour Organization formula of 15 to 64 years[20]. In village life economic
activity can start as soon as a boy can control a donkey
or mule during harvest - at about ten years old - and a
girl can work at rice transplanting - until the villager
is physically incapable of further work - at perhaps 70
years old.   Overall information on the general employment
situation in rural Dezful is contained in the 1956 and 1966
National Census Reports and a summary of the data is
presented in Table 63.   The census definitions assume anyone ten years and over (including those over 70 years) as
active and do not distinguish between permanent and
temporary employment.
The data show that there was a general decline in formal
employment between 1956 and 1966 - a trend which should
be treated with caution since there is much casual and
informal employment in peasant agriculture.   However, it
could be related to a rapid population and labour force

TABLE 63

Employment Status of Population of Rural Dezful

Status of Population		First Census [a] (1956)	Second Census [b] (1966)
Total Population	Male	60,244	38,214
	Female	68,095 [c]	34,751 [d]
	Both sexes	128,339	73,965
Household	Number	24,432	13,700
	Average size	5.3	5.3
Economically Inactive Category (10 years)	Both sexes	46,320	27,085
	" % of total population	36.1	37.1
	" average per household	1.9	1.9
Economically Active Category (10 years)	Male population	39,543	23,821
	" % of total male population	65.6	62.3
	" average per household	1.6	1.7
	Female population	42,476	22,059
	" % of total female population	62.4	63.5
	" average per household	1.7	1.6
	Both sexes	82,019	45,880
	" % of total population	63.9	62.9
	" average per household	3.3	3.3
Employed	Male employed	34,033	18,215
	" % of male econ. active	86.1	76.5
	" average per household	1.4	1.3
	Female employed	3,087	1,459
	" % of female econ. active	7.3	6.6
	" average per household	0.1	0.1
	Both sexes	37,120	19,674
	" % of total population	45.3	42.9
	" average per household	1.5	1.4

Sources: a. General Statistical Department of the Ministry of the Interior,
Gozaresh Mashrich Hozeh Sarshomary Dezful, Vol 19 (Tehran, Iran:
General Statistical Dep., 1959) p 23.

b. Iranian Statistical Centre, Plan Organization National Census of
Population and Housing November, 1966, Vol 77, Dezful Shahristan
(Tehran, Iran: Statistical Centre 1968) p 32.

Notes: c. Includes the population of Andimeshk and Shush.

d. Includes the population of Shush.

TABLE 64

Bonvar Hossein Population Employment Profile, 1973–74.

Employment	Status	Landholder No.	Landholder %	Landless No.	Landless %	Total No.
Total Population	Male	120	83.3	24	16.7	144
	Female	117	77.5	34	22.5	151
	Both Sexes	237	80.0	58	20.0	295
Household	Number	38	76.0	12	24.0	50
	Average Size	6.2	–	4.8	–	5.9
Economically Inactive Category	Both Sexes	93	79.5	24	20.5	117
	Both Sexes % of total population	39.2	–	41.4	–	39.7
	Both Sexes Average per Household	2.5	–	2.0	–	2.3
Economically Active Category	Male population	74	82.2	16	17.8	90
	% of total Male population	61.7	–	66.7	–	62.5
	Males – Average per Household	2.0	–	1.3	–	1.8
	Female population	70	79.5	18	20.5	88
	% of total female population	59.8	–	52.9	–	58.3
	Females – Average per Household	1.8	–	1.5	–	1.8
	Both Sexes	144	80.9	34	19.1	178
	% of total population	60.8	–	58.6	–	60.3
	Both Sexes Average per Household	3.8	–	2.8	–	3.6
Permanent Employment (Full-Time)	Male Employed	48	85.7	8	14.3	56
	% of males – economically active	64.9	–	50.0	–	62.2
	Males – Average per Household	1.3	–	0.7	–	1.1
Temporary Employment (Part-time Work)	Male employed	23	74.2	8	25.8	31
	% of males – economically active	31.0	–	50.0	–	34.4
	Males – Average per Household	0.6	–	0.7	–	0.6
	Female employed	25	83.3	5	16.7	30
	% of females – economically active	35.7	–	27.8	–	34.1
	Females – Average per Household	0.7	–	0.4	–	0.6
	Both Sexes	48	78.7	13	21.3	61
	Both Sexes – % of Econ. Active Population	33.3	–	38.2	–	34.3
	Both Sexes – Average per Household	1.3	–	1.1	–	1.2
Unemployment	Male Unemployed	3	100.0	–	–	3
	% of Male Economically Active	4.1	–	–	–	3.3
	Males – Average per Household	0.8	–	–	–	0.6
	Females Unemployed	45	77.6	13	22.4	58
	% of Female Economically Active	64.3	–	72.2	–	65.9
	Females – Average per Household	1.2	–	1.1	–	1.2
	Both Sexes	48	78.7	13	21.3	61
	% of Economically Active Population	33.3	–	38.2	–	34.3
	Both Sexes – Average per Household	1.3	–	1.1	–	1.2

Source: Field studies.

increase which probably exceeded rural labour demand.
Furthermore the 1960s agrarian reform measures have caused
somkar and **rabani** to become unemployed, and the new irrigation system has made traditional **bildars** (canal cleaners)
redundant. The recent expansion of urban and rural
construction has provided some new employment opportunities.
Women play very little part in economic rural life because
permanent agricultural work and employment outside the
village, have traditionally been limited to men. Details
of employment patterns are more clearly revealed by an
examination of the three villages, Bonvar Hossein, Chogha
Sorkh and Shalgahi Sofla.

7.7   The Traditional Village of Bonvar Hossein.

Table 64 presents the main economic characteristics and
employment situation in the village whilst the types of work
done are shown in Table 65. Table 66 shows the type of
work undertaken by families without land in the village.

7.8   The Farm-Corporation Village of Chogha Sorkh

Since June 1972 Chogha Sorkh, together with five neighbouring villages, has been incorporated into the Shamsabad
Farm Corporation. This has meant that the villagers have
had to transfer their land rights to the Corporation, and
on the basis of the value of their lands they received a
corresponding number of shares. The village land is now
being cultivated and managed by a government manager,
and the peasants, as 'stock-holders', receive a dividend.
The employment situation is summarized in Table 67. Table
68 describes the types of employment available and Table
69 indicates how those families who did not have land rights
have found employment.
Fewer males are permanently employed than in Bonvar
Hossein, because the peasant **juft**-holders have become wage
earners or are unemployed. The Farm Corporation has not
been able to provide adequate alternative employment for
those peasants who, under the traditional farming situation,
were either self-employed or full-time family helpers.
Although the majority of self-employed peasants would have
been under-employed, the traditional system was semi-
subsistence in nature and most peasant farmers needed no
additional employment to supplement their modest income.
Now with no land to cultivate, an increasing number of
peasants of Chogha Sorkh are looking unsuccessfully for
salaried employment with the Farm Corporation. Employment
for landless peasants of Chogha Sorkh, differs from that
available to landless peasants in Bonvar Hossein, in that
temporary employment is not found within the village.
Instead, the unemployed look to those villages which are
still traditional, local farm corporations or agribusinesses.
Five former **juft**-holders are employed on land retained

TABLE 65

Occupations of Economically Active Male Population
in Bonvar Hossein, 1973-74.

Type of Employment (Permanent)	No. of peasants involved			
	Land-holding	Landless	Total	%
A. **Agriculture**	45	2	47	52.2
Self-employed **juft**-holders a	(39)		(39)	
Farm Labour (unpaid family helpers)	(4)	(1)	(5)	
Shepherd (salary earners) b	(2)		(2)	
Herdsman (salary earner)		(1)	(1)	
B. **Non-agriculture** (outside the village)	3	6	9	10.0
Government employment				
Sabz-ab Railway Station	(2)	(2)	(4)	
Dezful Air Base	(1)	(2)	(3)	
Private construction companies				
(road builders and watchman)		(2)	(2)	
C. **Non-employed**	26	8	34	37.8
Students				
Students with summer jobs	(11)	(2)	(13)	
Students with no summer jobs	((11))	((2))	((13))	
Non-students	-	-	-	
Non-students with part time work	(15)	(6)	(21)	
Non-students with no work	((12))	((6))	((18))	
	((3))		((3))	
Total male population 10-69 age group	74	16	90	100.0

Source: Field studies

Notes: a.Two **juft**-holders (½**juft** each), sons of the former **kadkhoda** have migrated to Dezful. In the 1973-74 agricultural
          year, one leased his land to a local farm (with a ½ **juft**, making his total holding one **juft**) and the other one
          rented his ½ **juft** to a farmer from outside the village. The two other sons of the **kadkhoda** with ½ **juft** each, have
          formed one single household, pooling their income and expenditure.
          b.The two shepherds are members of the two major sheep-owning households who also hold **jufts.**

TABLE 66

Employment Situation of the Landless Households in
Bonvar Hossein, 1973-74.

Hh. No.	Total Members No.	Econ. In-active	Econ.Active Male	Female	Total	No. of Workers (Male)	Occupation	No. of Workers Male	Female	Occupation	Remarks
						Permanently Employed		Temporarily Employed			
1	1	1									A widow
2	1	1									A widow
3	1			1	1				1	Rice Transplanting	A widow
4	2		1	1	2			1	1	Rice Transplanting	A divorcee and son of 15
5	6	4	1	1	2			1	1	Rice Transplanting (man also working on other farm jobs)	Husband and wife working
6	4	2	1	1	2	1	Farm Labour				Wife has a baby of 7 months
7	3	0	2	1	3	1	Herdsman	1		Farm Work	Wife 60 years old not working
8	7	5	1	1	2	1	Watchman also temporary farm work				Wife has a baby of 2 months
9	7	5	1	1	2	1	Carpenter at the Air Base		1	Rice Transplanting	Wife working during rice transplanting
10	8	2	3	3	6	1	Construction Work at Air Base	2	1	Rice Transplanting and other farm work	A daughter of 14 works only during rice transplanting
11	9	2	4	3	7	2	Railways and road construction	2		Rice Transplanting	2 sons working during rice transplanting
12	9	2	2	5	7	1	Railways	1		Farm Work	
Total	58	24	16	18	34	8		8 13	5		

Source: Field studies

TABLE 67

Chogha Sorkh Population Employment Profile, 1973-74.

	Employment Status	Peasants With Land Rights No.	Peasants With Land Rights %	Peasants Without Land Rights No.	Peasants Without Land Rights %	Total No.
Total Population	Male	192	88.9	24	11.1	216
	Female	154	87.5	22	12.5	176
	Both sexes	346	88.3	46	11.7	392
Household	Number	52	81.3	12	18.7	64
	Average size	6.7		3.8		6.1
Economically Inactive Category	Both sexes	138	87.9	19	12.1	157
	Both sexes % of total population	39.9		41.3		40.1
	Both sexes average per household	2.7		1.6		2.5
Economically Active Category	Male population economically active	110	88.7	14	11.3	124
	% of total male population	57.3		58.3		57.4
	Males - average per household	2.1		1.2		1.9
	Female population economically active	98	88.3	13	11.7	111
	% of total Female popilation	63.6		59.1		63.1
	Females - average per household	1.9		1.1		1.7
	Both sexes economically active	208	88.5	27	11.5	235
	% of total population	60.1		58.7		59.9
	Both sexes - average per household	4.0		2.3		3.7
Permanent Employment (Full-time)	Male employed	37	82.2	8	17.8	45
	% of males - economically active	33.6		57.1		36.3
	Males - average per household	0.7		0.7		0.7
Temporary Employment (Part-time work)	Male employed (including students)	65	92.9	5	7.1	70
	% of males - economically active	59.1		35.8		44.6
	Males - average per household	1.3		0.4		1.1
	Female employed (including students)	31	86.1	5	13.9	36
	% of females - economically active	31.6		35.7		32.4
	Females - average per household	0.6		0.4		0.6
	Both sexes (including students)	96	90.6	10	9.4	106
	Both sexes - % of econ. active population	46.2		37.0		45.1
	Both sexes - average per household	1.8		0.8		1.6
Unemployed	Male unemployed	8	88.9	1	10.1	9
	% of males - economically active	7.3		7.1		7.3
	Males - average per household	0.2		0.1		1.4
	Female unemployed	67	89.3	8	10.7	75
	% of females - economically active	68.4		61.5		65.8
	Females - average per household	1.3		0.7		1.1
	Both sexes	75	90.4	8	9.6	83
	% of economically active population	36.1		29.6		35.3
	Both sexes - average per household	1.4		0.7		1.3

Source: Field studies.

TABLE 68

Occupations of Economically Active Male Population
of Chogha Sorkh, 1973-74.

Type of Employment (Permanent)	No. of Peasants involved			
	With land rights	Without land rights	Total	%
A. Agriculture	28	6	34	27.4
Self employed, flock keeping	(6)	(1)	(7)	
Shepherds (unpaid family helpers)	(5)		(5)	
Shepherd (salary earner)		(1)	(1)	
Shepherds (Shamsabad Farm Corporation)	(2)		(2)	
Herdsman (salary earner)		(1)	(1)	
Farm labour (Shamsabad Farm Corporation)	(9)		(9)	
Farm labour (Dez Project)		(1)	(1)	
Farm labour (Private farms and gardens)	(6)	(2)	(8)	
B. Non-Agriculture	9	2	11	8.9
Self-employed, driver	(1)		(1)	
Private Construction Companies (driver, road building, store keeping)	(6)	(1)	(7)	
Clerical and typing (Shamsabad Farm Corporation)	(2)	(1)	(3)	
C. Non-employment (permanent)	73	6	79	63.7
Students	(19)	(1)	(20)	
Students with summer jobs	((14))		((14))	
Students with no summer jobs	((5))	((1))	((6))	
Non-Students	(54)	(5)	(59)	
Non-Students with part time work	((51))	((5))	((56))	
Non-Students with no work	((3))		((3))	
Total male population 16-69 age group	110	14	124	100.0

Source: Field studies.

TABLE 69

Employment Situation of Landless Households,
Chogha Sorkh, 1973-74.

Hh. Number*	Total Members Number	Household Composition — Econ. Inactive Members	Active Male	Active Female	Active Total	Permanently Employed No. of Workers (Male)	Permanently Employed Occupation	Temporarily Employed No. of Workers Male	Temporarily Employed No. of Workers Female	Temporarily Employed Occupation	Remarks
1	4	2	1	1	2			1		Rice transplanting and other farm jobs	Wife has a 2 yr. old child
2	4	2	1	1	2	1	Farm labour (private veg. farm)				Wife has a 1 yr. old child
3	2		1	1	2						A 60 yr. old widow and a son of 10 (student) mother unemployed.
4	5	2	1	2	3	1	Driver		2	Rice transplanting	Wife and mother both work during rice transplanting
5	3	1	1	2	3	1	Farm labour (DIP)		2	Rice transplanting	Wife and mother-in-law both work during rice transplanting.
6	5	3	1	1	2			1	1	Rice transplanting (man also works on other farm jobs)	
7	5	3	1	1	2	1	Shepherd				Wife has a 2 yr. old child
8	5	2	2	1	3	1	"Typist" in Shams-abad Farm Corporn.	1		Rice transplanting and other farm jobs	Wife unemployed
9	4	2	1	1	2			1		moqani digging or repairing wells	Wife has a 1½ yr. old child
10	1			1	1						Widow
11	4		3	1	4	2	Herdsman (father) Farm labour (son) (private veg.farm)	1		assistant herdsman	Wife unemployed
12	4	2	1	1	2	1	Flock keeper				Wife has a 1 yr. old child
	46	19	14	13	27	8		5	5		
								10			

Source: Field studies

Hh. *: Household

by the old landlords on a 'modified' sharecropping basis. The landlord provides land and water and the peasants have cultivation rights for the summer rice crop season only. The peasants also supply the seed and labour in return for 50 per cent of the harvest. Interestingly, the Shamsabad Farm Corporation, like two nearby farm corporations, is also re-leasing land on a temporary and modified share-cropping basis similar to that used by the landlords.

7.9   The Village of Shalgahi Sofla

Shalgahi Sofla is one of 100 of 169 villages in the DIP area where lands and houses were purchased by the KWPA for release to the Iran Shell Cotts Agribusiness Company, one of four agribusinesses in the area. The operation began in 1971 and was eventually to encompass 31 villages - some 15,000 hectares. In 1973-74 village cultivation stopped and the land was levelled by Shell Cotts. The villagers will eventually be evacuated and resettled in one of the **shahraks** planned for the area.

The main economic and employment features of Shalgahi Sofla are summarized in Table 70 and Table 71, whilst Table 72 describes the situation of families which originally had had no land rights. The most striking feature is that un-employment is double that of Bonvar Hossein and that, in addition to the usual opportunities for temporary employment, there is one unique source - **kar-e gil** (mud work). This involves erecting mud walls to enclose newly established citrus gardens. In summer 1974, 25 Shalgahi Sofla peasants were employed in **kar-e gil**, nearly one quarter of all peasants in temporary employment. **Kar-e gil** has now become 'institutionalized' and generally an experienced peasant contracts for the construction of a wall. He, in turn, recruits other peasants to work for him on a daily piece-work basis.

The peasant 'sub-contractors' organize themselves into a team of six or seven, and each person undertakes a specific task. One man breaks up the ground with a pick-axe and a second brings buckets of water which is mixed with the earth by a third person who then works the mixture to the required consistency by treading straw into it with his bare feet. Three people, usually school-age boys, are involved in carrying workable quantities of the finished mixture to the 'master builder' who lays down and shapes the layer with his bare hands.

When all the layers have been completed, a thin finishing coat of mud with a higher proportion of straw is applied over the whole wall to cement the layers together and improve its appearance. A wall constructed in this tradi-tional manner, is extremely resistant to the climate and it is not uncommon to find examples of similar walls in rural Dezful which have remained in good condition for over 100 years.

Payments made to the peasants engaged in **kar-e gil**

TABLE 70

Shaigahi Sofla Population Employment Profile, 1973-74.

Employment Status		Peasants With Land Rights		Peasants Without Land Rights		Total
		No.	%	No.	%	No.
Total Population	Male	210	76.4	65	23.6	275
	Female	184	71.9	72	28.1	256
	Both Sexes	394	74.2	137	25.8	531
Household	Number	59		26		85
	Average Size	6.7	69.4	5.3	30.6	6.2
Economically Inactive Category	Both sexes	159	76.1	50	23.9	209
	Both sexes % of total population	40.4		36.5		39.4
	Both sexes average per household	2.7		1.9		2.5
Economically Active Category	Male population economically active	122	73.5	44	26.5	166
	% of total male population	58.1		67.7		60.4
	Males – average per household	2.1		1.7		2.0
	Female population economically active	113	72.4	43	27.6	156
	% of total female population	61.4		59.7		60.9
	Females – average per household	1.9		1.7		1.8
	Both sexes economically active	235	73.0	87	27.0	322
	% of total population	59.6		63.5		60.6
	Both sexes – average per household	4.0		3.3		3.8
Permanent Employment (Full-time)	Male employed	30	71.4	12	28.6	42
	% of males – economically active	24.6		27.3		25.3
	Males – average per household	0.5		0.5		0.5
Temporary Employment (Part-time work)	Male employed (including students)	68	70.8	28	29.2	96
	% of males – economically active	55.8		63.6		57.8
	Males – average per household	1.1		1.1		1.1
	Female employed (including students)	16	78.9	4	21.1	20
	% of females – economically active	14.2		9.3		12.8
	Females – average per household	0.3		0.1		0.2
	Both sexes (including students)	84	67.4	32	32.6	116
	Both sexes – % of econ. active population	35.7		36.8		36.0
	Both sexes– average per household	1.4		1.2		1.4
Unemployment	Male unemployed	24	85.7	4	14.3	28
	% of males – economically active	19.7		9.1		16.9
	Males – average per household	0.4		0.2		0.3
	Female unemployed	97	71.3	39	28.7	136
	% of females – economically active	85.8		90.7		87.2
	Females – average per household	1.6		1.5		1.6
	Both sexes	121	75.9	43	24.1	164
	Both sexes – % of econ. active population	51.5		49.4		50.9
	Both sexes – average per household	2.1		1.7		1.9

Source: Field studies.

TABLE 71

Occupations of Economically Active Male Population
of Shalgahi Sofla, 1973–74.

Type of Employment	No. of Peasants involved			
	Previously with land rights	Without land rights	Total	%
A. Agriculture	20	7	27	16.3
Self employed , farming + gardening (rented land)	(3)		(3)	
Self employed, flock keeping	(3)	(1)	(4)	
Shepherds (unpaid family helpers)	(2)	(1)	(3)	
Shepherds (salary earners)	(2)	(1)	(3)	
Herdsman (salary earner)	(1)		(1)	
Farm Labour (Shell Cott Agribusiness)	(4)		(4)	
Farm Labour (Iran-America Agribusiness)	(1)		(1)	
Farm Labour (Dez Project)	(2)		(2)	
Farm Labour (private farms and gardens)	(1)	(2)	(3)	
Tractor and Bulldozer Drivers	(1)	(2)	(3)	
B. Non-Agriculture	10	5	15	9.0
Self employed, driver	(1)		(1)	
Watchmen (Shell Cott)	(4)	(1)	(5)	
Watchmen and Guards (private)		(2)	(2)	
Baker	(2)	(1)	(3)	
Cook	(1)		(1)	
Plumber		(1)	(1)	
Private Construction Companies (road building)	(2)		(2)	
C. Non-employment (permanent)	92	32	124	74.7
Students	(35)	(4)	(39)	
Students with summer jobs	((23))	((3))	((26))	
Students with no summer jobs	((12))	((1))	((13))	
Non-Students	(57)	(28)	(85)	
Non-students with part-time work	((45))	((25))	((70))	
Non-students with no work	((12))	((3))	((15))	
Total	122	44	166	100.0

Source: Field studies.

TABLE 72

Employment Situation of Landless Households, Shalgahi Sofla, 1973-74.

Hh. *	Total Members Number	Household Composition Econ. Inactive Members	Econ. Active Members Male	Female	Total	Permanently Employed No. of Workers (male)	Occupation	Temporarily Employed No. of Workers Male	Female	Occupation	Remarks
1	6	4	1	1	2			1		Wall construction and casual farm work	Wife has a 6-month old baby.
2	6	4	1	1	2			1		" " "	Wife has a year old child
3	6	1	1	4	5			1		" " "	Wife has a 1-month old baby, a sister is blind, another sister and mother unemployed
4	8	1	2	5	7	1	Watchman, village	1		: :	All household females unemployed
5	7	2	2	3	5	1	Watchman, Ahwaz	1		: :	Wife jas a 5-month old child, sister student, mother unemployed
6	7		4	3	7			4		Rice transplanting and casual farm work	Son student (with summer job) all household females unemployed
7	5	3	1	1	2			1	1	Wall construction. Wife, a village baker	
8	6	4	1	1	2			1		Rice transplanting and casual farm work	Wife has a year-old child
9	6	4	1	1	2			1		" " "	Wife has a year-old child
10	6		3	3	6			3		Wall construction and casual farm work	Son student (with summer job) daughter student, wife and mother unemployed
11	9	3	4	2	6	1	Plumber	2		: :	Brother & all household females unemployed
12	6	4	1	1	2	1	Flock keeper (self-employed)			: :	Wife unemployed
13	4		3	1	4	1	Shepherd "	2		: :	Wife unemployed
14	3	1	1	1	2			1	1	Rice transplanting. Wife, part-time grocer	Son student (unemployed) Wife has 2-months old baby
15	7	4	2	3	5	1	Tractor driver (private farm)				
16	9	4	3	2	5	1	Farm labour (private farm)	2		Rice transplanting and casual farm work	Son student (summer employment) all household females unemployed
17	2		1	1	2			1		Casual farm work	Mother unemployed
18	3		1	2	3			1		Wall construction	All household females unemployed
19	2		1	1	2						Widow is blind and daughter student
20	5	3	1	1	2	1	Farm labour (private farm)				Wife unemployed
21	1	1									Widow
22	1	1									Widow
23	11	2	5	4	9	1	Herdsman	3	1	Rice Transplanting	Wife has a year-old child, a son and two daughters unemployed
24	2		1	1	2	1	Watchman, (Shell Cotts)				Wife unemployed
25	2		1	1	2	1	Bulldozer driver (private farm)				
26	7	4	2	1	3	1	Baker, Andimeshk	1	1	Rice Transplanting	Wife unemployed
Total	137	50	44	43	87	12		28 [a]	4		

(Temporarily Employed total: 28 [a] + 4 = 32)

Source: Field studies   Note: a. Includes three students with summer jobs only.

Hh *: Households

average about 200 rials per metre of finished wall - 100 rials ($1.40) less than the amount of money which the contractor himself receives. The profit to the peasant contractor is, therefore, a lucrative 50 per cent - only at the expense of his relatively underpaid fellow workers - which undermines the myth that peasants themselves are innocent of the exploitative nature of urban-style business practice or entrepreneurship.

7.10   Changes in Traditional Employment Structure.

The differences between the three field study villages are summarized in Table 73. However, another factor must be considered - differing job opportunities (especially for males) are directly related to the physical proximity of centres for labour demand.

The most important cause, however, for the differences arise from the changeover from traditional peasant agriculture to non-peasant large-scale mechanized farming. Farm corporations and agribusinesses have changed self-employed peasant workers to wage-earners, a transition not welcome to older peasants who have found it difficult to work under younger foremen. Others find employment as shepherds, herdsmen and farm labourers - in private market gardens or, in a few cases, as tractor and bulldozer drivers. The latter occupation is regarded by some peasants as conferring status and prestige.

Although the majority are still employed in the agricultural sector, there has recently been an increase in non-agricultural employment. However, the majority can only take jobs requiring little technical skill or training and are thus at a disadvantage with their more skilled urban counterparts. Full employment in villages seems unlikely until the government introduces comprehensive vocational training programmes, geared to the labour demands of new mechanized large-scale farming, a process that has only just begun with the creation in 1972 of an elementary vocational training school near Shamsabad.

The most drastic change in Shalgahi Sofla has been the employment of women as **moziri** or **mozdi** (wage-earners outside their own village) - unheard of under the traditional system. However, today women find work outside their own village as **pakhtar**, weeding sugar beet fields (farm corporation), cotton picking (agribusiness), or harvesting onions, garlic or broad beans (private market garden). This has been made necessary by reduced real family earnings, since produce which would have been grown on the land must now be bought. In addition temporary work for men is not always sufficiently available. Market prices are often prohibitive and, habitual food intake may have to be reduced. In Shalgahi Sofla, the peasants are extremely pessimistic about their personal future in agriculture. Many former **juft**-holders have purchased houses in Dezful, with the average of 60,000 rials paid by the KWPA for a

TABLE 73

Summary of Employment Status in Bonvar Hossein, Chogha Sorkh and Shalgahi Sofla, 1973-74.

Employment Status of Peasants	Bonvar Hossein (Traditional)			Chogha Sorkh The Shamsabad Farm Corporation			Shalgahi Sofla (Shell Cott Agribusiness)		
	With land rights	Without land rights	Total	With land rights	Without land rights	Total	With land rights	Without land rights	Total
Population Male	120	24	144	192	24	216	210	65	275
Female	117	34	151	154	22	176	184	72	256
Both sexes	237	58	295	346	46	392	394	137	531
Households No.	38	12	50	52	12	64	59	26	85
Average size	6.2	4.8	5.9	6.7	3.8	6.1	6.7	5.3	6.2
Population Inactive %	39.2	41.4	39.7	39.9	41.3	40.1	40.4	36.5	39.4
Active %	60.8	58.6	60.3	60.1	58.7	59.9	59.6	63.5	60.6
Employment									
Permanent Male %	64.9	50.0	62.2	33.6	57.1	36.3	24.6	27.3	25.3
Temporary Male %	31.0	50.0	34.4	59.1	35.8	44.6	55.8	63.6	57.8
Temporary Female %	35.7	27.8	34.1	31.6	35.7	32.4	14.2	9.3	12.8
Unemployment									
Male %	4.1	-	3.3	7.3	7.1	7.3	19.7	9.1	16.9
Female %	64.3	72.2	65.9	68.4	61.5	65.8	85.8	90.7	87.2

Source: Field studies

juft and the 10,000 to 15,000 rials paid for a village house. Clearly, peasants affected by agribusinesses have directed their attention towards the town where they believe their future lies. There is also little urban appreciation of the difficulties faced by the peasant in cultivating land in severe climatic conditions with summer temperatures often reaching 40 degrees centigrade. As one peasant now living in Dezful said "we (the peasant farmers) are regarded as little better than **supurs** (dustmen)". Unless urban dwellers become aware of the potential contribution of the peasantry to the national food supply, and peasant status is increased, there seems little hope that Dezfulli peasants will make a spirited and significant contribution to national agrarian development.

7.11 Per Capita Income in Iran

Changes in agricultural activity will also mean changes in rural income and income distribution. Official records over the last two decades, although inadequate, indicate that the national average **per capita** income, is steadily rising. The rise has been greater in the urban than in the rural sector and in 1976 and 1977 attempts have been made to eliminate the disparity between the town and village(21).

Accurate surveying of a peasant economy is extremely difficult because of its semi-subsistence nature. No record is kept of domestically consumed produce or of labour input by the family unit. Also, some of the factors involved are permanent in nature – price structures – and others are transient – crop pest or disease. Their effects on income must be carefully distinguished. In Dezful, factors such as livestock reduction because of pasture restriction or the introduction of water charges have reduced incomes, while rising price levels have created the illusion that incomes have increased. The overall result is perhaps that **real** income (at constant prices) rather than monetary income has changed very little.

Most past estimates of average national **per capita** income have been based on current rather than constant prices, thus making comparison difficult. Pesaran suggested that the average **per capita** income at constant prices 1959–60 was $155 and had risen to about $304 by 1971–72(22) – an average annual growth rate of 8.3 per cent, despite a population growth rate of over three per cent. In 1973 the **per capita** income was 48,863 rials ($717)(23) and by 1974–75 was $1,274 (24). Thus, **per capita** income has increased nearly nine times since the early sixties and by 1976 was estimated to have reached $1,700(25). However, the differentials are as staggeringly large as the income figures themselves. In Tehran for example, with 14 per cent of the total Iranian population of over 30 million in 1973/74, the average **per capita** income exceeded $1,075(26). If Tehran were excluded, this figure would drop to $338.

TABLE 74

Estimated Income Distribution , Khuzestan Plain, 1957-58

Per Household (a)		Income Bracket Annual		Per Capita		%
Rials	US Dollar equivalent ($ = 75 rials)	Rials		$		of population (2,000,000)
Under 36,000	Under 480	Under 6,000		Under 80		80
36,000 – 107,999	480 – 1,339	6,000 – 17,999		80 – 239		15
108,000 – over	1,340 – over	18,000 – Over		240 – Over		5

Source: Adapted from Nederlandsche Heidemaatschappij, "Report on the Dez Irrigation Project, Supplement No 1" June 1959, (Unpublished), p III – 14.

Notes: (a) Assumed six persons per household.

Income differentials within an area such as Khuzestan are considerable. The **per capita** income in 1957-58 was estimated at $100 -$120 (27), but 80 per cent of the total province population had an income **below** this. "In Khuzestan roughly 80 per cent of the population belongs to the so called third class, with an income per FAMILY not exceeding 3,000 rials per MONTH. The majority of this group have a family income of 1,800 rials or less. For about 15 per cent of the population, the family income amounts to from 3,000 rials to 9,000 rials a month, while only five per cent have incomes exceeding 9,000 rials" (28). ($1.00 = 75 rials in 1957-58). The Development and Resources Corporation (D & R) suggests that "annual farm income **per capita** for Iran as a whole has been estimated approximately at 6,000 rials ($80) and Khuzestan farming incomes are probably not significantly different (29). Other estimates are considerably lower than the D & R one given above. Lodi in 1965 estimated the approximate annual income of a farmer's family at 20,000 rials ($265) (30). On the assumption of six persons per average household, this would amount to about 3,300 rials ($44) per person.

7.12   Estimates of Dezfulli Peasant Income

Dezfulli peasants are reluctant to reveal information and generally underestimate their earnings. As a result indirect methods of gathering information must be used. The estimated cost and returns of an average **juft** in a traditional village like Bonvar Hossein in 1973/74 (current prices) is made up as follows:

```
CROP FARMING
      Gross Return (per average juft)        182,000 rials
   -  Direct costs                            70,500
      Seeds                     (13,700)
      Fertilizer                (11,020)
      Labour (Hired)            (21,260)
      Services (tractor)        ( 9,830)
      Payment for land          (14,600)
   -  Crop Farming Net Income                111,500 rials

STOCK RAISING
      Gross Return (per average juft)         37,400 rials
   -  Direct costs (Herdsman)                  2,500
   -  Stock Raising Net Income                34,900 rials

   FARMING NET INCOME per juft              146,400 rials
```

In the above calculation the value of the products consumed on the farm is included in the net income. Moreover family labour costs are not included in production costs.

In villages like Chogha Sorkh, which are attached to a farm corporation, ex-**juft**-holders now have two sources of income: dividends from the Farm Corporation and earnings from salaried jobs. Dividends from the Farm Corporation

TABLE 75
Household Income Distribution,
Bonvar Hossein, 1973–74.

Household Income Bracket, Annual　　　　　　　　　Landholding　Households

Rials	US Dollar equivalent $=70 rials	Household No.	%	Population No.	%	Average size Hh. *	Mean Hh. * Income Rials	Per Capita Income Rials
Under　36,000	Under　514	–	–	–	–	–	–	–
36,000 – 71,999	514 – 1,028	– b	–	–	–	–	–	–
72,000 – 107,999	1,029 – 1,543	24	63.2	127	54.0	5.3	73,400	13,850
108,000 – 143,999	1,544 – 2,057	3	7.9	24	10.2	8.0	128,700	16,010
144,000 – 179,999	2,058 – 2,571	9 c	23.7	65	27.7	7.2	151,300	21,010
180,000 – over	2,572 – over	2	5.2	19	8.1	9.5	225,600	23,740
Total		38	100.0	235	100.0	6.8	104,000	16,800

Household Income Bracket, Annual　　　　　　　　　Landless　Households

Rials	US Dollar equivalent $=70 rials	Household No.	%	Population No.	%	Average size Hh. *	Mean Hh. * Income Rials	Per Capita Income Rials
Under　36,000	Under　514	6 a	54.5	15	27.3	2.5	11,300	4,520
36,000 – 71,999	514 – 1,028	1	9.1	7	12.7	7.0	46,500	6,700
72,000 – 107,999	1,029 – 1,543	3	27.3	24	43.6	8.0	83,300	10,410
108,000 – 143,999	1,544 – 2,057	–	–	–	–	–	–	–
144,000 – 179,999	2,058 – 2,571	1	9.1	9	16.4	9.0	166,600	18,500
180,000 – over	2,572 – over	–	–	–	–	–	–	–
Total		11	100.0	55	100.0	5.0	48,300	9,650

Household Income Bracket, Annual　　　　　　　　　Total　Households

Rials	US Dollar equivalent $=70 rials	Household No.	%	Population No.	%	Average size Hh. *	Mean Hh. * Income Rials	Per Capita Income Rials
Under　36,000	Under　514	6	12.3	15	5.2	2.5	11,300	4,520
36,000 – 71,999	514 – 1,028	1	2.0	7	2.4	7.0	46,500	6,700
72,000 – 107,999	1,029 – 1,543	27	55.1	151	52.1	6.0	74,500	12,410
108,000 – 143,999	1,544 – 2,057	3	6.1	24	8.3	8.0	128,700	16,010
144,000 – 179,999	2,058 – 2,571	10	20.4	74	25.5	7.4	152,900	20,660
180,000 – over	2,572 – over	2	4.1	19	6.5	9.5	225,600	23,740
Total		49	100.0	290	100.0	5.9	91,500	15,500

Source:　Field studies　　　Notes:　a. Includes three households with only a single
　　　　　　　　　　　　　　　　　　　　member (widows)
Hh. * = Households　　　　　　　　b. Each household with half a juft.
　　　　　　　　　　　　　　　　　c. Each household with a full juft

amount to 410 rials per share (118 shares per **juft**), thus ex-**juft**-holders receive about one third of the income from agriculture that is earned by **juft**-holders in traditional villages.

Salaried income is more difficult to estimate. However typical 1973/74 wage rates are given below:-

i.	Unskilled farm labour (permanently employed)	80-120 rials
ii.	Temporary **barzegar**: labour employed for grain harvesting	200 rials
iii.	Tractor, bulldozer and rural truck drivers	150-200 rials
iv.	**Kar-e bil-o-kolang**, work with spade and pickaxe ie. building and road construction work	100-120 rials
v.	**Kar-e gil**, mud work, garden wall construction (piece work) average daily payment	100-150 rials
vi.	**Moqani**, well diggers and plumber	200 rials
vii.	Assistant baker, baker, cook	150-200 rials
viii.	Watchman and field guard	80-100 rials
ix.	Clerk and typist (employed by farm corporations)	120 rials

It should be noted that the estimates of the **per capita** income given here deliberately exclude income arising from investment in property or similar cases.

It might be noted that in most traditional villages payment of daily wages is not a common practice for certain jobs. For instance, the communal herdsman and the shepherd are hired annually and rice transplanters are paid seasonally on a piece work basis (see chapter 5). In Bonvar Hossein the annual salary of herdsman and shepherd in 1973-74 amounted to 70,000 rials and 32,000 rials respectively. The rice transplanter wage varied from one village to another, ranging from approximately 4,000 to 8,000 rials for women and 6,000 to 8,000 for men.

Household and **per capita** income calculations for the three field study villages of Bonvar Hossein, Chogha Sorkh and Shalgahi Sofla are given in Tables 75 – 80 and can be compared with the figures for Khuzestan as a whole in Table 84.

The **per capita** income in Bonvar Hossein at $220 (current prices) is only one sixth of the 1974-75 national average, but it has risen considerably from the 1958 national rural average. However, there is a considerable income differential between landholding householders and landless ones. The mean income of the former is 104,000 rials ($1,886) while among the latter it is less than half – 48,300 rials ($690). This feature is also shown in Chogha Sorkh which is part of a farm corporation scheme. However the differential on a **per capita** basis is only 8.3 per cent – insignificant in comparison with Bonvar Hossein where the corresponding difference is 73.9 per cent. This is primarily because the

TABLE 76

Per Capita Income Distribution, Bonvar Hossein, 1973-74.

Income Bracket (Per Capita, Annual) Rials	US Dollar equivalent ($ = 70 rials)	Land Holding Population			Landless Population			Total Population		
		No	Vert. %	Horiz.	No	Vert. %	Horiz.	No	Vert. %	Horiz.
Under 6,000	Under 85	–	–	–	14	25.4	100.0	14	4.8	100.0
6,000 – 11,999	85 – 169	70	29.8	68.6	32	58.2	31.4	102	35.2	100.0
12,000 – 17,999	170 – 254	67	28.5	100.0	–	–	–	67	23.1	100.0
18,000 – 23,999	255 – 339	49	20.9	84.5	9	16.4	15.5	58	20.0	100.0
24,000 – 29,999	340 – 424	40	17.0	100.0	–	–	–	40	13.8	100.0
30,000 – 35,999	425 – 510	–	–	–	–	–	–	–	–	–
36,000 – over	510 – over	9	3.8	100.0	–	–	–	9	3.1	100.0
Total		235	100.0	81.0	55	100.0	19.0	290	100.0	100.0
Average Per Capita Annual Income		16,800 rials ($240)			9,660 rials ($138)			15,500 rials ($220)		

Source: Field studies.

TABLE 77

Household Income Distribution
Chogha Sorkh, 1973–74.

Household Income Bracket, Annual   Households With Land Rights

Rials	US Dollar equivalent $=70 rials	Household No.	%	Population No.	%	Average size Hh. *	Mean Hh. * Income Rials	Per Capita Income Rials
Under – 36,000	Under 514	2	3.8	11	3.2	5.5	25,000	4,550
36,000 – 71,999	514 – 1,028	18	34.6	81	23.4	4.5	51,300	11,400
72,000 – 107,999	1,209 – 1,543	17	32.7	123	35.5	7.2	87,000	12,020
108,000 – 143,999	1,544 – 2,057	10	19.3	91	26.3	9.1	125,800	13,820
144,000 – 179,999	2,058 – 2,571	3	5.8	23	6.7	7.7	165,200	21,550
180,000 – over	2,572 – over	2	3.8	17	4.9	8.5	196,200	23,080
Total		52	100.0	346	100.0	6.7	88,400	13,290

Household Income Bracket, Annual   Households Without Land Rights

Rials	US Dollar equivalent $=70 rials	Household No.	%	Population No.	%	Average size Hh *	Mean Hh. * Income Rials	Per Capita Income Rials
Under 36,000	Under 514	5	41.7	17	37.0	3.4	19,600	5,760
36,000 – 71,999	514 – 1,028	5	41.7	20	43.5	4.0	50,400	12,600
72,000 – 107,999	1,029 – 1,543	1	8.3	5	10.8	5.0	89,000	17,800
108,000 – 143,999	1,544 – 2,057	1	8.3	4	8.7	4.0	126,500	31,600
144,000 – 179,999	2,058 – 2,571	–	–	–	–	–	–	–
180,000 – over	2,572 – over	–	–	–	–	–	–	–
Total		12	100.0	46	100.0	3.8	47,100	12,270

Household Income Bracket, Annual   Total Households

Rials	US Dollar equivalent $=70 rials	Household No.	%	Population No.	%	Average size Hh. *	Mean Hh. * Income Rials ·	Per Capita Income Rials
Under 36,000	Under 514	7	10.9	28	7.1	4.0	21,100	5,290
36,000 – 71,999	514 – 1,028	23	36.0	101	25.8	4.4	51,100	11,640
72,000 – 107,999	1,029 – 1,543	18	28.1	128	32.7	7.1	87,100	12,250
108,000 – 143,999	1,544 – 2,057	11	17.2	95	24.2	8.6	125,900	14,570
144,000 – 179,999	2,058 – 2,571	3	4.7	23	5.9	7.7	165,200	21,550
180,000 – over	2,572 – over	2	3.1	17	4.3	8.5	196,200	23,080
Total		64	100.0	392	100.0	6.1	80,700	13,170

Source: Field studies   Hh. * = Households

TABLE 78

Per Capita Income Distribution, Chogha Sorkh, 1973-74

Income : Bracket (Per Capita, Annual) Rials	US Dollar equivalent ($ = 70 rials)	Population with Land Rights			Population without Land Rights			Total Population		
			%			%			%	
		No	Vert.	Horiz.	No	Vert.	Horiz.	No	Vert.	Horiz.
Under 6,000	Under 85	18	5.2	85.7	3	6.5	14.3	21	5.4	100.0
6,000 – 11,999	85 – 169	143	41.3	86.7	22	47.8	13.3	165	42.1	100.0
12,000 – 17,999	170 – 254	133	38.4	90.5	14	30.5	9.5	147	37.5	100.0
18,000 – 23,999	255 – 339	32	9.2	91.4	3	6.5	8.6	35	8.9	100.0
24,000 – 29,999	340 – 424	6	1.7	100.0	–	–	–	6	1.5	100.0
30,000 – 35,999	425 – 510	9	2.6	69.2	4	8.7	30.8	13	3.3	100.0
36,000 – over	510 – over	5	1.5	–	–	–	–	5	1.3	100.0
Total		346	100.0	88.3	46	100.0	11.7	392	100.0	100.0
Average Per Capita Annual Income	13,290 rials ($190)				12,270 rials ($175)			13,170 rials ($188)		

Source: Field studies

TABLE 79

Household Income Distribution,
Shalgahi Sofla, 1973-74.

Household Income Bracket, Annual   Household Previously With Land Rights

Rials	US Dollar equivalent $=70 rials	Household No.	%	Population No.	%	Average size Hh. *	Mean Hh. * Income Rials	Per Capita Income Rials
Under 36,000	Under 514	23	39.0	96	24.4	4.2	22,500	5,400
36,000 - 71,999	514 - 1,028	23	39.0	156	39.6	6.8	49,300	7,260
72,000 - 107,999	1,029 - 1,543	8	13.5	82	20.8	10.0	79,500	7,760
108,000 - 143,999	1,544 - 2,057	5	8.5	60	15.2	12.0	129,460	10,790
144,000 - over	2,058 - over							
Total		59	100.0	394	100.0	6.7	49,700	7,450

Household Income Bracket, Annual   Household Without Land Rights

Rials	US Dollar equivalent $=70 rials	Household No.	%	Population No.	%	Average size Hh. *	Mean Hh. * Income Rials	Per Capita Income Rials
Under 36,000	Under 514	13	50.0	53	38.7	4.1	20,900	5,130
36,000 - 71,999	514 - 1,028	7	26.9	41	29.9	5.9	50,600	8,640
72,000 - 107,999	1,029 - 1,543	4	15.4	23	16.8	5.8	75,500	13,120
108,000 - 143,999	1,544 - 2,057	2	7.7	20	14.6	10.0	129,500	12,950
144,000 - over	2,058 - over							
Total		26	100.0	137	100.0	5.3	45,600	8,660

Household Income Bracket, Annual   Total Households

Rials	US Dollar equivalent $=70 rials	Household No.	%	Population No.	%	Average size Hh. *	Mean Hh. * Income Rials	Per Capita Income Rials
Under 36,000	Under 514	36	42.4	149	28.1	4.1	21,900	5,300
36,000 - 71,999	514 - 1,028	30	35.3	197	37.1	6.6	49,600	7,550
72,000 - 107,999	1,029 - 1,543	12	14.1	105	19.8	8.8	78,200	8,930
108,000 - 143,999	1,544 - 2,057	7	8.2	80	15.0	11.4	129,500	11,830
144,000 - over	2,058 - over							
Total		85	100.0	531	100.0	6.2	48,500	7,760

Source: Field studies   Hh. * = Households

TABLE 80

Per Capita Income Distribution, Shalgahi Sofla, 1973–74.

Income Bracket (Per Capita, Annual) Rials	US Dollar equivalent ($ = 70 rials)	Population previously with Land Rights			Population without Land Rights			Total Population		
		No	Vert. %	Horiz. %	No	Vert. %	Horiz. %	No	Vert. %	Horiz. %
Under 6,000	Under 85	128	32.5	76.2	40	29.2	23.8	168	31.6	100.0
6,000 – 11,999	85 – 169	216	54.8	76.3	67	48.9	23.7	283	53.3	100.0
12,000 – 17,999	170 – 254	45	11.4	63.4	26	18.9	36.6	71	13.4	100.0
18,000 – 23,999	255 – 339	5	1.2	71.4	2	1.5	28.6	7	1.3	100.0
24,000 – 29,999	340 – 424	–	–	–	–	–	–	–	–	–
30,000 – 35,999	425 – 510	–	–	–	–	–	–	–	–	–
36,000 – over	510 – over	–	–	–	2	1.5	100.0	2	0.4	100.0
Total		394	100.0	74.2	137	100.0	25.8	531	100.0	100.0
Average Per Capita Annual Income		7,450 rials ($106)			8,660 rials ($124)			7,760 rials ($111)		

Source: Field studies

population of Chogha Sorkh has greater access to salaried
employment, despite their smaller returns from the agricultural sector.

The income differential between the landholding and landless peasants is not limited to rural Dezful; it is a pheno-
menon of traditional Iranian peasantry.   Ajami, in his study
of the villages in Fars Province, in south western Iran
has made reference to it (31).   However, Shalgahi Sofla is
an exception to this general income distribution pattern.
Here there is no significant income differential between
previous landholding peasants and landless ones and income
levels are far below those in Bonvar Hossein and Chogha
Sorkh.   Indeed the average **per capita** income of peasants
previously holding land and now working as hired labourers
(7,450 rials), is 14 per cent less than that of the landless
ones (8,660 rials).   However, the majority of the former
landholding peasants have some investment income arising
from purchase of property in Dezful and from money lending
within the village.   The value of income from such sources,
although often not considerable, influences the peasant **per
capita** income.

A crude but culturally compatible method of 'measuring'
village economic prosperity is to compare the percentage
of village population who, in any given year, make the
pilgrimage to visit the tomb of Imam Reza.   In Bonvar
Hossein, 19 (6.5 per cent) of the total population of 295,
made the pilgrimage during 1973–74.   The corresponding
number in Chogha Sorkh was 12 (3.1 per cent) of the total
population of 392, and in Shalgahi Sofla, the figure was
seven (3.1 per cent) of the total population of 531.   These
findings support the hypothesis that the initial land reform
programme in rural Dezful has been more conducive to the
economic prosperity of the peasantry than were the subsequent introduction of farm corporation schemes or agribusiness enterprises.

Chapter Notes

1. Talcott Parsons, "Some considerations on the theory of social change", **Rural Sociology**, No 26, pp 219-239.

2. FAO, **Report to the Government of Iran on the development of land and water resources in Khuzestan**, op. cit., p 1.

3. Reader Bullard (ed.), **The Middle East: A Political and Economic Survey**, (London, UK: Oxford University Press, 1958), p 393.

4. Adams, **op. cit.**, p 118.

5. Layard, **op. cit.**, p 87.

6. Interview with A. Khoban, The Forestry Officer for the Dezful Shushtar Region, 7th August 1974.

7. **Kayhan,** No 9245, 10 Ordibehasht 1353 (30 April 1974)

8. K. Eghbal, "Possibilities of agricultural mechanization in Iran", in **Farm Mechanization in Iran** (Reading UK: University of Reading, Department of Agriculture, 1969), p 9.

9. **Kayhan,** 6 Bahman 1352 (26 January 1974)

10. J.H.Neville, "The current trends and prospects for farm mechanization in Iran" in **Farm Mechanization in Iran** (Reading UK: University of Reading, Department of Agriculture, 1969), p 5.

11. Personal Interview with Hossein Darvish, former (1940-41) Director-General of Khuzestan Agriculture Office and Manager of the Hosseinabad Estate Farm (since 1947), Tehran, 29 September 1974.

12. Nederlandsche Heidemaatschappij, "Report on the Dez Irrigation Project", **op. cit.**, p III-22.

13. **Ibid.**

14. **Ibid** p III-5.

15. Personal Interview with Darvish, **op. cit.**,

16. Nederlandsche Heidemaatschappij, "Report on the Dez Irrigation Project", **op. cit.**, p III-22.

17. Lambton, **Landlord and Peasant in Persia, op. cit.**, p 254.

18. Personal Interview with Abdulkarimi, General Manager of the Southern Agricultural Company, Ahwaz, 21 September 1974.

19. Institute for Economic Research, "Rural Economic Problems of Khuzestan", **Tahqiqat-e-eqtesadi**, Vol III, Nos 9 and 10, 1965, p 192.

20. Mahmoud Setoudeh-Zand, "The consequences of rapid population growth on the labour force of Iran", in the proceeding of the International Union for the Scientific Study of Population, Sydney Conference, (Sydney, Australia, 1967) p 144.

21. Kayhan Havaii, 15 Ordibehesht 2535 (5 May 1976)

22. H. Pesaran, "Income distribution trends in rural and urban Iran", a paper presented at the International Conference on the Social Sciences and Problems of Development, Persepolis, Iran, June 1-4, 1974, p 24.

23. Mahmoud Tajdar, "Growth and regional diffrences in Iran", a paper presented at the International Conference on the Social Sciences and Problems of Development, Persepolis, Iran, June 1-4, 1974, p 4.

24. Kayhan Havaii, 3 Esfand, 1353 (21 February 1975), quoted Houshang Ansari, The Minister of the Economy and Finance.

25. Kayhan Havaii, 12 Khordad 2535 (2 June 1976), quoted Mansur Rohani, The Minister of Agriculture and Natural Resources.

26. Kayhan, 29 Modad 1353 (20 August 1974), quoted the findings of an economic research group of the University of Tehran.

27. D & R, The Unified Development of the Natural Resources of the Khuzestan Region, op. cit., p 3.

28. Nederlandsche Heidemaatschappij, "Report on the Dez Irrigation Project, Supplement No 1", op. cit., p III-14.

29. D & R, The Unified Development of the Natural Resources of the Khuzestan Region, op. cit., p 48.

30. Lodi, op. cit., p 1.

31. Ajami, "Social classes, family demographic characteristics and mobility in three Iranian villages", op. cit., pp 62-72.

PLATE 8   Mechanized sugar cane harvesting at Haft Tappeh

8 FARM CORPORATIONS, AGRIBUSINESSES AND SHAHRAKS

8.1 Introduction

Since the late 1960s and up to the 1979 Revolution the government has adopted two different approaches to increasing agricultural productivity - the consolidation of small plots into agricultural corporations, and the purchase of private holdings for release to large agribusiness companies, replacing peasant agriculture by large-scale mechanized farming. Both of these approaches have involved further changes to the rural land holding situation of rural Dezful.

8.2 The Creation of Farm Corporations

National economic planners have repeatedly questioned the economic validity of peasant farming since the mid-1960s. Their arguments have been based on the fact that irrigated farming land was very limited (20 million hectares - 12.0 per cent of the total 165 million hectares) and thus measures to increase agricultural productivity were essential to national development. Farms were divided into uneconomic units, especially through inheritance(1). The planners suggested that this could be overcome by consolidation into farm corporations (agricultural shareholders' companies) (2) and this was authorized on 24th January 1968, on a five year (1968-72) experimental basis. The farm corporations were "to bring business methods, sophisticated finance, skilled management and the latest agricultural techniques into the newly emancipated Iranian village"(3). The units were to be established in 'suitable' rural areas to engage in the following activities:

- " The exclusive and permanent use of land belonging to shareholders;

- Creating all possible opportunities for the use of farming machinery and making the fullest efforts to

- establish the most modern methods of operation;

- Preventing the division of the land into small and uneconomic portions after the decease of a shareholder and promoting the most effective ways of using the land, water, operating facilities and manpower.

- Reducing the costs of production;

- Establishing the correct methods of administration in production and exploitation of the land by co-ordinated application of all the basic principles of management;

- Expanding the area of land under cultivation in the region of operations, by making use of infertile, uncultivated and waste land;

- Establishing handicrafts and cottage industries and developing the same with a view to preventing un-employment and putting to work the surplus manpower available in the rural district concerned, and increasing the income of shareholders and bringing abour the means of insuring those shareholders who are engaged as manual labourers in corporation; and

- Assisting and co-operating in promoting the execution of development and social programmes in the rural areas" (4).

The following procedure was followed when a Farm Corporation was established. Firstly, the Ministry of Co-operation and Rural Affairs indicated where the farm cor-poration units were to be established. Potential for expansion was an important consideration here, in which the proximity of the State land and water supply were them-selves special criteria (5). The area of a farm corporation could exceed 1,000 hectares and could include from two to 20 villages and farms. Secondly, the majority of local farmers had formally to request the Ministry to establish a farm corporation in their locality, although in practice such requests were usually made on the advice of official agents. The Ministry then arranged for the formation of an 'evaluation committee' consisting of three members – two elected by majority vote of landowners and peasant culti-vators and the third appointed by the Ministry. The evaluation committee appointed land surveyors to determine the area to be incorporated and appraise the value of the land and other factors of production for each peasant holding – water rights, farm machinery and oxen. The evaluation committee then reported to the Ministry which in turn determined the shares allocable to each owner and "invites all the interested landowners and peasant cultivators to sign the Articles of Association, hold their first meeting and elect Directors" (6).

At this initial official meeting, landowners and peasant cultivators transferred their land rights to the corporation receiving a corresponding number of 1,000 rial shares in

return. Farm Corporation shares were not transferable to
non-members and could only be sold to another shareholder
or inherited upon the shareholder's death.

The organization chart of a 'typical' farm corporation
is shown in Figure 20. At the first general assembly the
shareholders elected from amongst themselves two persons
to act as 'inspectors' to 'supervise' the operations of the
corporation and three persons to serve on the Board of
Directors. The Board in turn chose its chairman and sec-
retary from among its three members and also selected the
Farm Corporation Managing Director from three Ministry
nominees. In practice however, the Board simply endorsed
the most suitable candidate recommended by the Ministry.

The Managing Director was usually an agricultural university graduate and a Government employee directly responsible
to the Farm Corporation Central Supervisory Unit of the
Ministry in Tehran. He co-ordinated his activities with
the local **Shahristan** Office of Co-operation and Rural Affairs.
In the field his main tasks were to consult the Board of
Directors to plan and implement the operational programme
of the Farm Corporation. He also directly supervised the
administrative and field staff – semi-professional accountant,
book keepers, clerks, typists, storekeepers and a tea man
and one or more agricultural college graduate farm specialists, technicians (usually high school graduates and
members of the Extension and Development Corps), and
permanent and temporary field workers respectively. Farm
labourers were usually hired from amongst the shareholders.

A shareholder could hold three different positions within
the same farm corporation. As an 'ordinary' shareholder,
he might also be a hired field labourer in charge of irrigation or weeding and at the same time he might also be
a member of the Board of Directors or an 'inspector' partly
responsible for management. Most peasants engaged in this
'triple-role playing' situation were uncertain of where one
set of duties begins and the other ends. Colleagues also
found it difficult to interpret their activities and consequently could not make the necessary adjustments in
relationships with them – not only as 'triple-role' occupiers
but also perhaps as relatives, friends or neighbours.

The salaries of the managing director, agricultural
specialists and accountants (who are normally civil servants)
were paid by the government. The government also made
itself responsible for the construction of various buildings
and it provided essential transport vehicles. In addition,
the Ministry provided the corporations with a loan at four
per cent annual interest. In 1968-69, the overall government
'grant' to 14 farm corporations amounted to 214,376,865 rials
($2,858,358) (7) . Individual grants ranged from 525,600 rials
($7,008) to 133,800,000 rials ($1,911,429) to the Shahabad
Qaenat Farm Corporation in Birjand **Shahristan**, bordering
Khurasan and Sistan Provinces. On average, each farm
corporation received a free government grant of 12,085,856
rials ($161,145). A further government concession has been
exemption from income taxes, registration fees or other

FIGURE 20

Organization Chart of a 'Typical' Farm Corporation

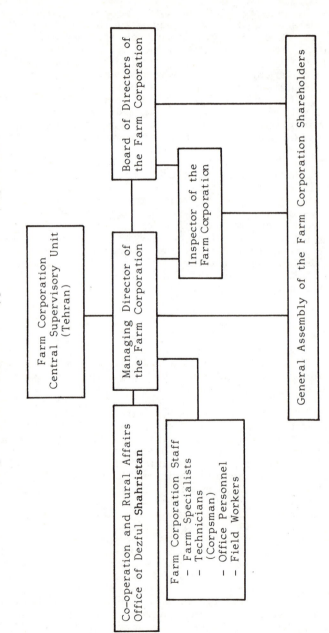

Source: Field studies.

expenses paid by private companies (8).
Each farm corporation prepared an annual **bilan** (financial statement). This was submitted to the farm corporation inspectors and the Farm Corporation Supervisory Unit of the Ministry of Co-operation and Rural Affairs. Upon Ministry approval, the corporation's net profit was determined and distributed in the following manner:

- At least 15 per cent was placed in the corporation's reserve account;

- A small part could be appropriated to cover doubtful claims;

- A small part could be appropriated for the operating account for the next year;

- Part, upon approval by the general assembly, might be paid as bonuses to the members of the board of directors, manager, inspector and employees of the corporation; and

- The balance was divided among the shareholders in proportion to their shares (9).

The number of farm corporations increased very rapidly from their inception in 1968. In the first year 14 farm corporation units were established. Two years later, (1970) 13 more were founded, and by the end of 1972, there was a total of 52 in operation. Since then, 23 more have been founded, bringing the total to 75 by 1975. It was anticipated that by the end of the Fifth Development Plan in 1978, there would be 140 such corporations in the country. (10). There is much variation in size - the Aryamehr Farm Corporation near Shiraz has a total of no more than 80 family heads as shareholders whereas the number of shareholders of the Shahabad Qaenat Farm Corporation in Birjan exceeds 1,200 (11).

8.3 Farm Corporations in the Dez Project Area

In 1970, the Development and Resources Corporation (D & R) was requested to submit a proposal analysing the applicability of farm corporations in the future Dez project developments.

The D & R appraisal report which was submitted in August 1970 recommended the introduction of farm corporations in the DIP area and considered a farm corporation to be "an instrument which combined the principal social benefits of land reform and the economic improvements resulting from large-scale consolidated agriculture " (12).

The area originally designated was a large 9,000 hectare tract to the north of the Project which was later enlarged to 13,000 hectares. This particular location was chosen because of the fertility of the land, the abundant water supply and a 365-day growing season for crops. In other

words the area was suitable for large-scale intensive agriculture. A further factor was the parallel presence of agribusinesses in the same area which would facilitate a
comparative evaluation of the performance of both systems
operating under relatively equal physical conditions. The
D & R report maintained that "this area was selected by
the Ministry of Water and Power as the best place in which
to try to unify the two methods of developing the project
lands so as to achieve soon a modern, commercial agriculture
through engaging the local farmers in intensive, irrigated
farming and full use of the land and water resources.
(13). However, the tract was relatively populous with many
villages in which population pressure on land was higher
than that of any other location within the DIP area. In
this respect it was 'unsuitable' for the agribusiness alternative for it would involve major problems in finding
suitable alternative employment for the large number of
peasant cultivators who would have been displaced.

The 1970 D & R report was accepted by the Plan Organization and the Ministries concerned with certain modifications
and since 1971 four farm corporations Dez, Dezful, Shamsabad
and Shush have been established in the DIP area. They
cover 33 villages (Table 81) and include six independent
farms not attached to any specific village. The general
characteristics of the farm corporations are given in Table
82.

The Dez Farm Corporation was officially formed on 25 May
1971 and is the oldest corporation in Dezful. It incorporates
eight villages with a total of 222 peasants with land rights
who formerly held 151 **jufts** between them. Their land rights
were transferred to the Corporation and in return they
received 15,423 shares – on average 11 shares for each
hectare of land transferred (each hectare was valued at
11,000 rials). Thus the initial capital amounted to 1,543,000
rials ($220,329). In the eyes of the peasant shareholders,
the economic performance of the Dez Farm Corporation has
not been a success, for in its initial operating year (1971-
72) the annual dividend per share amounted to from 12 rials
to 132 rials ($1.9) per hectare. However, in the 1973/74
cropping year, this was considerably improved and approached 240 rials. In the Dez Farm Corporation, as in the
three other farm corporations in the DIP area, not all
dividends were paid in cash. Part was given in kind
(usually in wheat).

The physical and economic situation of the Dezful Farm
Corporation was less favourable than that of the Dez Farm
Corporation , for the Dezful Farm Corporation was situated
only four kilometres from the town of Dezful and had to
compete for labour with nearby market gardeners and fruit
growers as well as various construction companies operating
in Dezful itself. The Dezful Farm Corporation, which was
established on 4 September 1972, consisted of two villages
and six independent farms. Although the total land area
of the farm corporation was relatively large, part of it was
not suitable for farming. A total of 269 shareholders owned

2,947 shares between them (seven to nine shares per hectare). In 1973-74, the dividend paid per share was 100 rials which was the lowest dividend of any of the four corporations.

TABLE 81

The Number of Villages in the Dez Project Area
Incorporated in the New Agricultural Schemes,
1974

Type of Scheme	Frequency of occurrence among the DIP villages	
	No	%
Haft Tappeh sugar cane project	3[a]	1.8
Agribusinesses:	100[b]	59.2
Iran-America	(25)	(14.8)
Iran-California	(19)	(11.2)
Iran Shell Cotts	(31)	(18.4)
International (Hawaiian)	(18)	(10.7)
Allocated, not assigned	(7)	(4.1)
Farm Corporations:	33	19.5
Dez	(8)	(4.7)
Shamsabad	(6)	(3.5)
Dezful	(2)	(1.2)
Shush	(17)	(10.1)
Traditional villages not included	26	15.3
Mixed villages	7	4.1
Haft Tappeh + Agribusiness	(3)	(1.7)
Haft Tappeh + Traditional	(2)	(1.2)
Agribusiness + Farm corporation	(2)	(1.2)
Total	169	100.0

Source: Field studies

Notes: a. Two of these villages have been demolished
         b. 22 of these villages have been demolished.

Shamsabad Farm Corporation, which was founded on 24 May 1972, was considered by the local peasants as the most successful of the four since it provided its shareholders with the highest dividend (410 rials per share in 1973-74 cropping year). It included six villages of which Chogha Sorkh was one. The 235 shareholders have exchanged their land rights for 16,211 shares – an average of between 11 to 12 shares per hectare. This relatively favourable 'rate of exchange' was a reflection of the quality of the land in the Shamsabad Farm Corporation as compared with that of the Dezful Farm Corporation.

TABLE 82

General Features of the Farm Corporations in the Dez Project Area

Name of Farm Corporation	Farm Corporation Headquarters (Name of the Village)	Distance from the Town of Dezful (km)	Date of Formation	Composition		Approximate Ha.		Population Total 1973	No. of share-holders	No. of shares		Share Capital '000 Rials	Dividend paid per share Rials 1972-73
				No. of Villages	No. of Farms	Gross Ha.	Farm Land Ha.			Per Ha.	Total		
Dez	Qaleh Sheikh	7	25 May '71	8		b	1,400	1,795	222	11	15,423	15,423	240
Shush	Qaleh No Askar	16	16 May '72	17 a		2,819	2,800	2,770	357	11	22,832	22,832	310
Shamsabad	Chogha Sorkh	8	24 May '72	6		b	1,400	3,035	235	11-12	16,211	16,211	410
Dezful	Qomash-e Momenan Farm	4	4 Sep.'72	2	6	2,900	b	1,054	269	7-9	25,122	25,122	100
Total				33	6			8,654	1,083		79,588	79,588	

Source: Field studies.

Note: a.   This figure includes three villages of Dacheh Sadat, Boreh Laton and Boreh Abdol Naby which were incorporated into the Shush Farm Corporation in March 1974. The data on Shush Farm Corporation exclude these three villages.

          b.   Data not available.

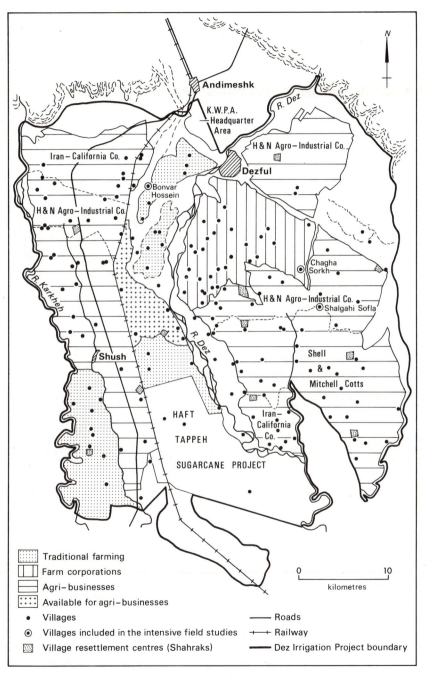

MAP 5   Agribusinesses, farm corporations and traditional
villages in the Dez Project area

The performance of the Shush Farm Corporation was also considered 'fair' by the peasant shareholders for the amount of dividend allocated to each share (in 1973/74) was relatively high (310 rials) as compared with the 100 rials dividend given by the Dezful Farm Corporation. The Shush Farm Corporation, which was founded on 16 May 1972, originally included 14 villages with a total of 357 shareholders. The shareholders received 22,832 shares at 11 shares per hectare. Shush Farm Corporation in addition to its 14 original villages, has, since March 1974, included three more villages, bringing the total number of villages to 17 which makes it the largest farm corporation in terms of both hectarage and number of shareholders.

8.4   The Problems of the DIP Farm Corporations

Ideally, the farm corporation could be viewed as a means of involving the peasant cultivators in large-scale farming by consolidating the individual peasant holdings into a single farming unit. The peasants as a group would cultivate and eventually manage this unit for the corporate good of all and, as an added incentive, the government would initially inject considerable capital and technical know-how into the corporation.

However, field enquiries and observations of the operation of the four farm corporations in the DIP area indicate that they have not been successful in achieving these aims. The greatest stumbling block seems to be the attitude adopted by peasant shareholders towards their involvement in the running of the corporation. The peasants feel that they have lost their newly acquired land rights to the farm corporations and the significance of the shares which they received in exchange has not been fully accepted by them. Consequently there is a lack of a sense of corporate unity between the peasants on the one hand and the managerial technical staff on the other. The peasants feel alienated from the organization and see themselves as hired labourers with no concern for the end product of their labour. They feel that any increased productivity will not benefit them directly and, as a result, they do not put as much effort into the work as they did when they were working as freeholders or even as sharecroppers.

The managements in all four farm corporations studied were fully aware of this indifferent attitude held by the majority of the peasant shareholders and as a result had organized the cultivation of some crops on a modified sharecropping basis – the corporation provides the seeds, land, water and machinery and the peasants provide the labour. The harvest is then divided according to a mutually agreed rate. The adoption of this centuries-old practice has contributed towards the 'financial success' of these farm corporations.

To many of the peasants the manager represented a substitute for their former landlord and in this respect they petitioned him to intervene as an arbitrator in settling domestic family disputes. The manager's inability as a government employee, to act in this paternalistic manner served to widen the distance between management and peasant shareholders.

Another major problem connected with farm corporations relates to their limited labour requirement. This often means unemployment for a number of previously self-employed peasant cultivators. In a 1973 study of the Dez Farm Corporation, it was suggested that the Farm Corporation had improved the employment situation of the villages incorporated into it. The report stated that in 1972-73 the Dez Farm Corporation was able to offer employment totalling 110,700 'man-days'. Of this amount, 90,000 man-days were allocated to the peasant shareholders and the remaining 20,700 were offered to traditionally landless (non-shareholder) peasants in the incorporated villages or to workers from outside. The report maintained that under the old sharecropping system, the total man-day requirement for the eight incorporated villages had amounted to 51,179 man-days. This figure was less than the total number of man-days available - 300 able-bodied peasant workers working for 300 days a year amounting to 90,000 available man-days. Thus, under traditional cultivation there would have been a loss of 38,821 man-days which means that the 'average' peasant would have worked for 170 days in a year and would have been idle for the remaining 130 available working days. From these calculations the report concluded that the employment situation of the eight villages had improved as a result of their incorporation into the Dez Farm Corporation, for the Farm Corporation offered employment for 300 man-days as opposed to the 170 required under the traditional farming system (14).

However the concept of a 'man-day' cannot be realistically applied to traditional farming in rural Dezful. It is true that under the traditional farming system the peasant had a long season of underemployment or perhaps unemployment, but it should be noted that during the seasons of peak labour demand his work-day far exceeded the eight hours conventionally adopted as the equivalent of one man-day. Furthermore, the concept of a 'man-day' is not a measure of productivity, nor does it recognize that a peasant working on his own plot is more likely to increase his efforts than a peasant working for an organization or another individual. There is evidence that fuller employment is provided in those villages which were and have remained traditional than in those which have been incorporated into farm corporations.

In addition to the problem of employment, there are also indications that some of the shortcomings of the farm corporations stemmed from the attitude of the management. More specifically this relates to the management's excessive concern for competition with neighbouring farm corporations. This sometimes led to the adoption of short-term developmental strategies which provided impressive production records - initially important to gain the confidence of the peasant shareholders who were disappointed with their production-related dividend payments. Occasionally this desired increase had partly been obtained by the heavy application of fertilizer which may ultimately be detrimental to soil conditions.

Furthermore, some of the farm corporations have been faced with technical problems arising from a mechanized farming operation. Lack of availability of spare parts for farm machinery has meant that a tractor can remain idle for as long as two months while awaiting the delivery and install- ation of a needed spare part. Moreover, lack of a supporting market intelligence agency has meant that, for instance, a crop of tomatoes harvested by the Dez Farm Corporation in May 1974 was unable to realise its full market value and had to be sold locally at a reduced price in order to prevent the loss of the entire crop through spoilage.

These two examples, illustrating the lack of supporting services in rural areas, demonstrate that a large-scale farming operation cannot be run in isolation but must be integrated within overall agricultural development strategy with provisions for the improvement of all aspects of agri- cultural production, processing and distribution.

8.5 Acquisition of Land for Agribusinesses

Water has always been the most serious factor limiting increases in agricultural production in Iran. To increase the water supply, several large dams have been built and to promote the effective utilization of available water a law nationalizing all of the country's water resources came into effect on 5th October 1967(15). However, in those areas where a regulated water supply has been available, increases in agricultural production have been less than expected.

By the end of the Third Plan in 1967 it was found that the national annual agricultural growth rate had been only 2.5 per cent as opposed to the target of 4.0 per cent. (16).In the Fourth Plan therefore a new approach for intensive farming on a strictly commercial basis was proposed. The budget was directed towards the creation of large farming and animal husbandry units to be operated by advanced techniques. A sum of $147 million, out of a total of $800 million was assigned to creating 34 large agricultural units – either farm corporations or agribusiness enterprises. Official circles supported the idea that the best means of reaching the required growth rate was through the establish- ment of agribusinesses.(17). A distinction is made here between agribusinesses and agro-industries. An agribusiness farming unit involves the setting up of a large-scale (usually over 1,000 hectares) mechanized and capital intensive farming operation, whose activities are horizontally integrated – growing a variety of crops. When the farming operation takes the form of a unit including both producing and pro- cessing; it is referred to as agro-industry whose activities are thus vertically integrated, such as the Haft Tappeh sugar cane plantation which undertakes both the cultivation and the refining of the sugar cane. In the DIP area, with the exception of the latter, the remainder of the large-scale commercial farms are agribusinesses.

On 27th May 1968, the Law Establishing Companies for Utilization of Land Downstream of Dams came into effect. Under this law, the Ministry of Water and Power was authorized to purchase individual holdings in areas irrigated by dams and to consolidate the holdings for release to agricultural companies for rapid development and utilization (18).

8.6 Agribusinesses in the Dez Project Area

The agribusiness law was first implemented in 1969 in 68,000 hectares of the Dez Irrigation Project area (54.4 per cent of the total 125,000 hectares). However, large-scale commercial farming had first made its appearance in what is now the DIP area as far back as the early 1950s, when a few landowners and land leaseholders established large-scale mechanized farms near Shush.

Government interest in the possibilities of large-scale farming in the DIP area was first aroused by the recommendation of a feasibility study undertaken by D & R. In selecting the DIP area for agribusinesses, the government was influenced by the fact that it was an area in which considerable investment had already been made in dams and irrigation networks. It had been believed that peasant users of the new facilities would be able to afford the charges for this service out of the extra income to be derived from the expected increase in production, but production expectations were not attained and water charges were not paid. The government therefore considered agribusinesses as the alternative means for increasing agricultural production and paying the necessary water charges.

Another reason behind the government's decision to set up agribusinesses in the DIP area was the desire of national planners to introduce modern, large-scale farming systems into the agricultural sector. Success would be more likely if an area already well endowed with fertile land and water were used and the DIP area seemed well suited in this respect. The Khuzestan Water and Power Authority (KWPA) therefore invited landowners and peasant proprietors in the villages and farms involved on 17th July 1969 to contact the KWPA office in Dezful to sell their holdings to the government. Between July 1969 and June 1973, the government 're-purchased' 40,000 hectares in the designated areas. The remaining part of the total 68,000 hectares allocated for agribusinesses was to be re-purchased by March 1974 (19).

At the same time potential foreign and domestic large-scale investors were invited to visit the DIP area and to submit feasibility reports on creating large-scale mechanized farming units there. The reports were to be reviewed by the Ministry of Water and Power and, if approved, a specific area was made available to the investor. A comprehensive

TABLE 83

Agribusiness Units in the Dez Project Area

Name of Company	Total Capital Mn.Rials ($= 70 rials)	Field Head-quarters	Distance from the town of Dezful km	Date of Formation	No. of Villages Incorporated	Hectarage			Under Cultivation 1973-74		Field Labourers (July 1974)	
						Allotted Ha	Leased Ha	Land Levelled Ha	W. Crops Ha	S.Crops Ha.	Permanently Employed	Temporarily Employed
H.N.Agro-Industry of Iran and America	800 ($11.4)	Safiabad formerly village of Kutian	10	12 Dec. 1969	25	20,267	14,367 (Jan. 1974)	3,411 (Jan. 1974)	5,668	2,614	203	710
Iran-California Agri-business Company	230 ($3.3)	Bonvar Nazer	15	June 1970	19	10,536	5,267 (Jan. 1974)	3,795 (March 1974)	3,726	842	214	174
Shell Cotts Agri-business Co. of Iran	400 ($5.7)	Biatian Arshad	20	18 Jan. 1971	31	14,736	4,262 (March 1974)	3,800 (Feb. 1974)	1,365	2,891	408	86
International Agri-business Co. of Iran	1,120 ($16.0)	Town of Shush	50	10 June 1973	18	16,680	4,241 (Jan. 1974)	1,250 (Jan. 1974)	2,014	197	203	196

contract was signed between the two parties which spelled
out the responsibilities of both the investor and the government.

Under the contract, the government undertook to provide
a certain amount of land to the investor (usually several
large tracts made available according to a specific time-
table and not all at the same time). The government would
also construct the main irrigation canals, the secondary
canals for the delivery of water to each 100 hectare plot
and access and service roads to each 1,000 hectare tract.
In addition, it would also provide electric power (at the
consumer's expense) and would exempt the investor from
tax on any farm machinery he used (20). Ventures backed
solely by foreign investment were not authorized, for it was
government policy to encourage joint Iranian-foreign
ventures.

The investor had to agree to invest 80,000 rials ($1,143)
per hectare during the first five years of operation, and
thereafter he was expected to keep the annual gross product
value at about 60,000 rials ($857) per hectare. The minimum
area of a tract of land made available to an investor was
1,000 hectares and all land levelling was deemed to be the
investor's responsibility, together with the construction of
tertiary irrigation canals, ditches, drainage and field roads.
Furthermore, the investor had to agree to employ one man
for every ten hectares of land leased and after the first
five years to reduce the number of his foreign staff to three
per cent of his total personnel. In addition, he had to
offer one apprenticeship for every 500 hectares leased (21).

The contract was binding for a period of 30 years and
the annual land rental charge for the first two years after
land levelling was fixed at between 12,000 and 15,000 rials
per hectare. Thereafter it was to be calculated annually
at 1.75 to 2.25 per cent of the gross annual farm product.
In addition a water charge of 0.2 rials per cubic metre
was also levied on delivery from the turnout gate in each
100 hectare plot.

By 1974 four agribusinesses were operating in the DIP
area, as joint ventures between foreign and domestic
investors. The number of villages included in these four
agribusinesses is given in Table 81 and general data on
the four companies are included in Table 83.

Of the four companies, H.N.Agro-Industry of Iran and
America (often called the Iran-America Agribusiness) began
operation in 1969, and its original major shareholder was
an emigrant Iranian, Hashim Naraqi, now a naturalized
American and one of the biggest almond growers in the USA
(22).Of the total 20,000 hectares allotted to the company,
14,000 hectares have actually been handed over of which
a quarter was levelled originally. However, by utilizing
unlevelled land in the 1973-74 cropping year, the company
had nearly 5,700 hectares under winter crops and 2,600
hectares under summer crops. The winter crops were mainly
wheat grown in the fertile dry farming area of Sabili, north-
west of Dezful. The company has also established several

large citrus orchards covering a total area of about 550 hectares (23). It was claimed by managers of neighbouring agribusinesses that by being the first agribusiness to be established in the area, Iran–America Agribusiness acquired the best land, suitable for alfalfa and vegetables, particularly asparagus, primarily for export purposes.

The total number of labourers employed by the company was nearly 1,000 of which only one fifth were permanent staff. The company has not yet established the canneries specified in its contract (24). It has, however, established alfalfa presses for cattle–cake, a cotton gin and a weighbridge on the road from Andimeshk to Ahwaz.

The second agribusiness, Iran California Agribusiness Company, was founded in June 1970, as a partnership between the American–based Trans–World Agricultural Development (25) and the agricultural development Bank of Iran. Initial investment shares were in the ratio of 46 per cent Iranian and 54 per cent American. The first project manager was 78 years old George Wilson, who from 1951 to 1955 had headed the California Farm Bureau Federation. Apparently his initial interest in acquiring land in Khuzestan led to the formation of the Iran–California Agribusiness. The total land allotted to the company was about 10,000 hectares of which nearly half had been leased by January 1974 and approximately 3,800 hectares were levelled by March 1974. In 1973–74, the company had nearly 3,700 hectares under winter crops and 840 hectares under summer crops. They were growing a wide variety of crops but had not built a proposed cannery and packing plant. An interesting feature of land use by this company was the sub–lease of 100 hectares of its land to Isfahani migrant peasant workers on a modified sharecropping basis. Part of this company's labour requirement is drawn from the previous **juft**–holding local peasants who were paid an hourly rate of ten rials per hour in summer 1974. Hourly rates payment is completely alien and incomprehensible to peasant field workers who are accustomed to organizing their work time–table to coincide with sunrise and sunset.

Shell–Cotts Agribusiness of Iran, established on 18th January 1971, was initially a triangular partnership between Iranian investors, The Royal Dutch/Shell group and the British holding company of Mitchell Cotts. (26). The company was allotted a single tract of about 14,700 hectares in the south of the Project Area. By March 1974, about 4,260 hectares had been leased and 3,800 hectares levelled. In the 1973–74 cropping year, the company had 1,365 hectares under winter crops and 2,891 hectares under summer crops of which 1,940 hectares were cotton. In proportion to the amount of land released to it, Shell Cotts employed a higher ratio of permanent labourers than any of the other companies.

The most recent agribusiness company to be established in the DIP area was the International Agribusiness Company of Iran on 10 June 1973. 60 per cent of the investment is of foreign origin and 40 per cent of domestic origin. One of the foreign investors was the Hawaiian Agronomic Company

which acted as a major participant in establishing the Haft
Tappeh sugar cane plantation in the late fifties and early
sixties.   A Japanese concern held 15 per cent of the shares.
The Ahwaz Sugar Refinery Company also had a 15 per cent
share.   Out of its total land allocation of 16,680 hectares,
the company had received 4,240 hectares, by January 1974,
of which 1,250 had been levelled.   The Company experimented
with the introduction of sturdy beef cattle breeds for intensive meat production.

8.7   The Problems of Agribusinesses

Agribusinesses in the DIP area have not been the success
which had been anticipated.   Within less than a decade
of their establishment, the initial enthusiasm of many of
the foreign investors has given way to disappointment and
a desire to disentangle themselves.   In 1970, Naraqi had
guaranteed the success of agribusiness in the DIP area.
"With enough water for irrigation, enough power for processing plants and enough insecticides and fertilizers from
the petrochemical plants nearby, success is almost guaranteed here ... Anyone who cannot make it in Khuzestan has
no business being a farmer"(27).   Wilson too was quoted as
being impressed with the favourable physical conditions of
the farming areas of Khuzestan and wished to participate
in the agricultural activities of the region.   "I saw those
big rivers and that land laying there ... and it looked
'God-durned good' to a farmer like me.   I thought then
I'd like to have a piece of it someday" (28).   Yet by 1975
both had sold the greater part of their shareholding to the
Iranian Agricultural Development Bank.   In some cases, rent
and water charges running into several million rials have
not been paid.   The other two companies have fared little
better and foreign investors slowly withdrew their support,
leaving the finance of agribusinesses more and more in the
hands of the Iranian Agricultural Development Bank who
found that their technical and managerial duties have
increased beyond acceptable limits.   The details of losses
incurred up to 1978 are given in Table 84.
There are a number of reasons for the agribusinesses'
lack of success.   First, they all suffered from a lack of
sufficient field supervision to cover their large tracts of
land.   This inevitably led to misuse and wastage of expensive inputs, thus adding to the cost of the operation.   Field
observations reveal that although advanced technical know-
how was available there was a noticeable absence of **delsozi**,
(enthusiasm and devotion to duty) on the part of the field
technicians and workers.   This attitude of indifference is
probably the result of a feeling of bitterness felt by many
peasants who lost their newly-acquired land rights to the
agribusinesses established on their farm land.   The cultivators' short-lived period as peasant proprietors had offered
them hope for the future which was quickly dashed by the
advent of agribusiness.   It is not surprising that this

TABLE 84

Financial Situation of the Four Agribusinesses in
the Dez Irrigation Project Area, 1977-78.

Agribusiness	Area originally allocated Hectares	Land Leased Hectares	Land Levelled Hectares	Land under cultivation Hectares	Costs per hectare Rials	Income per hectare Rials	Cumulative losses Mn. rials	Capital paid Mn. rials	Debts to Ag. Dev. Bank Mn. rials	Debts to others Mn. rials
Iran-California	10,600	10,600	4,700	6,300	48,095	31,587	308	230	555	131
Iran-America	20,200	15,000	5,500	9,000	a	a	224	458	528	263
Iran-Shell Cott	15,700	6,200	5,600	5,500	65,090	29,272	998	600	621	453
Iran-International	16,700	12,000	6,000	5,000	96,000	65,000	527	860	552	500
Total	63,200	43,800	21,800	25,800 b	-	-	2,057	2,148	2,256	1,347

Source: Data issued by the Agricultural Development Bank of Iran, Committee Report
on the Survey of the Agricultural Situation in Dezful, May 1979.

Notes: a.   Costs and income per hectare not available for 1977-78,
            for 1976-77 costs and income per hectare were 41,777 rials
            and 38,075 rials respectively and the corresponding
            cumulative losses amounted to 198 million rials

        b.   Includes 4,300 hectares of unlevelled land sub-leased to local peasants
            and Isfahani migrant workers for growing summer crops.

bitterness and resentment is expressed in a reluctance to give whole-hearted support to their new employer. The feeling is well-known to the employers, who have recently found it expedient to employ outsiders with no vested interest in the land rather than local peasants. This has exacerbated the deteriorating employment situation in the DIP area, particularly for ageing peasants with limited employment opportunities outside the agricultural sector.

Moreover, the agribusinesses have been 'transplanted' from technologically sophisticated societies with capital intensive economies into a society which only a few years before had followed an age-old semi-subsistence form of sharecropping farming system. From the outset, the organizers seemingly ignored the possibility that there would be a 'cultural lag' to qualify any apparent success and a disproportionate amount of capital (29), and machinery were introduced. A more moderate approach, such as the 'support **boneh** farming' approach, would have been more appropriate. In any case if the agribusinesses were really necessary, they could have been encouraged to invest in developing virgin land rather than taking over existing peasant farms. This would have provided new areas to absorb labour and foster large-scale farming, rather than expelling farm labour as actually happened (30).

8.8   The New Resettlement Centres

Concurrent with the land purchasing programme for agribusiness use, plans were drawn up to replace villages involved in the agribusiness scheme with new resettlement centres or **shahraks** ('small towns').

A total of 13 **shahraks** had been planned to replace the 100 villages involved, and they were intended to serve as sources of labour for the agribusiness companies and as nuclei for programmes "to improve the finances, education and physical health of the existing villages."(31). Between 1972 and 1974 five resettlement centres were constructed, three in the Pilot area and two in the north-western part of the Project area. The major features of these centres are summarized in Table 85. Since 1972, three of these **shahraks** have been occupied by the inhabitants of 25 villages whose land has been purchased for agribusinesses. 22 of the villages were demolished after their evacuation and the remaining three were still partly inhabited in summer 1974. In Table 86 the villages that were evacuated together with their respective populations, are listed.

The resettlement centres have been provided with services and facilities which are not usually available in the traditional villages. These include piped water, electric power supply, a large school, a clinic, public bath houses, 'modern' shops, a slaughter house and a mortuary. The Dez Irrigation Project Authority is currently operating these services and facilities, mainly because the new **shahraks** do not correspond to the official definition of towns and

TABLE 85

Features of the five Shahraks in the DIP Area, Summer 1974

| Name of Shahrak | Location | | No. of villages included in resettlement | Occupation date | Resettled population a | Number of Housing Units | | |
	Nearest Previous Village	Distance from Dezful km				Occupied	Vacant	Total
Kavous	Kutian	16	7	24.04.72 to 26.06.74	2,250	429 at 2.03.74	21	450
Khusrou	Khusrouabad	20	10	7.08.72 to 4.01.74	1,800	321 at 2.03.74	11	332
Sasan	Shamoun	30	8	2.04.72 to 20.01.74	2,190	440 at 4.04.74	10	450
Babak b	Seyheh	20				250	–	250
Bahram b	Chichali Hermushi	35				250		250

Source: Field studies

Notes: a. Not all village evacuees have resettled in the new shahraks.
        b. Since 12th September 1974, the Babak and Bahram Shahraks have been occupied by the Kurdish refugees from Iraq.

villages.   Each **shahrak** has a population of less than 5,000
and cannot therefore be classified as a town.   On the other
hand, no farm land is attached to any of the centres so
they cannot be considered as villages.   Furthermore, no
administrative provision has been made for the administration
of **shahraks** and no adjustments have been made since they
came into existence in 1972.   This has led to a lack of
services – except for education – which would normally be
expected in towns or villages, nor is there **kadkhoda** or
mayor.   Thus, the DIP administration has appointed members
of its staff as temporary 'unofficial' **shahrak** supervisors.

8.9   The Residential Area of the Shahrak

The typical residential area of each **shahrak** consists of
a series of rows of four-housing units, with a maximum
capacity of 500 units.   Each of these units is designed for
occupation by one household and consists of two main rooms
(6 x 4 and 2 x 3 square metres) and a plot of approximately
700 square metres of land.   The 'houses' are not fenced
and no provisions have been made for the new peasant
settlers to keep more than two or three farm animals on
their premises, so as to avoid health hazards and the potential 'danger' to agribusiness crops.   A peasant informant
indicated that owners of cattle which stray near the agribusiness farms are fined 700 rials ($10).   Figure 21 shows
the plan of a typical village resettlement centre.
The **shahraks** bear little resemblance to traditional
villages.   The living quarters are smaller, and the brick
and metal materials used produce houses which are not
particularly pleasant in the summer months, with an inside
temperature frequently above 40°C.   To make the new houses
more habitable, some peasants have made their own modifications, usually by constructing additional and more suitable
living/sleeping rooms often in mud and straw, erecting walls
round the house for privacy and protection and constructing
animal shelters next to the living quarters.   Some of these
physical modifications, such as enclosing the house, can
be seen as indications that peasants still desire security
and feel a need to protect themselves in case of emergency.

8.10   Socio–economic Consequences of the Shahrak Resettlement Programme

The socio–economic effects of the new programme mainly
relate to the consequences of the amalgamation of heterogeneous villages and to the employment opportunities available to the new residents.   From the population background
of the villages assigned to each of these **shahraks**, it
appears that the policy has been to bring together villages
of different ethnic origins.   This may have been an attempt
to weaken individual tribal associations, which have long
been connected with nomadic or semi–nomadic life.

FIGURE 21   A 'typical' Shahrak village resettlement centre in the Dez Project area

TABLE 86

Villages Included in the New
Resettlement Centres, 1972–74.

Name of Shahrak	Villages Included in Resettlement	Ethnic Background	Evacuated [a] Pop 66	Hh.66 [*]	Date of Resettlement
KAVOUS	Farrash	Dezfulli/Arab	278	48	9.05.72
	Balenjoon	Arab/Dezfulli	196	20	25.11.73
	Hosseineh				
	Balenjoon	Arab/Dezfulli	287	45	26.06.74
	Deylame Olia [b]	Arab	315	60	8.01.74
	Boneh Khapel [b]	Arab	127	24	25.06.74
	Kutian	Dezfulli	772	135	25.04.72
	Nadjafabad	Dezfulli	650	115	24.04.72
Total:	7 Villages	–	2625	447	–
KHUSROU	Khairabad (East)	Lur Sagvand	194	34	15.01.73 to 15.03.73
	Biatian Arshid	Bakhtian/Arab	486	112	30.04.73
	Qaleh Abbas	Dezfulli/Lur Sagvand	213	40	14.04.73
	Boneh Tileh	Dezfulli	120	20	3.05.73
	Boneh Nabhan	Arab	104	19	30.09.72
	Boneh Seyd Taher	Arab	91	16	8.10.72
	Boneh Chary	Arab	117	17	12.09.72
	Khusrouabad	Bakhtiara/Arab	599	96	6.11.72 to 4.01.74
	Qaleh Abde Shah [b]	Arab/Dezfulli	790	136	17.12.73
	Azizabad	Lur Sagvand	119	22	7.08.72
Total	10 villages	–	2833	512	–
SASAN	Deylama Sofla	Arab/Dezfulli	537	109	2.03.72
	Shamoun	Lur Sagvand/ Dezfulli	517	97	2.03.72 to 10.02.73
	Boneh Alvan	Arab	303	53	12.03.72
	Boneh Younes	Arab	91	15	20.03.72
	Boneh Rahlmeh	Arab	356	62	20.01.74
	Salarabad	Lur Sagvand/Arab	528	105	13.05.72 to 20.08.72
	Sardarabad	Lur Sagvand/ Dezfulli	333	61	20.08.72
	Qaleh–Now Sardarabad	Lur Sagvand/ Dezfulli	240	44	10.05.72
Total	8 Villages	–	2905	546	–
GRAND TOTAL	25 Villages Resettled	–	8363	1505	–

Source: Field studies   Notes: a. Not all resettled in the shahraks
                                        b. Not yet demolished

Hh. [*] = Households

Patricia Rosenfield who visited these **shahraks** in 1973 and 1974 also refers to this development and maintains that:

> "To provide better living conditions for farm laborers, all of the villagers in the DPIP area are being moved to new-town developments, **shahraks**. (Note, however, that those DPIP villages under farm corporations are excluded from the resettlement scheme.) Old villages are then plowed under. Traditional, established village relationships have been broken; persons from the same village, even from the same family are sent to different **shahraks**. No matter whom one consults nor how one considers this changing of set patterns of behavior, it is a drastic innovation - particularly in Iran, where the extended family is the basic social organization, performing economic, medical and religious functions. Engineers on the project consider this mixing of Arab and Persian population within the **shahraks** essential for progress. They maintain that it introduces change to people whose daily existence has never varied." (32).

However, there is no official information available on underlying objectives of the **shahraks** so it is difficult to form a definite conclusion. The migration of members from heterogeneous village communities and their amalgamation into the new resettlement centres, has given the **shahraks** characteristics similar to those described by Duncan Mitchell as "open disintegrated communities" (33).

In the new **shahraks** everybody lives on his own, and life is segregated rather than communal. With the exception of family and kinship, there is little group activity. Even the village elders, who in the traditional village were active in settling local disputes, take a passive role of 'wait and see'. Meanwhile, conflicts amongst the residents of **shahraks** over acquiring a few metres of extra land or using a neighbour's courtyard for grazing, escalate. These conflicts are not only limited to neighbours who were originally strangers to each other, they also occur between close members of the same family. For instance, two brothers with their own families, on being resettled in a **shahrak** had decided to live as two separate households. But the unit which they were to share had two rooms of different sizes and they could not agree who should occupy the larger one. Finally through the mediation of the **shahrak** supervisor, they drew lots and the younger brother occupied the larger room. According to the supervisor of one of these centres, many recent conflicts in **shahraks** have been related to spatial restrictions which the peasants have rarely experienced before.

Some members of **shahraks**, who have had no alternative to evacuating their village, show resentment by constantly neglecting **shahrak** regulations. For instance, in **Shahrak** Khusrou, a number of water taps have been installed for communal use. According to the regulations, their use should be limited to obtaining drinking water. But some of the peasants not only disregard this restriction by using it lavishly for washing their clothes and dishes, but even leave the water running when they have finished.

Another problem of resettlement appears to be finding adequate employment for the older peasants. The agribusiness establishments prefer to hire more able members from the shahraks. This leaves the older members with no alternative but to join the "Dez Project Special Fund Employment Scheme" receiving a wage of 60 to 80 rials a day in 1974 for casual work - odd jobs such as making cement bricks or assisting in shahrak maintenance. These tasks are seen by the authorities to be a means of supplying the older members with an income rather than as a means of actually accomplishing specific tasks. This wage is claimed by the shahrak authorities to be comparable to the peasant farmer's income prior to the introduction of the agribusiness scheme. However many peasant farmers argue that when they were cultivators they supplied their household with basic foodstuffs, which were not reflected in their net cash income. Now they have to pay for these food items at retail market prices which are considerably above the level that an average household with five or six members can afford.

However, it should be mentioned that some illusory indicators of economic prosperity exist in these new centres. According to shahrak supervisors, the availability of electricity has enabled a few relatively well-off peasants to acquire luxury items such as television sets, refrigerators and gas stoves. This has led some peasants on low incomes to copy the lifestyle of their privileged neighbours, buying some of these items on long-term credit rather than for cash. The peasant's indebtedness at a time when he has limited employment opportunity and income restricts the domestic budget and often leads to a less adequate diet. To a stranger visiting these shahraks for the first time, possession of refrigerators, gas stoves and television sets gives a false impression of an improvement in the peasant's standard of living.

8.11 Village Polarization Scheme

In addition to the rural settlement scheme, the government initiated a programme of village polarization. Since many scattered villages are sparsely populated and their physical and social services are poor, the government began to establish several hozeh omran rustai, (rural development poles) after 1973. The programme consists of concentrating the physical and social services in fewer, but more viable villages - villages with larger populations and with the potential for further expansion to serve the needs of other satellite villages lying within their catchment areas. It was expected that the country's 55,000 villages would eventually be merged into 4,000 - 5,000 large rural poles and resettlement centres (34).

The present rural population of approximately 19 million is expected to increase to 23.2 million by 1990 (35). If the rural centralization programme were to have been completely implemented by that date, the larger rural settlement centres would have had an average population of about 5,000 compared to the 1976 average village population of approximately 380. It would also have led to the disappearance of nearly 50 per cent of existing villages, more than half of which have a population of less than 250 – a population limit below which villages would not officially be considered viable and their amalgamation would therefore be inevitable.

During the Fifth Development Plan (1973–78), it was expected that 1,180 rural development poles would be established throughout the country and would affect some 13,320 villages (nearly 25 per cent of the total)(36).Of this total,110 centres were planned for Khuzestan Province of which seven would be established in the region administered by the Dezful **Shahristan**. Of the latter, two would be located within the Dez Project area, possibly one near Shuhan and one close to Khalaf Moslam. The other five were to be established outside the Project area near the villages of Seyyed Nor (Sharqi Subdistrict), Saleh Davoud and Dosuq (both on Sorkheh Subdistrict), Sardasht and Mahvareh (both on Sardasht Subdistrict).(37). These seven rural development centres would be constructed in addition to the 13 **shahraks** being sponsored by the Dez Project Authority and the four large rural centres to be built for the Farm Corporation Scheme.

Each rural development unit would consist of a central village and ten or more satellite villages containing 5,000 – 6,000 people. The villages incorporated into a regional development pole would be distant from a town and thus without urban services. The central village would have to have a room for future expansion, be easily accessible to the inhabitants of the satellite villages (a maximum of eight kilometres away) and it would have a minimum population of 500.(38). A budget of 30,000,000 rials ($428,570) would be allocated for each unit. The fund would be used to provide a wide range of physical facilities, including piped water system, public bath house, mortuary, slaughterhouse, health clinic, crop storage facilities, veterinary service office, power supply system, library, **dehsra** (village communal house) and post office. The establishment of large regional rural poles and centralization of rural inhabitants are in line with "government plans to improve living conditions of villagers through better and less expensive distribution of services."(39).

However, the earlier problems in agricultural development, coupled with the events of the Iranian Revolution in February 1979, have called all these plans into question. Recent revelations of the costs and failures of the agribusiness and agro-industry schemes have made it unlikely that earlier plans will be continued, particularly given popular resentment against them.

Chapter Notes

1   Denman, **op. cit.**, p 210.

2.   Wolfgang Ule, "Land reform in Iran and the develop-
     ment of agricultural shareholders' companies" in
     Klaus-Peter Treydle and Wolfgang Ule (eds.)   **Agri-
     culture in the Near East,**   (Bonn-Bad   Godesberg,
     Germany: Verlag Neue Gesellschaft G m b H, 1973),
     p 116.

3.   Denman, **op. cit.**, p 210.

4.   **Farm Corporations Formation Law and Statutes,**(Tehran,
     Iran: Ministry of Co-operation and Rural Affairs,
     1971), p 20.

5.   Denman, **op. cit.**, p 213.

6.   John Freivalds, "Farm corporations in Iran: an
     alternative to traditional agriculture", **The Middle
     East Journal,** Vol 26, No 2, 1972, p 187.

7.   Denman, **op. cit.**, p 230.

8.   Freivalds, **op. cit.**, p 188.

9.   **Ibid.**

10. Nosratollah Khatibi, "The development of Garmsar
     (Iran) farm corporation: A case study", **Oxford
     Agrarian Studies,** Vol IV, No 1, 1975, p 20.

11. Denman, **op. cit.**, p 215.
     William E. Warne was the first Director of the Techni-
     cal Co-operation Mission of the USA (Point IV Prog-
     ramme) in Iran.   The programme was initiated in
     January 1952.

12. **Farm Corporations for the Dez Irrigation Project,**
     op. cit., (Enclosed letter from David E.Liliental to
     the Minister of Water and Power, August 5, 1970,
     p 1.).

13. **Ibid.**, p 9.

14. Mehdi Norozi, "Baresi Moq-adamati Sherkat Sahami
     Zerai Dez", (Preliminary study of the Dez farm cor-
     poration), (Tehran, Iran: Research Centre, Ministry
     of Co-operation and Rural Affairs, 1973, p 2).

15. Lambton, **The Persian Land Reform 1962-1966, op. cit.,**
     p 357.

16. Michael Field, "Agro-business and agricultural plann-
     ing in Iran", **World Crops,** Vol 24, No 2, p 69.

17. Liz Thurgood, "Agribusiness - The short cut to
     prosperity of the land", **The Times,** 22 May 1973.

18. D & R, **Farm Corporations for the Dez Irrigation Project, op. cit.**, p 9.

19. Agro-industry and Settlement Department, "Faaliat-hai Kesht va Sanat va Asarat-e an dar Barnameh-e Keshavarzi-e Mamlekat", (Activities of agro-industry and their impact on the national agriculture), May 1973.

20. **Ibid.**, pp 7-9.

21. **Ibid.**, p 9.

22. Bagley, **op. cit.**,p 33.

23. "Faaliat-hai Qasmat-e Kesht va Sanat va Eskam" Mordad Mahe-e 1353 (Activities of the agro-industry and settlement department of the KWPA during July 1974) (Unpublished), p 1.

24. **Kayhan,** 2 Azar 1348 (12 December 1969).

25. Trans-World Agricultural Development was founded in 1965 by 15 farmers engaged in irrigated agriculture in the Californian Imperial Valley.   Bagley, **op. cit.**, p 33.

26. Mitchell Cotts Group Limited is a British Mercantile firm which owns numerous subsidiaries engaged in engineering, manufacturing, agriculture and transport. a) The company has experience of agricultural development in Sudan and Ethiopia b). a) "Iran-Shell Cotts Operating Agreement" 1971 (Unpublished). b) Bagley, **op. cit.**, p 33.

27. Griggs, **op. cit.**, p 128.

28. **Ibid.,**

29. Field, **op. cit.**, p 71.

30. Bolster, **op. cit.**, p 17.

31. D & R, **Dez Irrigation Project Stage II, Feasibility, op. cit.**, p 54.

32. Patricia L. Rosenfield, **Development and Verification of a Schistosomiasis Transmission Model with Data from Bilharziasis Control Project and Dez Pilot Irrigation Project, Khuzestan Province, Iran.** (Washington DC, USA: Agency for International Development Department of State, 1975), p 82.

33. G. Duncan Mitchell, "Depopulation and rural social structure", **The Sociological Review,** Vol 42, 1950, section 4.

34. **Kayhan,** 1 Khordad 1350/22 May 1971.

35. Khazaneh and Sadat Darbandari, **op. cit.**, p 27.

36. Plan and Budget Organization, **Gozaresh Barnameh Omrani Panjum Keshvar** (Report on the Fifth Develop-

ment Plan) (Tehran, Iran: Plan and Budget Organization, 1352/1973), p 31.

37. Personal interview with Naqashpour, Head of the
     Khuzestan Department of Rural Development and Re-
     construction, Ahwaz, 13 October 1973.

38. Personal interview with Naqashpour, op. cit.,

39. Kayhan International, 16 February 1974.

PLATE 9   Boy transporting harvested rice to threshing ground

9 OTHER CAUSES OF CHANGE

9.1 Introduction

In addition to the major changes in Dezfulli rural life
wrought by land reform and the Dez Irrigation Project over
the last two decades, exogenous factors, usually inspired
by the government, have changed many other aspects of
village organization and local life.   The most important
of these aspects are the physical and social services, health
and education, agricultural credit and product marketing
and, finally, the various technical assistance services that
development planning has introduced into rural society.

9.2 Physical and Social Services

Up to the 1950s, physical and social services were very
poor in almost all of the 55,000 villages in Iran.   In a
few villages the community itself provided rudimentary
services - a communal bath house or a **maktab** (informal
school) - sometimes with the help of the landowners.   The
landlords only provided credit services that directly affected
their income from the land.   Government-sponsored services
at village level were limited to security and administration
through the gendarmerie, who were responsible for conscription notices, the issuing of summonses and the routine
policing of persons and property.   In a few major villages
the government also provided elementary schools.
In the early fifties village councils were established and
allocated funds to be used for local improvements in
amenities such as piped drinking water and communal bath
houses.   Until the 1960s, however, such improvements were
piecemeal because of a chronic lack of funds.   Since then
government involvement at village level has increased
through financial assistance and advisory services.   Basic
services have improved but there are so many villages in
Iran and the conditions are often so poor that official intervention has done little more than scratch the surface of

this overwhelming problem. In addition, the limited funds
available have narrowed the scope of rural services and
have led to their unequal distribution over the country and
local regions such as rural Dezful.

The creation of village equity courts and of rural cultural
centres was intended to improve the quality of rural life
and social conditions. These programmes in rural Dezful
have a very limited coverage at present, but they could
prove to be effective instruments for assisting the peasantry
to achieve a socially enriched life. The village equity
courts using trustworthy local men with a knowledge of local
affairs as judges would be the soundest, simplest and most
economic way of resolving local differences. Similarly, the
rural cultural centres aim at developing athletic, artistic
and technical potentialities and, if co-ordinated with other
government-sponsored services could contribute towards social
well-being.

9.3 Health Services

Until 30 years ago, modern medical services existed only
in a few major cities. Smaller towns and rural areas were
served by **hakimbashies** and specialists in folk medicine.
In recent years, however, nation-wide medical care has
become a major national objective but it has been difficult
to realize because of the fast growing population and the
inadequate number of doctors who are unequally distributed
between town and country - 60 per cent of the population,
who live in the countryside are served by just over ten
per cent of all available doctors.

Health problems in rural Dezful were very serious before
the 1960s - malnutrition was prevalent and communicable
and parasitic diseases were widespread. In addition,
peasant housing was poor and overcrowded while sanitation
and health education were non-existent. Provision of medical
facilities and a health education programme must form an
essential part of an overall and balanced rural development,
since lack of them leads to enormous economic losses consequent on the incapacity of the active population through
disease and death.

Even in 1973-74, field studies showed that a large number
of Dezfulli peasant communities are still without any kind
of medical facility or service. Of the 41 physicians working
in the area, only one doctor is actually in the sole permanent rural clinic. Even though three health programmes
have been introduced nationally since the 1960s to compensate
for the inadequacy of rural medical services the programmes
do not yet benefit the Dezfulli peasantry on a large scale.

The Health Corps, consisting of men and women liable
to military service, was formed in 1964. 11,000 people have
been involved, 20 per cent of them physicians. Corps
members serve rural communities through mobile health units
or stations. In the Dezful **Shahristan** two of these units
were in operation in 1973-74, serving 30 or so villages

outside the DIP boundaries. A national rural insurance scheme was started in 1969 – a peasant is entitled to free medical consultation and similar services on payment of 365 rials. In Dezful the scheme has been limited to 32 villages (22 per cent of 145 villages in the DIP area) involved in the four farm corporations. Since 1972 a new pilot programme has been successfully tried out in a few rural and nomadic communities of Fars and West Azarbayjan provinces but has not yet been extended to Dezful. This new approach involves medical auxiliaries recruited and trained on the spot to provide essential health care to rural and nomadic communities. One year of basic training enables the auxiliaries to diagnose simple illnesses, dispense medicine, carry out family planning, immunization, disease detection and similar services. It seems that this new approach, using local people to carry out primary health care in their own communities, may become an effective, simple and economical source of health care in many villages long deprived of even the most rudimentary medical services.

9.4   Education

Although Dezful is famed as the home of Iran's most ancient institution of higher learning, in 1956 98.8 per cent of its rural inhabitants were illiterate. By 1966 this figure had dropped at a rate of less than one per cent per annum to 90.9 per cent and does not seem to have substantially changed in the intervening years up to 1974. In only one quarter of all villages surveyed did the literacy rate exceed 15 per cent. However, during the past 50 years education has been transformed from informal religiously biased schooling to a formal secular educational system.

At the start of the 20th century, the entire educational facilities, mainly for teaching Islam, of the Dezful region consisted of 27 **maktabs** (elementary schools) and **madresehs** (secondary schools). State participation began in 1910 when the Ministry of Education was formed. In 1943 compulsory education was started, but even ten years later half of primary-school age children in Iran still had no formal education. Formal educational facilities were also disproportionately distributed among urban and rural areas and in 1964 the percentage of urban children in schools was more than double that in rural areas.

The major campaign against rural illiteracy was started in 1962 with the formation of the Literacy Corps consisting of conscripted high school graduates. Since 1968, women have also been included in another corps. The work of these two corps, together with the intensive rural school construction programme of the early seventies, has extended the availability of free education to rural children previously without this opportunity. As a result, the gap between the provision of elementary educational facilities in rural and urban areas has been considerably narrowed.

Adult literacy schemes have not been as successful as

those for children.   Between 1967 and 1972 a jointly sponsored by UNESCO and Iran-Work Oriented Adult Literacy
Programme was carried out in several villages in the Dez
Project area but field studies in 1973 and 1974 showed that
most adult peasants are still illiterate.

9.5   Rural Credit

Many Dezfulli farmers require financial assistance, but
government-sponsored credit facilities are inadequate so the
peasantry tends to sell produce in advance of harvest to
secure credit from private sources.   Advance selling involves
a price differential of often more than 100 per cent and
moneylender terms are usually little better, with interest
rates of 50 or even 75 per cent.   Town shopkeepers and
bazaar merchants offer credit at rates usually lower than
those of the moneylender in the village but usually only
to the relatively prosperous to avoid the risk of bad debt.
Government aid is limited to the village co-operative credit
scheme but in rural Dezful, these functions often exist only
in theory and have rarely been effective in providing
adequate credit.   In 1973, a nationwide merger programme
was introduced to consolidate and improve these societies.
The amalgamated co-operatives also operated as retail outlets
for a wide range of consumer goods.   However, in 1973 and
1974 enquiries suggested that most Dezfulli villages used
neither the credit nor the retail facilities of the co-operative
mainly because the loans were inadequate and no credit
was offered in the retail outlets.
A major weakness of the Iranian co-operative movement
has been a failure to make peasant members fully aware
of the co-operative's objectives and functions.   The co-
operatives have only recently begun and still require
considerable government financial support.   Nevertheless,
if members could properly understand the function of their
co-operative, more peasants would participate and benefit
from the services available.   The village co-operative could
free the peasants from advance selling and massive indebtedness, as well as causing an increased investment of labour
and capital in land, which in turn would benefit national
agricultural productivity and peasant income.

9.6   Market Outlets

Traditionally, Dezfulli agricultural marketing was dominated by the landowners' harvest sales – the peasant's
usually being too small to market – and comprised wheat,
rice and sesame.   Wheat was mainly sold to the government
and rice and sesame to local merchants.   Fruit and vegetables were produced by owner-cultivators and marketed
through the local **barfurush** – a simple and efficient system
but financially unattractive to the producer because of the
high commission and handling charges.

Significant changes have occurred in the past two decades because of government intervention through guaranteed prices and subsidies, and because of improvements in communications. Government intervention has often reduced the number of middlemen and thus reduced the gap between the producer's selling prices and the retail prices. An extension of a programme to cover perishable produce as well as cereals and industrial crops would guarantee the farmer a fair, stable income, and the consumer a reliable supply of farm products at reasonable prices.

The new rural road system has not only changed the peasant's trading pattern, but has also led to social changes, such as the adoption of urban style dress. Moreover, the improved road and telecommunication network has allowed local fruit and vegetable producers to expand production because of a guaranteed market in the major urban centres which are now within reach, rather than just local markets in Dezful town.

The quality of Dezful citrus fruit and vegetable is good because of fertile soil, ample water and proper climatic conditions. If grading, packing and loading were improved, local producers could compete with imported products as well, particularly as Dezful is favourably located to three of Iran's major consumer markets – Ahwaz, Khurramshahr and Abadan – and for export to some Gulf States. The national market has been expanding, because of the improved urban economic position. Dezful could become a leading fruit and vegetable producing centre for Iran – but only if national policies can provide more security for private producers and facilitate the participation of experienced local agriculturalists.

9.7 The Village Production Service

The Village Production Service developed from the Khuzestan Fertilizer Programme in 1962 and gradually widened its scope to stimulate rapid increases in agricultural production in the 58 villages of the Dez Pilot area. Although the Service only lasted about seven years it extended its programmes to 22 villages outside the Pilot area in the last three years of its existence. The objectives and the tasks were predetermined by the developmental agency and were achieved by offering local cultivators temporary incentives and, in some cases, by supervision through agricultural agents. The Service emphasised mass application of fertilizer, use of farm machinery and the cultivation of new crops. Many ideas were eventually widely accepted, such as the use of fertilizer, although others, such as alfalfa cultivation were less popular.

During field studies it was noted that although in Bonvar Hossein the former landowners no longer dominated farming activities, the peasants had continued the traditional practices. They did adopt fertilizer and Berseem clover in the rice lands however, and cultivators in Chogha Sorkh had also adopted these two practices before 1970. These two villages were relatively representative of the area, and it was clear that Dezfulli peasants were, and most probably still are, cautious over adopting new farming practices. They only responded to the items which were compatible with their inherited agrarian system.

The experience of the Village Production Service shows that when agricultural programmes are planned without due consideration and involvement of the peasants, the outcome is rarely beneficial to the local or national economy. Primary emphasis in agricultural planning should be placed on obtaining the effective co-operation of native cultivators. As Lambton suggests "unless the goodwill and the co-operation of the peasant is enlisted and his confidence won, production is unlikely to increase" (1). An experienced old farmer in Bonvar Hossein once said that "we could grow very good crops only if we had **del-ba-stagee** (wholehearted attachment to our cultivation)" - a view reflected by the majority of local peasants and landowners. More importantly such a peasant-oriented programme would improve economic prosperity in rural communities which would benefit the urban population and reduce rural migration to the already over-crowded cities - Ahwaz (286,000 in 1972), Tehran (4,500,000 in 1976) thus relieving urban unemployment.

9.8   Extension Services

In the early fifties, several foreign agencies carried out pilot village developmental projects and in consequence of their apparent success a countrywide extension programme was launched in December 1952. Subsequently an agricultural extension service was established in 1953 designed to assist in the adoption of improved practices to increase agricultural productivity and earnings.

Initially the US Point IV Technical Assistance Agency provided guidance and the extension programme was in part patterned on the American Co-operative Extension System. The family-oriented extension programme was carried into the rural communities by village level agrcultural and home economics extension agents, backed by provincial and national extension specialists and supervisors. In March 1968, the home economics sector was transferred to a new Ministry, a strict division of responsibilities was created at all levels between the two extension organizations. However since in traditional rural society each family member works in close co-ordination with his fellows, a co-ordinated extension programme would have been more effective than this compartmentalized approach.

Since 1964, the extension agent has been supplemented by the members of the Extension and Development Corps, created to improve rural living standards. Unlike the Literacy Corps and Health Corps, the work of this Corps seems to be more difficult and complex for it involves persuading and instructing farmers to adopt new practices.

Progress has in consequence been slow.

Since the late 1960s, the Agricultural Extension Service has been modified twice. The pilot village extension project which covered 155 villages throughout Iran, involved intensified extension work linked with the Ministry of Agriculture and aimed at promoting modern farming technology at the village level. The Impact Programme on Selected Crops has included a series of production incentives and subsidies intended to increase national agricultural productivity.

In general, the Agricultural Extension Service has been very limited. Its total annual field staff numbers have always been well below 1,000 and it has only reached ten per cent of all Iranian villages. In the Dezful area, because of the existence of the DIP-sponsored Village Production Service, Ministry of Agriculture extension activities were even more limited – there were never more than five village-level agents in any one year. The impact of their work was very little, if any. This ineffectiveness is multi-dimensional. Dezfulli peasant farmers were, and mostly still are, habit-bound, illiterate and relatively poor. This combination renders them extremely cautious in adopting new practices unless such practices are proven to be visibly superior to traditional methods. In any case such superiority would have to be undertaken by an authority acknowledged by them as mature, experienced and trust-worthy – deserving of respect and confidence. The extension service has not sufficiently allowed for this in appointing its agents; instead it has organized itself on an 'imported' model which is ineffective in rural Dezful in particular, and, most probably, in rural Iran in general. Basically, extension work has not evolved from within the agrarian social structure of Iran but it is an alien incompatible graft which in any case did not receive the attention that such a delicate operation really requires. It is not surprising that extension work has failed to bear fruit.

Alternative experimental rural development approaches have been conducted in Iran such as the endogenous integrated pilot project in Alashtar where an attempt has been made to utilize the existing informal, traditional village hierarchy – based on deference to age, experience and trust-worthiness rather than wealth – as a channel of communication to multiply and support **bonku** use of improved agricultural practices. The field agent would be selected from among local progressive farmers of sufficient stature to persuade fellow members of the hierarchy to adopt new agricultural techniques. Furthermore, successful compatible innovations, such as Isfahani migrant peasants should be used to demonstrate more productive methods of farming.

9.9 A Tentative Conclusion

A common view of land reform might suggest that traditional village social structure, dominated by the authority

of the landlord and his agents, was well integrated and
relatively 'stable', consisting of interdependent, mutually
reinforcing social organizations. Changes arising in any
of these would create needs for readjustment in other
component social organizations within the village. Land
tenure reform would be considered to have altered village
land tenure organization and to have acted as a 'disruptive
factor', upsetting traditional social equilibrium. To restore
stability, services supporting the creation of suitable new
social organizations would be needed. However, the actual
replacement services provided do not fully correspond to
village requirements and thus the village is in a state of
'instability'. It requires appropriate social services which
could facilitate new social organizations which themselves
would restore 'stability' to village social structures. This
view was supported by reports of a number of students of
agrarian reform which underlined the impact of the land
reform programme on agrarian social structure, but did not
emphasised the inter-relationships between the impact of the
land reform programme and other concurrent agrarian and
social developments.

This study seeks to suggest, however, that in rural Dezful
and perhaps in rural Iran overall specific changes in
village social structure cannot be related exclusively to
land tenure reform, or indeed to any other single development. In fact, over the past 25 years there has been a
complicated pattern of changes in rural Dezful, of which
the land reform programme contributes a major but not an
isolated element. The concurrency and inter-relationships
of elements of change in rural Dezful make it difficult, if
not impossible, to isolate the impact of land reform in the
village social structure.

The effects of endogenous and exogenous changes too,
cannot always be identified. Although major and direct
effects of some of them on the village social structure were
distinguishable - for example, the 'disappearance' of the
landlord was a direct consequence of the land reform programme - there were other changes whose effects were diffused
and so closely inter-related with other factors that it was
impossible empirically to distinguish them. An indvidual
example illustrates this well. Abdullah, from Bonvar Hossein
changed from being an unpaid family farm labourer to being
a taxi driver in Dezful, as the result of a complex set of
interactions. The use of a tractor to cultivate village lands
(impact of farm mechanization) meant that there was no
opportunity for employment on the family **juft** for him.
However, since he was literate (impact of rural education
programme) and held a driving licence (impact of his
military training) he was able to find employment as a taxi
driver in the town of Dezful (impact of urbanization). His
subsequent marriage to the daughter of an army sergeant
instead of his **dokhtar amu**, (patriparallel first cousin) -
a further consequence of urbanization - has weakened his
relationship with his family in the village. Now his whole
lifestyle is the product of a complex of changes. Indeed,

Abdullah typifies the cumulative effect of farm mechanization, rural education programme, military service and urbanization on peasant work, family, kinship and marriage institutions. However, the impact of a single factor in this on the village social structure cannot be isolated, except for the fact that the sequence of events was triggered off by the introduction of a tractor into peasant cultivation.

The dynamic nature of village social structure makes analysis of the impact of a single social or economic reform measure even more difficult. The social structure and system of a village, and village social organizations which are interdependent, may be regarded as approximating to a 'field' and the 'regions' or 'groups' or 'individuals' or other elements within a field (2), where "the members of a group constitute a dynamic field such that change in the behavior of one member can induce a change in behavior of other members."(3). Field enquiries in DIP villages support this view in so far that changes in one village social organization often lead to changes in the structure and functions of others. This idea of 'social dynamism' is also emphasised by contemporary sociologists, for "change in one direction produces changes elsewhere " (4).

Given the complexity of the elements of socio-economic change in rural Dezful and the dynamic nature of village social structure, it is more realistic to abstain from analysis of the impact of individual elements of change and, instead, to regard the impact of any change as being part of a complex whole, formed from diverse influences arising from endogenous and exogenous aspects of change. The impact of the land reform programme cannot be isolated from the impact of all the other concurrent changes; and new hypotheses must take the complex nexus of change, as well as the dynamic nature of village social structure into account. This is particularly important, given the vast political changes that Iran has undergone in the past two years. Indeed it may be a long time before a true balance of rural change can be drawn up and before the real effect of development planning up to the end of 1978 on the Iranian countryside can be clearly seen.

Chapter Notes

1.   Lambton, **The Persian Land Reform 1962–1966, op. cit.,**
      p 281.

2.   Kurt Lewin, **Field Theory in Social Science** (New York,
      NY, USA: Harper, 1951).
      See also – Merton Deutsch, "Field Theory in Social
      Psychology", in Gardner Lindzey and Elliot Arenson
      (editions). **The Handbook of Social Psychology,** second
      edition, Vol 1, (Reading, Mass., USA: Addison-Wesley
      Publishing Co., 1968).

3.   Quoted in Vernon J. Nordby and Calvin S. Hall, **A
      Guide   to   Psychologists   and   their   Concepts,** (San
      Francisco, Calif., USA: W.H.Freeman and Co.,   1974),
      p 115.

4.   W.J.H.Sprott,   **Sociology**   (London,   UK: Hutchinson
      University Library, 1969), p 166.

10 POSTSCRIPT

The imaginative scheme for the creation in Khuzestan of a total river basin development area on the model of the TVA was implemented more or less continuously from the early 1960s. But physical development of the land and water resources of Khuzestan was rarely as thoroughly researched as the original concept demanded. Construction of reservoir dams and irrigation systems proceeded at a pace far greater than research into problems of soil salinity and alkalinity, into the long term effects of intensive agriculture on re-claimed lands and into the economic viability of agriculture within the development zone. In particular, those engaged in the agricultural programme within the KWPA and its successors were slow to study indigenous cropping and irrigation practices, to establish how far constraints existed, or the means devised to circumvent or mitigate them.

In the foregoing chapters it will have become amply apparent that those in charge of development in Khuzestan had little regard for local farming. Over much of the development area traditional villages were swept away together with existing cultivated areas and the farming practices which sustained them in a difficult physical environment. Changes made to the agrarian structure of Khuzestan within the KWPA development zone were irreversible in so far as the original farmers and tenants were largely moved away from their former lands and, in the main, found alternative employment in fields other than agriculture or in the **shahraks** set up for the agricultural corporations in the area.

This postscript will endeavour to trace the trends in agriculture in Khuzestan since 1976 and establish the degree to which the themes elaborated in this volume have been continuing factors and whether the pessimism for the future of agriculture in the area has been justified by events during the period to 1980. There were important changes affecting the whole of the Iranian economy in the period 1973-76, some of them representing the culmination of processes begun earlier but visible in sharper contrast, and some deriving from events occurring in the period after 1976. The course of and effects of these vicissitudes in Iranian fortunes were important in so far as they affect agricultural prosperity in general and the position of agriculture in Khuzestan in particular.

During the 1970s Iran became increasingly an oil economy. While the direct impact of the oil industry remained limited, especially as expressed through levels of employment even in Khuzestan, the flow of oil revenue was much augmented and the role of oil revenues in total government income, in foreign exchange earnings and in contribution to the national income became greatly enhanced. Rising income per unit of oil exported, resulting from the Organization of Petroleum Exporting Countries negotiations with the international oil companies, made notable increases in the level of Iranian oil earnings from the last quarter of 1973.

The direction and rate of expenditure of increasing oil income after 1973 had a deep impact on the nature of economic development and not least on the course of agricultural progress. Abandoning the existing economic development plan prepared for the period 1973 to 1978, in which generous if reluctant provision had been made for agriculture (approximately $2,215 million of investment funds), the government adopted a new and much larger development plan in which agriculture received an improved level of funding ($4,580 million of investments) but was relegated in importance vis-a-vis other sectors of the economy. At the same time, the government increased its outlays in every other area and especially in its current budget, defence, and a large number of new projects not originally in the development plan. The effects of so rapid a rise in investment and consumption were acknowledged by the authorities to have been disasterous. Severe bottlenecks in the ports, in the transport systems, in the domestic productive sectors and in labour supply produced accelerating inflation in prices, a boom in urban construction and a rapid growth in levels of wages.

A profound change was wrought in the distribution of population in Iran as a consequence of the economic boom from 1973. The census of 1976 showed that only 53.2 per cent of the population remained in rural areas against 61 per cent a decade previously and 69 per cent in 1956. Provisional estimates for mid-1978 suggested that the rural population had sunk below half the total. Employment in agriculture fell much faster than the rate of decline of rural population as country dwellers changed sectors of occupation if not their places of permanent residence. The attraction of rural people to urban residence and non-agricultural employment was occasioned above all other factors, it would seem, by the rapid rise in wages in the construction industry and by the great growth in employment opportunities as domestic consumer expenditure rose. In those areas of the country where returns from agriculture were low, and this was the case over large areas as a result of both constraints

of a physical nature and the government's pricing policy
for agricultural products, the small farmer had little to
discourage him from leaving the land to pursue higher wages
and less onerous work elsewhere.   The full extent of, and
regional variations in ,losses of people from agriculture were
not known with certainty, though the 1976 census indicated
that only 33.9 per cent of the employed poulation was
engaged in agriculture by November 1976 against 49.0 per
cent in 1966 and 56.3 per cent in 1956.

Among the important changes brought about by the period
of rapid economic development beginning in the mid-1960s
and running through to 1976/77 (but especially after 1973)
was a severe deterioration in the relative incomes of
agriculture against other sectors.   The agriculturally
employed in 1975/76 numbered some 2.98 million and shared
in 9.4 per cent of GDP while in 1965/66 approximately 3.55
million agriculturally employed persons shared 26.2 per cent
of GDP.   In broad terms agricultural work received a reward
of some 50 per cent of the average wage in 1965/66 but only
some 30 per cent in 1975/76.   In conditions of labour
shortage during the 1970s the poor ratio between agricultural
wages and industrial (including construction sector) pay
served to accelerate departures of manpower from agriculture
to such an extent that there were peak season labour
shortages in a number of major agricultural areas which
drew in labour from adjacent countries and notably
Afghanistan.

The very poor rewards to be gained in agriculture, the
flight of labour and, to an extent, capital from the land,
together with inept bureaucratic interventions at all levels
of operations in the sector brought stagnant or declining
production of most crops.   Official claims of substantial
increases in production of agricultural crops during the
early and mid-1970s have been generally discredited, even
within Iran.   During the same period rising incomes brought
an increased total demand for foodstuffs and a pattern of
consumption of foodstuffs of a changing kind, including new
items and products of better quality than previously demanded.   Production capacity of domestic agriculture proved
totally incapable of matching the new levels of demand.
Imports of agricultural goods rose sharply.   Iranian imports
of agricultural goods rose from $926 million in 1974/75 to
approximately $2,550 million by 1977/78 after the oil boom
against an average of less than $200 million in the three-
year period preceding 1973.

The government was slow to concede that its policies
for agriculture were inappropriate in the difficult years
1974 to 1976.   Modernization of agriculture through continuing and enforced change of the agrarian structure, in
which peasant farming was replaced by government controlled
farm corporations and production co-operatives and new
private sector agro-industries had been of questionable value
before the intense pressures of the boom period came into
play after 1973.   Government interference had bred a

corrosive degree of uncertainty which militated against long-term private investment in agriculture and stimulated a mood of insecurity that fostered migration of the peasant farmer community from many areas (eg. Stobbs observations in Nahavand 1976 *). Fear, insecurity and depressed levels of reward from agriculture in the years after 1973, situations exacerbated considerably by government policies, were active stimuli for peasant abandonment of agriculture when there was a simultaneous expansion of job opportunities in other sectors and as wage levels elsewhere rose much more rapidly than in agriculture. Not until 1977, when most of the damage had already been done, did the government acknowledge its failures in agriculture and look around for alternative policies.

The Province of Khuzestan had a special role to play within government strategy for modernization of agriculture. Planning policies were concerned to raise production from agriculture rapidly and to bring the growth rate in that sector more into line with those being achieved in industry and services. It had been hoped that the annual rate of increase in value-added in agriculture would rise to some seven per cent in real terms during the period 1973-78 in contrast to the four per cent realized during the preceding five-year plan period. One of the main vehicles for promoting a more rapid rise in output was to be the agro-industrial unit, which was to combine a high level of capital investment per hectare with modern and imported technology. Management where possible was to be brought in from abroad. The land reclaimed under the Dez dam project was scheduled to be the first and largest of the agro-industrial areas in the country, a pilot project for the brave new agriculture which would sustain crop production as peasant traditional farming was deliberately run down and replaced by state-controlled corporations.

Initial costs and human difficulties created by the Khuzestan agro-industries have been described and analysed earlier in this volume. What was not clear in 1976 was the degree to which the expenses of and the suffering engendered by the land clearances and construction of the agro-industries were in vain. After 1976 the foreign partners in three of the largest agro-industries withdrew. With few exceptions the agro-industries were effectively, if not officially declared, bankrupt. Causes of the difficulties that beset the agro-industries were not hard to find. If the foreign companies investing in the area are to be believed there was little that went right for them. From the beginning there was too much expected from the units. Yet basic research into soils and their response to intensive cultivation under irrigation and into crop suitability was at an embrionic stage when the

---

* Stobbs, C.A., **Agricultural change in Western Iran,** Unpublished thesis, London University, 1976.

main project was begun.   The operating companies were
faced with a great measure of bureaucratic incompetence
arising from the multiplicity of government departments
responsible for various aspects of the scheme and its
services.   The Iranian authorities in Tehran were generally
lacking in knowledge of the very considerable problems
faced by the agro-industries and were either inactive or
unsympathetic to them during the vital infant stage of their
growth.   Management of the agro-industries was severely
criticized in Iran, especially in relation to labour management at field level.   At the same time, as has been made
abundantly clear in earlier chapters of this study, resent-
ments among the original farmers moved from their traditional lands to make way for the agro-industries were
expressed in non-co-operation with the new units and in
active opposition from time to time.

Two basic and related problems lie at the heart of the
failure of the agro-industries in Khuzestan.   First, the
physical environment imposed harsh constraints on agriculture and especially on irrigated agriculture using simple
surface water spreading techniques since soil quality
appeared to decline rapidly.   To overcome the inherent
difficulties of the area required more research and a higher
level of current expenditure than was ever foreseen.   It
is probable, too, that inappropriate technology was used
for the main part under pressure from the demands of rapid
reclamation of land required in the leases of the agro-
industrial companies.   A more generous contract would have
permitted experiment with a variety of systems and the
ultimate use of locally adapted though sophisticated technology for irrigation.   But whatever the balance of factors
which brought about the demise of many of the agro-industries, the aggregate cause of their failure was high costs
against low returns.   An inimical government pricing policy
and a belief that their enterprises could not forseeably
make a reasonable return on investments made precipitated
an abandonment of the area by the foreign companies, many
of which had proved elsewhere that they were efficient
companies of great integrity.

Second, the managements of the agro-industrial units
were caught in the same trends after 1973 as the rest of
the agricultural sector.   Costs of all inputs rose rapidly
and were often in short supply.   The shortage and high
costs of labour were also a major problem, especially since
these modern units relied on relatively skilled labour which
was most in demand in the expanding industrial and construction sectors.   At the same time, periodic shortages of
water and electricity made economic operation of the farms
extremely difficult.

In sum, the agro-industries were beset by difficulties
of a significant kind before 1973 and there were good
grounds for believing that their future even then was suspect.
Their fate was sealed by the effects of the oil boom after
1973, except where special circumstances prevailed such as
at Haft Tappeh sugar cane estate.   The unfortunate fact

was that all other forms of agriculture in Khuzestan were
adversely affected by mismanagement of the economy from
late 1973. The farm corporations, though propped up by
government subsidies, were no better means for modernization
than the agro-industries, while the neglect of traditional
farming areas, which had been least generously treated with
respect to credits and technical assistance and which had
been affected by insecurity over the future, resulted in these
zones too, declining in their contribution to agricultural
production.

The ultimate irony was that by 1978 the government was
offering lands formerly under the agro-industries back to
the peasants who had previously tenanted them but at a time
when most young and active farmers had already left either
farming or their villages or both. By the late-1970s, 20
years approximately after the inception of the Khuzestan
development scheme, and only ten years after the adoption
of the agro-industrial unit as a principal vehicle for agricultural modernization, agricultural production in the reclaimed
areas was little more and possibly somewhat less than had
been the case before the project began.

Such pessimistic findings could be mitigated slightly by
the conclusions drawn from experience of agricultural policy
in the 1970s by the Iranian Minister of Agriculture and Rural
Affairs. Speaking to a Symposium on Agricultural Policy
at the University of Shiraz, in 1978, the Minister conceded
that "under Iranian conditions one agricultural system is
not feasible. We need several agricultural structures adapted
to local conditions, including peasant farming, small group
farming, rural production co-operatives, agricultural corporations, agro-industries and commercial private farms." Such
a stance represented a significant change in official policy.
But the agricultural mismanagement of the Dez irrigation area,
Khuzestan, and the loss of local peasant and incoming
capitalist farmers alike was a high price to pay for so small
an advance in realism in the agricultural policy of the
central government in Tehran.

The failure of the shah's policies for agriculture played
an important part in his ultimate overthrow in February 1979.
Losses of rural poulation to the towns swelled the urban
unemployed. Up to a million workers moved from villages
to urban areas after 1973, often with their families, and
brought with them their religious commitment to Islam and
deep deference to the religious authorities. The rural exodus
played, therefore, a direct role in preparing the ground for
Muslim revolt against the shah. Knowledge of the collapse
of agriculture in many parts of the country contributed to
the growing belief among the educated that the cost of rapid
industrialization and modernization under the shah was being
purchased at the expense of agriculture, traditional village
society, and Islamic virtues enshrined in customary rural
practice. Increasing inability of the country to feed itself
confirmed not simply that the regime's agricultural policies
had failed but that it was prepared to permit Iranian
dependence on imports of foodstuffs, mainly from the USA,

in a way that reduced Iranian economic and political
sovereignty.
   The Iranian revolution of February 1979 brought with
it convulsions of a political and economic nature which
altogether precluded formulation of a coherent policy towards
national development.   In principle, the early revolutionary
governments were dedicated to agricultural regeneration of
the country.   Those agribusinesses of Khuzestan which had
survived, were formally abandoned in 1980 as part of a
policy designed to remove foreign and large enterprises from
the agricultural sector.   A land reform was prepared for
the entire country, which would create a small peasant
proprietor class through re-allocation of former crown lands
(khaliseh) and lands sequestrated from large landowners
or forfeited by members of the former regime.   By definition
it appeared as if the farm corporations and producer co-
operatives would be disbanded under the terms of the new
proposals.   The future for the new land reform was unsure
in mid-1980.   The **ulama** were divided on the legality of
the reform and the attitude towards it by the newly constituted **majlis** unclear.
   It will be apparent from the evidence presented in this
volume that peasant proprietorship as proposed by the 1980
land reform had much to recommend it.   Empirical work,
backed up by three village case studies indicated that the
structure of agribusiness companies and farm corporations
was incompatible with the welfare of the traditional agrarian
system in Khuzestan.   It was also shown that peasant
farming can improve the level of labour and land productivity where suitable village oriented services have been made
available.   The great question for Iran is whether the
revolutionary governments will be able, any better than
their predecessors, to draw up an appropriate policy and
efficient ground level organization to reinforce changes in
the size of farm and type of ownership called for in the
new reform programme or emerge naturally from the post-
revolutionary chaos.
   Agrarian policy in Iran has travelled through full circle
in less than two decades. Proposals for reform of agriculture
included in the 1962 legislation inspired by Hassan Arsanjani
were firmly based on the establishment of a peasant proprietor class.   The first phase of this reform was more or
less consistent with Arsanjani's objectives.   Thereafter, and
effectively from 1964, the small scale approach to landownership and farm businesses was abandoned.   From 1967/68,
the government became mainly concerned with concentrating
farm land into large scale units as a mechanism for stimu-
lating faster growth in agriculture, which lagged ever
further behind other areas of the economy.   Losses of people
from the land, the uprooting of entire communities within
the selected development zones as in the Dezful area, and
the blight of economic uncertainty in traditional farming
areas were ignored or misunderstood by the governments
in Tehran.   By 1978 large areas of Dezful and other regions

of the country were uncultivated for lack of labour, support
services and likelihood of a fair return.   Meanwhile, the
large scale agricultural units had themselves run into severe
difficulties and were making only limited contributions to
total farm production.   Faced with other problems in infrastructure and industry, the government appeared to have
no credible policies to which to turn.   Following the revolution, small scale farming came back into favour once more
in a land reform which, stripped of its revolutionary dressing,
was a return to the spirit and purpose of the Arsanjani
programme of 1962.

It remains to be seen whether the far reaching changes
in economic, politics and demography which affected rural
Iran in the period 1962-1980 will allow a return to peasant
farming.   It must be suspected that official policies will
need a flexibility of definition and a generous financial
support applied appropriately in each regional context that
will be too demanding for a country in the throes of revolution to accomplish.   Uncertainty of purpose at the centre
and insecurity in the regions will make attainment of agricultural prosperity difficult.   It is as true of post-revolu-
tionary Iran as it was for Iran before the 1962 agrarian
reform that

> "The question at issue is not the need for reform,
> which is abundantly clear, but the means by
> which it is to be carried out.   Any measures
> which fail to relieve the peasant of his poverty,
> to dissipate the prevailing distrust, or which
> neglect the importance of the provision of
> security for all are unlikely to succeed.   More-
> over, it is futile to suppose a movement for
> reform can be brought about by an act of the
> legislature alone." *

Certainly, the future of the Dezful area, with its difficult
physical conditions for agriculture and its legacy of disruption in the last 20 years, is as full of promise as ever
for the establishment of productive farming under small scale
peasant proprietor cultivation.   Prospects for fulfilment of
this promise would, in 1980, appear to be as distant as they
were in 1960 unless the conditions laid down by Professor
Lambton are created without too much delay.

---

*   Lambton, A.K.S., **Landlord and peasant in Persia**,
     Oxford UP, London, 1953, p 395.

INDEX